Along with Youth

ALONG WITH YOUTH

Hemingway,
The Early Years

PETER GRIFFIN

Oxford   New York
OXFORD UNIVERSITY PRESS
1987

Oxford University Press, Walton Street, Oxford OX2 6DP

Oxford New York Toronto
Delhi Bombay Calcutta Madras Karachi
Petaling Jaya Singapore Hong Kong Tokyo
Nairobi Dar es Salaam Cape Town
Melbourne Auckland
and associated companies in
Beirut Berlin Ibadan Nicosia

Oxford is a trade mark of Oxford University Press

First published 1985 by Oxford University Press, Inc.
First published as an Oxford University Press paperback 1987

British Library Cataloguing in Publication Data
Griffin, Peter, 1942–
Along with youth: Hemingway, the early
years.—(Oxford paperbacks).
1. Hemingway, Ernest—Biography
2. Novelists, American—20th century—
Biography
I. Title II. Hemingway, Ernest
813'52 PS3515.E37Z/
ISBN 0–19–282091–5

Printed in the United States of America
Bound in Great Britain
by Biddles Ltd, King's Lynn

Foreword

Readers of this book by Peter Griffin are in for a pleasant surprise, whether they are Hemingway buffs who have read every available word on the subject or merely the curious who want to know what recent scholarship may have revealed about a famous writer dead almost a quarter-century. I have been fortunate to have been in close touch with Peter since he first obtained Mary Hemingway's permission to attempt what he told her he thought he could do, bring life and feeling to a thoroughly researched and accurate biography of Ernest Hemingway. I believe he has done just that, and I believe it sorely needed doing. If this first volume is an indication, we will have a work significantly different from the first officially authorized biography which, while a monument to tireless research and hard work, seems to me to be about someone I never knew, someone without humor and, in short, without life.

If I need to check some date in Hemingway's life, there is no better tool than Carlos Baker's biography. It sometimes turns out to be inaccurate or incomplete, but on the whole it is a priceless reference work, and I am well aware of the toll its writing took on Professor Baker. Griffin's biography, while I believe it to be as accurate as anything I have ever read about my father's early years, is not written as a reference work. It has been written by a young man who has shown me insights into my own father's character and behavior I would not have thought possible in view of the time lapse between Hemingway's death and the research Griffin has accomplished. These insights and his innate skills have enabled him to bring a far different view of Hemingway as a developing human being. There aren't as many of the players around now as there were fifteen or more years ago, not as many witnesses. There are, however, fewer constraints as well. Ruffled feathers have for the most part been smoothed. Truths which would have caused pain then can now be voiced. Peter Griffin has voiced many of them, and some of them surprising in the extreme.

For my part, I made my mother's correspondence, which is now at the Kennedy Library, available to him early on, and he has skillfully quoted and translated their content into a rounding out of the courtship between my mother and father which portrays them and their time as truly as I think it can be done.

I was pleased to see Griffin's use of some examples of my father's early writing done at different times in those early years. They graphically illustrate what we should all realized, that good writing is not a gift but is arrived at by a combination of intelligence, clear thought, intuition, and hard work, as well as single-minded determination. That the young Hemingway had a long way to go is all too apparent, but there are indications, even then, of some of the requisite qualities. Furthermore, they are quite funny.

At the risk of seeming like Hemingway's good 1940s pal, Winston Guest, when he said halfway through reading "The Life of Christ" aboard the *Pilar*, "Papa, this is a wonderful story. I can hardly wait to find out how it ends," I will end by saying that this is a wonderful biography because it reads like a story, and you will very likely join me in wondering how it will all end in a future volume.

North of Ketchum   Jack Hemingway
1985

Preface

On October 28, 1977, I wrote a six-line note to Mary Hemingway. I told her I wanted to write my dissertation at Brown University on her husband because his works had meant a lot to me during the hardest times of my life. I said I knew most scholars agreed that Hemingway had been "done." But I said I could not find the author of *In Our Time*, *The Sun Also Rises,* and *A Farewell to Arms* in the biographies I had read.

Nine days later I found in my mail a small blue envelope, boldly addressed, with her address embossed in white on the back. Mrs. Hemingway wrote, "I must regretfully report that my program of various commitments is so full between now and early December that I cannot say something such as 'Come whenever you like.' I'll be here from late November onward. Why don't you ring me for a specific date?"

My wife and I visited Mary Hemingway six times the following year. During our hours of conversation, Mary told fascinating stories and made me understand I was not at work on a project—I was trying to learn about her husband, the most "decent" and the most complex man she had ever known. Mary also mentioned a friend who she knew had been close to Ernest when he was a boy during the First World War. His name was Bill Horne, and he lived outside Chicago.

I called Bill Horne on the night of July 3, 1979. He was eighty-eight years old at the time. There was a holiday celebration going on at his home, and it was hard for each of us to make the other understand. Eventually Bill was convinced that I appreciated Ernest Hemingway and suggested I come to Chicago. He had a lot to say.

My wife and I got to Bill and "Bunny" Horne's home in Barrington

Hills on July 7. Bill's beautiful black dog Lena sniffed around us as we rolled out of our rented Toyota. Bill, with twenties-style steel-rimmed glasses and a lifeguard whistle hung around his neck (to call Lena, I was later told), stood at the weather-worn screen door. A half-hour later, sitting on the veranda, sipping cocktails Bunny Horne brought in, the tape recorder turning away, I asked Bill my prepared questions: What were his first impressions of Ernest? What was life like for them in New York before embarking for Italy in 1918? Could we talk about Schio? What was life like in Milan at the American Red Cross Hospital? And how about Agnes Kurowsky, Ernest's first love? I had read Bill's letters to Ernest (now with the Hemingway papers at the John F. Kennedy Library) and, with a bit of priming, Bill's memory started to flow.

During his reminiscence of the Chicago years when he and Ernest lived together on North State Street, and then later when Bill lost his job and went home to New York and Ernest moved in with Kenley and "Doodles" Smith, Bill made a remark he immediately regretted. Then he said, "Speak only well of the dead," more to himself than to me. Bill denied the remark was true. "I was showing off for your wife, Pete, that's all." An hour later the interview came to a comfortable end, and my wife and I left for our hotel. But eight o'clock that night Bill Horne called. Could we come out to Barrington Hills the next day?

The eighth of July was overcast and threatened rain. The dog Lena greeted us at the car again, and Bill was at the door. This time though, after Bunny served us delightful cocktails, Bill said he was "going down cellar." A few minutes later he came back with a copper-coated tin box that looked as if it had once been a Whitman Sampler. Bill opened up the box and brought it over. "Take a look at this, Pete," he said. There was a cardboard-covered photograph album, some yellowed, sharply creased pages of typing, and, pressed flat by the weight of the album, letters that began "Horney Bill" and ended "Hemmy," " 'Oin," or "Hemingstein." He had been keeping this stuff, Bill said, because he once planned to write his own story of Hemingway. But it was too late now.

In his letters to Bill, Ernest opened his heart as he never had before, and, with the exception of his letters to his first wife, Hadley, never would again. He wrote of his love for Agnes Kurowsky, of his home in Oak Park, Illinois, of his parents, Clarence and Grace Hemingway, and of what he hoped to do with his life. (I noticed a letter dated March 13, 1919, the day Ernest heard from Agnes that she was engaged to an Italian duke.) As I looked at the photographs, Bill chuckled at the Fiat ambulances (they were top-heavy, threatening always to roll off the narrow mountain roads) and at the outside shots of the mess at Schio (Ernest, overweight, fooling with a bayonet against the chest of a friend). Bill sang an Italian air; he saddened at the photo of a town, shell-pocked and cratered, in the Dolomite hills. Take it all with you, Bill said. But my wife and I and Bunny Horne said no.

Bill spoke also that afternoon of Ernest Hemingway's funeral in Ketchum, Idaho. He was very proud to have been a pallbearer for his friend. Bill said he remembered many of the mourners with affection, but most of all he remembered Ernest's first son. Bill called him Bumby or, sometimes, Jack.

I met Jack Hemingway in Boston on July 29, 1979. He and his daughter Joan had come East for the internment of Jack's mother's ashes in Vermont. (Hadley Hemingway Mowrer had died in Florida in January, at eighty-eight.) As we sat talking in the bar of the Hilton Hotel at Logan Airport, Jack sipping a Campari, the sense of interview evaporated. Jack told some extraordinary stories. When he had worked for Merrill-Lynch in the mid-1950s, he said, he went through a time of severe depression. His father asked him to the home in Ketchum, Idaho. They would both work on what to do. Late one afternoon, after father and son had gotten purposively drunk, they bought a goat, slaughtered it, and Ernest, the goat on his back, climbed to the roof of his house and tied the carcass to the chimney. As the vultures flapped down, Ernest and Jack gave them twelve-gauge shotgun blasts instead of an evening meal. In an hour the rooftop was littered with the birds. Then Jack and his father made a pact about suicide. Each promised to call the other, first. But, Jack said, his father didn't keep his word.

I asked Jack about the early years. He said the great tragedy for his father was the broken heart Ernest's wartime love affair with his nurse in Milan, Agnes Kurowsky, had given him. How did Ernest feel about his mother, Grace? I asked. He always claimed he hated her, Jack said. Did Ernest love anyone in his first family? Yes, Jack said. Clarence, his father, and his sister, Ursula. Did Ernest really learn to box? He wasn't much in the ring, Jack said. (The trouble with Ernest's left eye had come during father-and-son bouts and the scoring Ernest's cornea had received from the lacing of Jack's glove.) But Ernest was a splendid bar fighter. He knew all the tricks, and he could hit very, very hard. Did your mother love your father all her life? I asked. Yes, Jack said. But when they were divorced she felt as if a millstone had dropped from her neck.

My meetings with Mary Hemingway, with Bill Horne, and with Jack Hemingway were the highlights of my two years of research. But only Bill Horne could give me details of Ernest's early life, and he knew only of the wartime experiences and of their months together in Chicago in

1920. For the rest I had to go to Oak Park, Illinois, where Ernest spent his first eighteen years, to Ernest's boyhood summer home, Windemere, on Walloon Lake in Upper Michigan, where I talked for hours with his sister Madelaine, and my wife and I lived in "The Annex," the small cottage Clarence Hemingway built for his children, and to Horton Bay four miles across the hills from Windemere where, after his ambulance service in Italy in World War I, Ernest lived in a little summer inn called Pinehurst.

I was fortunate to read, when the Hemingway collection at the John F. Kennedy Library was still a stack of boxes in a drab federal building in Waltham, Massachusetts, letters and diaries and manuscripts. As all of this was uncovered, I was struck by the early letters, ingenuous and senti- mental; the diaries Ernest's mother kept, too old and dry to be musty, filled with happy and sad family pictures, annotated in a lovely 1890s scroll; the manuscript fragments, one an unpublished 300-page novel from 1928, harshly edited by Ernest himself; and the story of Ernest's courtship of Hadley Richardson told in a thousand pages of Hadley's let- ters. After the dedication of the Hemingway Room at the new John F. Kennedy Library on Columbia Point, Dorchester, Massachusetts, I spent a delightful morning with Ernest's youngest sister, Carol.

Ernest Hemingway died in 1961, but as with all truly famous men, he lived on in the public imagination. In the glare of his personality, pioneering interpretations were done by Charles Fenton, Philip Young, and Carlos Baker. Now Hemingway is almost history. In the twilight of his "life" a biographer might see him more clearly.

Fall River, Massachusetts   P.G.
December 1984

To my wife,
Penelope

Acknowledgments

In writing this book, I enjoyed the generosity and kindness of many people. I am grateful to them and wish to acknowledge them adequately. But, as anyone who has read—or written—an acknowledgment page knows, that is impossible. Of the best fiction, Hemingway wrote, "the dignity of movement of an ice-berg is due to one-eighth of its being above water." The best this book has to offer is due to what is inexpressible here.

My thanks to: Jack Hemingway, Mary Hemingway, Bill and "Bunny" Horne, Curtis Church, George Monteiro, the late Milton Griffin, Anna Griffin, Arthur Lothrop, Theodore Voorhees, Henry M. Watts, Robert Rosenberg, Bertram E. Howard, George O'Brien, Robert O. Haley, Louise Keane, Rose Simon, Randy Kryn, Edward Wagenknecht, Lewis Clarahan, Susan Crist, Mrs. Ernest J. Miller, Carol Gardner, Wendy Warren Keebler, Bill Olhe, Carlos Baker, Maxine Davis, Polly Dow, Carolyn Raynor Scott, Warren Miller, Joan Ponton, Mrs. Arthur Burns, Al Gini, Rudy Clemen, Leslie Morris, Pat Julian, James Dilworth, Joseph Sciarra, Janice Motta, Eleanor Caton.

Invaluable to my research were: The John F. Kennedy Library, the Lily Library, the Kansas City Public Library, the Oak Park, Illinois Public Library, the Fall River, Massachusetts Public Library, the National Archives and Records Service, The Mary Institute, Oberlin College, Oak Park High School. My illustrations appear by courtesy of The John F. Kennedy Library, with the exception of numbers 14 and 15, which appear by courtesy of Theodore Voorhees and Mrs. Bill Horne.

Contents

Along with Youth

He was the sort of boy that becomes a clown and a lout as soon as he is not understood, or feels himself held cheap, and again is adorable at the first touch of warmth.

D. H. LAWRENCE
Sons and Lovers

❦ 1 ❧
Disorder and Early Sorrow

When he was six years old, Ernest Hemingway sat through a memorial service for his maternal grandfather, Ernest Hall. The First Congregational Church in Oak Park, Illinois, was hot, the organ seemed loud, the minister droned on and on. Reading from the obituary Grace Hemingway, Ernest's mother, had herself composed, he made Ernest Hall a cultured English gentleman, a lover of the arts, a student of history, a Christian of "fervent piety and a disciple's faith." Ernest Hall had "the dignity of a lord and the simplicity of a child," the minister said. "He was soldierly like Cromwell and saintly like Wesley. . . . He influenced men more than he was influenced by them." Confused no doubt by the service and by what he had seen at home, Ernest, that morning, told his mother, "I'm the son of the son of a better one."

Ernest Hall was born in Sheffield, England, in 1840. His father, Charles, was a silversmith, and the family well-to-do. When Ernest Hall graduated from St. Saviour's, an artisans' public school in London, he looked forward to university life and a professional career. But, in 1852, electroplating was invented, and the Sheffield silverworks went into a sharp decline. In 1854, Charles Hall packed up his family and emigrated to the United States. Instead of enjoying a freshman term at Cambridge or Oxford, young Ernest found himself tending sheep and cattle in Dyersville, Iowa.

For two years Ernest Hall worked hard on the family farm and, it seemed to his father at least, enthusiastically. Then late one afternoon, after they had been plowing all day, Charles Hall told his son to water the team before supper. That night Ernest Hall ran away, but not before he had driven his father's horses so far into the Little Maquoketa River that they were carried off and drowned.

3

4 ALONG WITH YOUTH

Ernest Hall spent the next four years working all along the Mississippi. He was a common hand on riverboats; he hired out for day labor; he enjoyed the pleasures of the St. Charles, a fine New Orleans hotel. With the start of the Civil War, however, he returned to Dyersville—the patriot and the prodigal son. As soon as he could, he enlisted in the First Iowa Cavalry and bought a good horse. He was made a corporal because of the horse.

While Mark Twain rode with his rebel irregulars in Marion County, Ernest Hall soldiered in Clinton, Missouri, across the state. In April 1862, according to his commanding officer, H. H. Heath, he received "a gunshot wound . . . during his term of service, but not in the regular discharge of his duties; though from an enemy in arms against the authority of the United States." (This last phrase kept him from being court-martialed.) The ball lodged on the inner side of the left femur. After five months in a hospital at Butler, Missouri, Ernest Hall was "still incapable of riding." He was given an honorable discharge. He sold his horse to the army for seventy dollars and went home.

Three years later, in 1865, Ernest Hall married Caroline Hancock. She was English-born, had been to the Australian gold rush with her sea-captain father, and with him had sailed around the Horn. She wrote poetry and played the piano well. Like Ernest Hall, she hated rural life. Immediately after the wedding, Ernest and Caroline moved to Chicago where, with his brother-in-law William Randall, they began a cutlery business. In October 1871, the Halls lost almost everything in the Great Chicago Fire. Nine months later, and after seven years of marriage, their first child, Grace, was born.

Perhaps because Ernest and Caroline Hall had once had dreams of their own, Grace became a willful and precocious child. She had blue-gray eyes, a sturdy little figure, blond hair, and fine "English" skin. At three years old, Grace could harmonize with the family quartet; at seven, she learned "by ear" to play the parlor organ. Once she took her brother Leicester's bicycle, a penny farthing, and, wearing a pair of his pants, shocked the ladies on the neighborhood streets.

Two illnesses did mar Grace's childhood. First, she had scarlet fever, and the disease left her blind for months. Then, one day while her parents were at church, Grace saw the outline of her fingers on the parlor organ keys. She prayed to God "very hard," and suddenly she could see. Grace never forgot the hug her father gave her and the feel of her mother's tears on her cheeks.

At fourteen, Grace contracted chorea, St. Vitus' dance. During her six-month convalescence she grew half a foot, none of her clothes fit her, and her mother, four feet ten inches tall herself, was alarmed. Yet Grace had also developed perfect pitch and a lovely contralto voice. Ernest Hall envisioned a career in opera for his daughter. He hired the finest voice instructors in Chicago and took Grace to every performance of the Chicago Opera Company.

As the years passed, Grace Hall became a local celebrity (she was the showpiece of the church choir) but nothing more. She would have to go to New York, Ernest Hall said, if she wanted serious study and a chance at real success. Four years after high school, when Grace seemed ready, fate intervened. One winter afternoon, Dr. William Lewis, the best internist in Oak Park, told Ernest Hall his wife Caroline was dying of cancer and had only a few months to live. Grace would of course nurse her mother. She must even learn to administer morphine.

Dr. Lewis, who visited his patient almost every day, brought with him a tall young man with thick crow-black hair, black piercing eyes, and a chin that Grace felt needed a beard. Dr. Lewis explained that Mr. Clarence Hemingway, who coincidentally lived in the gray house right across the street, was a student at Rush Medical College and that he had taken him under his wing. If all went well, Dr. Lewis said, Mr. Hemingway would be Dr. Hemingway next year.

In time, Clarence Hemingway took to stopping at the Halls' residence at 439 North Oak Park Avenue on his own. He and Grace sat in the mid-Victorian parlor—all plush and fringe—and drank her father's English tea. Clarence said he had heard her sing many times in the First Congregational Church and regretted that they had not been introduced before.

When it got warm enough in Oak Park to bring out the buds on the tree-lined streets and turn the broad lawns a tint of green, Clarence in his black, ministerial suit took Grace on afternoon walks. It would be good for her strained nerves, he said. Grace wore a picture hat to keep the sun off her skin and the glare from her fever-damaged eyes.

At first Grace did most of the talking. She asked questions about her mother's condition that day. How much was she suffering? Was there anything else after morphine? Then the talk turned to Clarence's own parents, Anson and Adelaide Hemingway. It was just the reverse in his family, Clarence said. His mother, Adelaide, with her bright agate eyes and curious serenity, was as healthy as a schoolgirl. She was six years older than his father, Clarence said, but Anson suffered from "pigeon breast" and had a bad heart. Was it from the war? Grace asked. Her father had been in the cavalry; he'd been wounded and was a hero. Anson Hemingway was no hero, Clarence said, but he had carried a fifty-pound pack for the Union infantry all over Mississippi and raised six children and had worked for the YMCA. Now his father was a realtor. Grace must have seen the office in the "Merchants' Block" downtown: "Hemingway Real Estate" the gold letters on the window read. Also, she must remember the tiny old house where their gray mansion, as he called it, now stood. Her father had graduated from a London public school, Grace said. He was a man of letters, turned to business by bad luck. Clarence remembered Grace in high school, though she was a class behind, and Grace said she thought she remembered him.

On some of their walks, Clarence took Grace Hall out to the prairie, where quail would at a stone's throw burst from cover or a red-tail fox would be prowling. Clarence told Grace he was a collector of arrowheads and spearheads, clay bowls and stone axes of the Pottawatomie Indians, all taken from the earthen mounds over by the Des Plaines River. He spoke of Indian friends he had made on a two-month visit to a mission school for the Dakota Sioux. Because of his extraordinary vision, the Indians called him Nec-tee-ta-la—"Eagle Eye." Why, Grace asked, was Clarence still in school at twenty-four? That's easy, he said. After three years at Oberlin College, he had failed and come home in disgrace.

Caroline Hall died on September 5, 1895, and by that time Clarence and Grace were engaged. Clarence asked for an early wedding, while he was still a student. But Grace had other commitments. Soon after the death of his wife, Ernest Hall had urged his daughter to try a season at the opera in New York; she was twenty-three; she might not get another chance. Clarence returned for his last term at Rush Medical College, still a bachelor. Grace headed east to the "famous" Madame Cappianni and took the stage name "Ernestine."

Grace Hall's months in New York the winter of 1895–96 were a heady experience. She met and was accepted by the cosmopolitan students of the Arts Students' League (Stephen Crane frequently visited there); she earned the confidence and support of Madame Cappianni; she had a flirtation with a young painter who did her portrait in a low-cut satin gown. Best of all, Grace had a successful debut at the old Madison Square Garden. Even her picture on the program, all flowery curls, was a hit. Nevertheless, in the spring of 1896, Grace returned to Oak Park. She told her father the harsh stage lighting hurt her weak eyes terribly. To console Grace, Ernest Hall at once proposed a European tour. Although she would not see Clarence Hemingway graduate, they did agree on a date for their wedding—October 1, 1896—and did decide where to live: with Ernest Hall.

On July 21, 1899, Grace Hemingway, attended by Dr. Lewis with Clarence handling the chloroform, gave birth to a second child. (The first,

Marcelline, had been born eighteen months before.) He was a robust, red-cheeked boy with his mother's complexion, her thick blond hair, and her blue-gray eyes. Dr. Lewis pronounced the baby perfect. Yet one Sunday in September while Grace was in Chicago, Clarence, without anesthetic, circumcised his son. At the First Congregational Church on October 1st, his parents' third wedding anniversary, the boy was named for Grace's father, then for her great-great-grandfather—Ernest Miller Hemingway.

In the Hall–Hemingway household, there was no doubt who was head of the family. Ernest Hall read the morning prayers, gave the five servants their orders, and sat down to a breakfast of crisp bacon, toast from an open rack, and Dundee orange marmalade, long after Clarence had begun his rounds. In the afternoon, Ernest Hall, who had retired at fifty, walked his Scottish terrier Tassels downtown to "see about my investments," he said. Like John D. Rockefeller, he wore a top hat and immaculate gray gloves and walked with his toes pointed out. He told Clarence, "Only red Indians walk toes straight ahead." At supper, "Abba" the biblical word for father as he insisted on being called—gave the blessing: "For what we are about to receive may the Lord make us truly thankful, for Jesus' sake, amen." Then, before dismissing the family (Clarence was "excused" if he had an emergency call), Ernest Hall would kneel at the center table in the parlor. His favorite, dark-eyed Marcelline, watched his gray mutton-chop whiskers and the pink baldness of her grandfather's head. Opening a small, thick book with gold-edged leaves bearing the inscription "Daily Strength for Daily Needs," he would read and read. Then all would rise, turn, and kneel down on the flowered Brussels carpet in front of their chairs—young Ernest, his hands folded on the black leather seat. Abba Hall would raise his head, his eyes looking upward, and through thin, pale lips speak "as though he were talking to God." Grace, stirred by emotion and habit, always thanked Abba for these performances with a "bear hug" and a kiss.

In a "Memory Book," leather-bound, the size of a family bible, Grace Hemingway kept a history of Ernest's first five years. (By his eighteenth birthday, she would fill four others.) Besides the conventional remembrances—Ernest weighed nine pounds, eight ounces at birth; he said "Papa" at five months and walked across the room at one year—she recorded, mostly without comment, some unusual behavior: "He sleeps with Mama and lunches all night. . . . He is *so* strong and well and loves his Mama so *tenderly*. . . . He plays 'Peek-a-boo' all by himself with the sheet . . . and cries with such heart broken sorrow when we all put on our things in the morning." After his grandfather led the morning prayers, Ernest would "play clown and turn summersaults to amuse the family." At night, after the inspirational ceremony, he would sing as loud as he could "Me!" each time the phrase "Jesus loves even me" occurred in the hymn. "If things were taken away from him, he would submit without a word," Grace noted. But later on he would "rush up" to his mother "and smile and in his rich, loving voice say 'Fweetie, Fweetie.' " Even if he were hurt severely, Ernest would not cry so long as "Mama would kiss it and make it well." If he displeased his "Mama," Ernest would "put away from his mouth sweets, puddings, and pastries" and ask for "plain bread and water instead." When he had done something he thought very wrong, Ernest would give himself a "whippy" "so Mama won't have to punish." Asked if he were afraid of the dark or of walking in the woods alone, Ernest would claim he was "afraid of nothing." But then he would cuddle around Grace's neck, asking to play " 'Kitty,' where Mama be the Mama kitty and strokes him and purrs." "He pats my face in the night," Grace wrote, "and squeezes up so close . . . and sings 'Ah' which is the way he loves."

When he was old enough to share a room with his sister Marcelline, Ernest sometimes asked his mother to stay with him and sing to him. Grace usually chose "Onward Christian Soldiers," the song she did first in choir. "When I get to be a big boy," Ernest would say, "I don't want to be an Onward Christian Soldier; I want to go with Dad and shoot lions and wolves." Yet, one Sunday at the First Congregational Church, Ernest waved "wildly" because the collection plate passed him by. When it returned, he dropped something in. On the walk home, Clarence Hemingway asked his son what he had been so anxious to contribute. "My gold penny, Daddy!" Ernest replied. "It was all that I had and I just had to give it." Grace knew that "this gold penny was so choice to him [it had been his father's Christmas gift] that he had cried bitterly when it was mislaid."

Grace called Ernest her "dutch bish dollie" and sometimes she dressed him in her own baby clothes. But when he insisted he was "Bobby" or "Punch" or "that Jake," she was pleased. "A boy's a boy for a' that," Grace would say. One morning, when he was five years old, Ernest crawled into Grace's bed. She told him the "happy secret" of the coming birth of his sister Madelaine. "He wanted to know all about it," Grace wrote, "so I explained and he felt the little one move." For weeks Ernest would smile slyly at his mother and whisper to her, "We know, don't we?" Yet a year later there was a curious brutality in the first letter he wrote:

Dear papa
    today Momma and the rest of us took walk We walked to the school house, Marcelline ran on ahead while we stopt at Clauses in a little wile

she came back she said thaat in the wood shed of the school house the[re] was a pocaipine, so we went up there and looked in the door, the pocaipine was asleep I went in a gave I[t] a wack with the axx. then I cave I[t] another and another. then I crouched in the wood. We came to Mr. Claus and he got his gun and . . . [the manuscript ends here].

The letter is on Windemere stationery. In the upper right-hand corner Ernest wrote to his father, "Hear [sic] some of the quills."

The Hall–Hemingway house in Oak Park had many rooms, and each family member seemed most comfortable in his own. For Grace it was the high-ceilinged parlor, with its fireplace, her upright piano, and windows so large the sidewalk oak seemed part of the room. For Ernest Hall it was the library behind mahogany doors, where he and his brother-in-law, Tyley Hancock, a jovial traveling salesman of brass beds, traded stories and smoked imported cigars. Clarence Hemingway also took one room for himself. Above the second-floor bedroom where Ernest was born, it was a turret attic with five windows and the brightest room in the house. Besides his Pottawatomie artifacts and the leather vest and moccasins he had gotten from the Dakota Sioux, Clarence kept a recent collection there. On shelves he had put along the walls, dozens of Ball jars held snakes and toads and salamanders bleached white in alcohol. One larger jar held a two-months' human fetus, still showing the primordial gills. After repeated trips with his father to the attic, Ernest could read the names on all the jars. He had a wonderful memory, Clarence thought, and the eye of a natural scientist. Because he showed no revulsion at the disgusting shapes in the jars, Clarence thought perhaps his son could be a doctor someday.

During these years, two more children were born to Clarence and Grace: their third, named Ursula, on April 29, 1902; their fourth, Madelaine, on November 28, 1904.

In August of 1898, the year before Ernest was born, Clarence and Grace Hemingway vacationed at a cottage owned by Grace's cousin, Madelaine Randel Board. The cottage was located on one of the small, many-armed lakes in the Petoskey region of northern Michigan, some eighty miles from the Canadian border at Sioux St. Marie. The lake, then called Bear but later Walloon, was spring-fed, cold, and very clear. Along the shore were birches and cedars; farther back, maples, hemlocks, and stands of pine. Twenty years earlier some of the land had been cleared by lumber

companies. But in 1898 only one small sawmill and a settlement of Ojib-
ways, who peeled hemlock bark for tanning, remained. On sunny days the
birches shone against the dark pine hills, and the lake turned a luminous
pale blue.

Clarence loved the good fishing in Bear Lake (pike, perch, and large-
mouth bass), the cool nights for sleeping, and the sound of wild ducks
calling across open water just before dawn. Before he and Grace left for
Oak Park, they bought one acre of land by a small bay on the north
shore. Two years later, Clarence built a cottage of his own on a part of
the lot cleared the summer before. To enjoy pure, fresh water while it
was still very cold, he had a well driven down directly from the kitchen
sink. Grace, in appreciation of her favorite author, Sir Walter Scott,
named the cottage Windemere.

When Ernest was old enough, he and Clarence swam and fished in the
lake, searched for bird nests and wildflowers in heavy foliage, made camp-
fires with flint and steel in the rain, and hiked along Indian-fashion, toes
straight ahead. (At five years old, Ernest hiked seven miles with his father and blistered his feet so badly there was blood in his socks and
shoes.) On the last day of each season, when, as usual, Clarence awakened
Ernest by holding onto his foot, there was always a long list of chores
they wanted to do together before the wood-burning lake steamer took
the Hemingways to the train at Walloon Village for the trip back to Oak
Park.

Seven years after his father's death, when Ernest had two young sons of
his own, he remembered Clarence in one of his finest short stories, "Fathers and Sons":

> His father came back to him in the fall of the year, or in the early spring
> when there had been jacksnipe on the prairie, or when he saw shocks of
> corn, or when he saw a lake, or if he ever saw a horse and buggy, or when
> he saw, or heard, wild geese, or in a duck blind; remembering the time an
> eagle dropped through the whirling snow to strike a canvas-covered decoy,
> rising, his wings beating, the talons caught in the canvas. His father was
> with him, suddenly, in deserted orchards and in new-plowed fields, in
> thickets, on small hills, or when going through dead grass, whenever split-
> ting wood or hauling water, by grist mills, cider mills and dams and al-
> ways with open fires.

On August 22, 1904, just before the Hemingways returned to Oak
Park, Ernest Hall applied to the Department of the Interior, Bureau of
Pensions, for the remittance his cavalry service had earned him. On the
notarized form, "Declaration for Original Invalid Pension," he wrote
that he suffered from "Sluggish circulation, disease of the kidneys, or

weak, and heart trouble." He assured the pension officer, "My disabilities
are permanent and in no way due to viscious habits. I am disqualified for
any occupation involving manual labor."

On October 15, 1904, Ernest Hall was granted six dollars per week for
"partial disability." Three weeks later he left for his usual vacation with
his son, Leicester, in Bishop, California. But in March, a month early, he
returned to Oak Park a very sick man. Dr. Lewis made the diagnosis. It
was Bright's disease.

For the next six weeks, Ernest Hall suffered the effects of kidney failure: he vomited; his skin turned brown; often he was delirious with fever. On cool spring nights, with the windows closed, the stench from his
room filled the house. When he died on May 10, 1905, the Hemingways
had lived with him for nine years.

In mid-June 1905, the Hemingway family made their annual trip from
Oak Park to Windemere. But this summer there was a different family
mood. Grace Hall-Hemingway, as she now signed her name, had inherited
the bulk of her father's estate, and she intended to make some changes.

First of all, Grace knew that for the past few years Clarence had had
his eye on a forty-acre former tenant farm directly across the lake from
Windemere. The meadow was all quack grass, the orchard girdled trees.
But in the summer of 1905, the farm was up for taxes, and this made it
a bargain Grace could not refuse. She named the property Longfield
Farm and bought the second rowboat Clarence said he needed.

While her husband worked hard replanting the orchards (he and Ernest
would row across the lake together, Ernest sitting amid saplings of Jona-
than apple and plum), Grace turned to more serious matters. For seventeen of her thirty-two years, she had lived in the house on North Oak
Park Avenue. But the gables, the veranda, the turret were all irretrievably
passé. Another resident of Oak Park, Frank Lloyd Wright, was creating
new designs everyone was talking about. They called them his "Prairie
Style." Now that Grace had her patrimony, she would have the old house
listed with Anson Hemingway's real estate office; buy a prized corner lot
at North Kenilworth Avenue and Iowa Street, one block away from
Wright's spectacular home; and hire the best builder in town. For the
rest of the summer at Windemere, Grace set to work designing her own
"modern" home.

When the Hemingways returned to Oak Park in September, Grace directed a general clearance of the furnishings her family had accumulated
over the years. Besides her mother Caroline's oil landscapes of the Des
Plaines River and Ernest Hall's small library—several Scott novels, an illustrated Gray's "Elegy," and a set of expensively bound "classics" still

looking new—Grace kept only her upright piano. One afternoon, as Ernest watched from the pantry window, a bonfire roared in the backyard.
Twenty years later, he wrote of what he saw that day in "Now I Lay Me"
for his book of short stories, *Men Without Women:*

> I remembered, after my grandfather died we moved away from that house
> to a new house designed and built by my mother. Many things that were
> not to be moved were burned in the back-yard. And I remember those
> jars from the attic being thrown into the fire, and how they popped in
> the heat and the fire flamed up from the alcohol. I remember the snakes
> burning in the fire in the back-yard.

In mid-August 1906, Grace and Clarence Hemingway, Marcelline, Ernest, Ursula, and Madelaine moved into their new house. It was three stories high, covered in light gray stucco with stark white trim. There were
many windows, some with latticework of the diagonal Elizabethan design. As in the Frank Lloyd Wright homes, there were large sheltering
overhangs at the edge of the roof, above the second floor and covering the
broad enclosed porch. Compared to the dark, mansard-roofed house across
the street, Grace thought her work looked strikingly alive.

In addition to some small flourishes (the living-room door, half in leaded
glass, had a family crest: a light blue H, the center bar of which was two
hands clasped, with a rising sun above, and a calla lily below), Grace was
most proud of the thirty-by-thirty-foot hall she called her music room.
There was a rug-draped platform in the center, and to its left stood a
Steinway grand piano. There were large radiators painted bronze, with
galvanized water-filled pots. Halfway up one wall, a balcony complete
with folding chairs faced an eighteenth-century portrait—full-length and
life-sized—of Grace's great-great grandfather, William Miller Hall. He
had been a pupil of Paganini, she believed.

In early September 1906, Grace enrolled Ernest at the Oliver Wendell
Holmes School on Chicago Avenue in Oak Park. It was a short walk from
the Kenilworth house, less than half a block away. Grace also insisted
that Ernest, at seven, and Marcelline, at eight and a half, should begin
school together.

About this time, Grace undertook her children's "cultural education."
There were trips to the opera, the symphony, and the theater in Chicago.
Grace did not discriminate among *Romeo and Juliet, Faust, La Bohème,
Aïda,* the operettas of Victor Herbert, and the "well-made" plays of Eu-
gene Scribe. On Saturday afternoons and sometimes after school, she took
Ernest and Marcelline, and later Ursula, to see the fine collections at the
Chicago Art Institute. On these visits Ernest saw works ranging from El

Greco's *Assumption of the Virgin* to the romantic landscapes of George Inness (*Home of the Heron* was one). Later Ernest recalled being impressed most by the lifelike bronze lions that stand at either side of the entrance to the Chicago Art Institute on three-foot-high pedestals.

During these years too, Grace was the director of the children's vested choir at the Third Congregational Church in Oak Park. She was pleased to discover that two of her daughters, Marcelline and Ursula, could sing. Ernest for a long time was a disappointment to her because, as she once said, "I needed a good voice and Ernest was a monotone." One day when he was twelve, however, Ernest was suddenly able to sing in a clear, pleasing alto. Grace was delighted, and she promptly made him a soloist in the vested choir. But a few months later his voice changed abruptly once again.

Because of his failure in the choir, Grace insisted that Ernest learn to play the cello for the family orchestra. To this end, she sent him to the music room to practice an hour every day. Unhappily, both Ernest and Clarence, who for several years practiced his cornet in the cellar, failed to become the musicians Grace had hoped for and always played the hymns and the Gilbert and Sullivan songs she preferred slightly off-key.

As Ernest moved up through the elementary grades at the Holmes School, he had to endure a special strain. He had to compete in the same grade with his older sister Marcelline. Since she was taller and stronger than Ernest and "predictable" in a way the teachers approved, he was usually second-best. When he developed myopia in the fifth grade, Ernest kept the problem to himself.

Perhaps because of his nearsightedness, Ernest read every chance he got. He advanced from the moralistic but frequently well-written tales in the popular boys' magazines (*Might and Main* or *Rough Riders' Weekly*, which contained "Stories for Boys Who Succeed") to works like Sir Walter Scott's *Ivanhoe* (received as a gift from his Uncle Leicester), Charles Dickens's *Christmas Stories for Children,* and Daniel Defoe's *Robinson Crusoe.* Later on he read Stephen Crane's *The Red Badge of Courage,* Rudyard Kipling's *Jungle Books,* and, over and over again, Mark Twain's *Life on the Mississippi.* From Twain, Ernest caught a bit of diction ("screed" for letter), a style of humor ("me trusty birch bark viacle"; "You have to part your hair in the middle to balance it"); and learned that with the mastery of technique courage can be acquired. In his thirties, Ernest would write his own *Life on the Mississippi* and call it *Death in the Afternoon.* The only friend he had in Oak Park during these years was Harold Sampson, a boy who was a year older and half a head taller. While Ernest was still hesitant, shy, and inarticulate, "Sam," as Ernest called him, was clever and playfully verbose. When Ernest felt the need to act grown-up, he usually tried to emulate Sam's style. And he invited him to Walloon Lake several times.

Of the seven years Ernest attended the Oliver Wendell Holmes School, he stood out from his class in only one. When he was in the seventh grade, in the 1911–12 school year, he was chosen for the lead in the class play (a production of *Robin Hood* just after the Christmas holidays) and to write the class prophecy in the spring. Unfortunately, *Robin Hood* was an ordeal for Ernest. He had to wear a wig, a velvet cap and tunic, and, despite his disproportionately large feet, velvet-covered shoes. Worst of all was the lip and eye makeup made necessary by the weak lighting. For both performances he carried a pitiful stage bow.

The class prophecy, however, was another matter. In this performance Ernest had the audience at his mercy. He himself could choose the victims and control the impression he made. A stridently independent Caroline was to be "President of a South American Woman's Suffrage Republic"; an idealistic Mary would become "a reformer who is trying to free the slaves and the school children"; an all too obvious Gertrude would someday write on "how to tell crows from crocus, fords from flowers, grass from trees."

Despite his demanding schedule, Clarence spent a surprising amount of time with his children during the nine months out of each year when the Hemingways were in Oak Park. In winter he took Ernest and his sisters to the Field Museum of Natural History, housed in the only remaining building of the Columbian Exhibition of 1893. Like his father, Ernest always found something exciting about the carefully assembled prehistoric skeletons, the fine examples of taxidermy, and the collections of semiprecious stones and antique coins. In spring, with warmer weather, there would be an annual trip to the Ringling Brothers Circus at the Chicago Coliseum. Ernest once infuriated the three-legged man by demanding that he show where the third leg was attached. On sunny Saturday afternoons, they all visited the Lincoln Park Zoo. One year Clarence took Ernest and Marcelline to see the state prison at Joliet, Illinois, and warned them that children who did not obey their parents ended up there. But occasionally Clarence took Ernest to the Forest Park Cemetery to visit the Black Angel Monument marking the Haymarket Square anarchists' grave. Ernest would ask to ride the "chute-the-chute" in the amusement park across the street on the way home. Clarence would always say no.

On July 19, 1911, Grace Hemingway, now thirty-nine years old, gave birth in her partitioned bedroom at Windemere to a fourth daughter, Carol. When her other pregnancies had come to term, in Oak Park, Grace had been terrified. There in the Michigan woods, "like an Indian," she said she was terrified again. But this time would be different, Clarence said. He would deliver his own child. After the birth, which went quickly and well, Grace told her husband that just as the baby came she had felt her spirit leave her body. Clarence told her not to be frightened, that it was not unusual and probably only the chloroform.

To their friends in Oak Park, the Hemingways appeared a model family. Clarence was sober and responsible, a devoted father, and a competent and respected physician. Having completed a four-month postgraduate course in obstetrics at New York's Lying-In Hospital in 1908, he expected to become head of that department at the new Oak Park Hospital. Grace, on her part, was an enthusiastic supporter of the local arts, a suffragette, and a disciple, she said, of the practical social Christian, Jane Addams. If all this made her a bit radical for Oak Park society, Grace's preference for the music of Chopin rather than Schönberg was sufficiently reassuring. Besides their personal attainments, Clarence and Grace had five healthy, attractive, and promising children. A sixth, Leicester, would be born on April 1, 1915, when Grace was forty-three.

And yet, despite appearances, there was trouble at 600 North Kenilworth Avenue. What the citizens of Oak Park took for serenity was only a surface calm. In his late thirties, Ernest wrote explicitly of the conflict and hypocrisy he had seen as a child at home:

He was married to a woman with whom he had no more in common than a coyote has with a white female poodle—for he was no wolf, my father. He was sentimental and like all sentimental people he was cruel; often he had too many emotions and when everything was gone to pieces he went in for martyrdom, and he went years before he discovered that the injustices a man suffers in his own home are only a proof of his weakness. There is only one thing to do if a man is married to a woman with whom he has nothing in common, with whom there can be no question of justice but only a gross fact of utter selfishness and hysterical emotionalism. And that is to get rid of her—he might try to whip her first but it would probably be no good. Whoever, in a marriage of that sort, wins the first encounter is in command and having lost, to continue to appeal to reason, to write letters explaining your position, to have it out again before the children—then the inevitable waking up, loser received by victor with some magnanimity, everything that had been told the children cancelled, the home full of love, and mother carried you, darling, over her heart, ah yes and what about his heart and where did it beat and who beats it now and what a hollow sound it makes.

Shortly before his birthday on July 21, during his fourteenth summer at Windemere, Ernest moved out of a three-bedroom cabin Clarence had built for the children just above the family cottage and pitched a sturdy two-man tent a few yards away. He slept on a cot, with a shotgun in a canvas case beneath; he had a kerosene lamp and piles of magazines. With the tent flap open, he could see the windows of his parents' separate bedrooms and the lake through a cluster of tall cedar trees. His sister Madelaine, who could not sleep well at Windemere, often saw Ernest's tent lit up late at night and decided that "he fancied himself a 'lookout' for all of us."

2

A Boy's Will

On September 6, 1913, Ernest and his sister Marcelline entered the freshman class at Oak Park High. The school was yellow brick, four stories
high, with two wings, an assembly hall, and a lunchroom. Costing three
hundred thousand dollars in 1903, it was the showpiece of the community. Before Clarence drove Ernest and Marcelline to school that day in
his black-curtained Model T (he was the high-school board chairman at
the time), he took their photograph on the front lawn. Marcelline was
dressed in a suit of plum-colored wool, ankle-length, with a tight skirt
slit up one side. Ernest wore britches, long black stockings, high shoes,
and a visored cap. His sister, at five feet eight and a half inches, was half
a head taller than he.

Ernest and Marcelline both took the college preparatory course their
freshman year at Oak Park High. Their subjects were Algebra, English,
General Science, and a foreign language. Marcelline chose Spanish. Ernest, because he knew Clarence wished it, signed up for Latin. Because
Grace had found Latin difficult during her own high-school years at the
old Lowell School, she immediately hired a tutor for Ernest.

Of the four subjects he studied in his freshman year, English was Ernest's favorite, in part because it was taught in an extraordinary room.
There were large-storied casement windows with stained glass, high-backed
chairs, a fretted beam ceiling, and a tile floor. On one side of the large
red brick fireplace, a line from the "Prologue" of Chaucer's *Canterbury
Tales* characterizing the "Clerk" ("And gladly wolde he lerne and gladly
teche") was inscribed on a low-relief scroll; on the other side of the fireplace, on a light stone shield, were the Greek words *"Ta Garista"* (sic),
the school's motto, meaning "The Best." The "design" was by John Cal-
vin Hanna, the former principal of Oak Park High. He proudly called it
the "Oxford Room."

Ernest also liked the wide-ranging reading list for Freshman English:
one hundred narrative poems (from the English ballads to *Sohrab and*

Rustum) the Greek myths, and stories from the Bible. The instructor,
Frank Platt, thought Ernest a bit dull (and Ernest thought Mr.
Platt a "friendly fool"), but he was touched by the way Ernest's eyes welled up
at the saddest stories, particularly when they were read aloud.

His first year at Oak Park High, Ernest joined a few activities. One, the
Rifle Club, he did not particularly mind. (Because nearsightedness kept
his scores embarrassingly low, he once punched holes in the bull's-eye
with his pencil before signing the target.) But others—like the Hanna
Club, Junior Achievers meetings where he was obliged to listen to an inspirational talk every week, and the school orchestra in which Grace insisted he play his cello—he found tedious and boring. In 1913–14, the
best part of Ernest's life came after school, with a boy two years older
than he, Lewis Clarahan.

In 1911, Lewis Clarahan had come with his family to Oak Park from
Newton Highlands, Massachusetts. His father was a postal inspector,
transferred from Boston to Chicago. Lewis became a freshman at Oak
Park High the year his family arrived. Ernest met Lewis by a series of
coincidences: Mr. Clarahan bought his house at 822 North Euclid Avenue through Anson Hemingway's real estate office; he chose Clarence for
the family's physician. And, because he had played a lot of tennis in the
East, he built a modest dirt court in the backyard. On warm spring afternoons in 1912, Ernest, who had gotten to know Lewis at Dr. Hemingway's office, began wandering over to 822 North Euclid to play. For a
while Ernest and Lewis shared little more than the tennis. (Though he
played hard, Ernest usually lost.) But Lewis eventually discovered he enjoyed Ernest's initiative and his taste for the outdoors, and Ernest found
Clarahan agreeable and sturdy.

In 1913–14, Ernest and Lewis "palled" together mostly on the outskirts
of Oak Park, on the North and South Prairie and by the Des Plaines
River. Besides the common things—fishing for carp from the North Avenue Bridge, flushing pheasants from the prairie brush, hiking sometimes
all the way to the drainage canal through Summit, and, in the late spring,
swimming nude at a secluded spot on the river—they had two "adventures." In the fall, Ernest insisted the boys investigate a gypsy encamp-
ment on the North Prairie. Yes, he'd heard the gypsies stole children, Ernest said. But he didn't care. The next spring, Ernest and Lewis took a
dozen small pickerel they had caught in the Des Plaines River up to Oak
Park's artesian water supply. Then they caught goldfish from a nearby
stock pond and brought them back in minnow buckets to make feed for
the pickerel. Ernest returned to the reservoir every year he lived in Oak
Park. In the deep water the "goldfish all turned silver or silver and black
mottled."

One incident did frighten the boys. On a hike with Lewis over the North Prairie, Ernest brought along his twenty-gauge shotgun. As they were walking in file, he triggered it accidentally and barely missed his friend.

By spring of 1914, Ernest was as anxious as ever to leave for northern Michigan. Perhaps even more so since Dr. Hemingway had been talking all winter about starting a vegetable farm on the forty acres at Longfield and had hinted Ernest might be put in charge. But in late May came what seemed to Ernest a stroke of bad luck. Marcelline was invited to a formal dance at the local Unitarian church house. Clarence, who always said, in front of his daughters at least, that dancing was the first step to perdition, was firmly against it. But Grace was for it, and Marcelline, who at sixteen had never had a date, was wildly excited when her mother announced she could go. Grace would have Marcelline's dress made of lavender and crème silk, and Ernest, who had grown less than an inch all year, would be his sister's escort.

After their five block walk together from North Kenilworth Avenue to the church house on Lake Street and the passage through the receiving line, Ernest left his sister with some of her friends and stood by the door. Unfortunately, Marcelline's night out was not the success she'd hoped for. Because she had never learned to dance, one partner after another abruptly returned her to her seat and excused himself. After a while, Ernest waited for his sister outside.

The summer of 1914 turned out the best of Ernest's young life. As he had expected, his father could spare only a few weeks from his new duties as head of obstetrics at Oak Park Hospital, and Ernest (at least after the initial planting was done) was in fact put in charge of Longfield Farm. But something else came as a wonderful surprise. Suddenly, in late June, Ernest began to grow. He could feel the difference each day, in a week it could be measured, and in a month everyone noticed the change. From five feet four inches in May, he grew to five-eight by his birthday and to five-ten by September. He also gained weight, going from one hundred ten to one hundred forty pounds.

To make the most of this blessing, Ernest invited his tall, quick-witted friend, Harold Sampson, up for July and August. The two boys lived in Ernest's tent, now on a cleared rise on Longfield Farm. Ernest began each day with a plunge in the cold lake and ended it with a swim off the dock at Windemere. For the first time in his life, he worked hard in the hot weather and loved the satisfying fatigue. By August, there was surplus enough from the farm—potatoes, beans, carrots, and peas—to supply a small hotel and several cottages around the lake. Ernest and Harold had frequent and sometimes bitter quarrels over trivial things that summer, and Ernest, now taller and stronger than Sampson, usually wanted to fight them out.

Grace Hemingway left Windemere in mid-August 1914 (Clarence had to close up the cottage in early September and take care of their three-year-old daughter, Carol, on his own) in order to continue what she had made a family tradition. As her children approached adolescence, Grace, as a sort of secular confirmation, had taken each to Nantucket Island, forty-five miles off the Massachusetts coast, where she and her parents had summered many times in the 1880s.

For Ernest, who had his trip in 1910, the month on Nantucket had been an unhappy experience. He spent most of his time with Grace's cousins, or at the First Congregational Church where Grace sang in the choir (her father had sung there twenty-five years before), or at suffragette meetings in the parlor of Miss Annie Ayres. Even his daily swims were unpleasant, because in the rough green water off Coatue Beach there were horseshoe crabs and slimy green kelp. Ernest's only relief had been the letters he wrote to Clarence (four in the first ten days), in which he fancifully reported sailing in "fine," "rough" weather on the open ocean (Grace would not permit any sailing because two of her cousins had drowned at it years before) and catching thirteen "sea trout" off a jetty. "The four biggest ones," he wrote, "supplied our table of six people."

That August of 1914, it was twelve-year-old Ursula's turn to make the trip.

Shortly after Ernest returned to Oak Park with his father, he got a postcard from Grace. He had news for his mother, too, he said, and answered right away:

Dear Mother—I got your card thanks very much. our train was 2:25 minutes late!! so no school. The program is all changed around lunch at a different time and a lot of other changes. There was a report circulating around that I was drowned and some of my pals thot I was a ghost. May I please have some long pants. Every other boy in our class has them, Lewis Clarahan, Ignatz Smith, and every other little shrimp. My pants are so small every time I wiggle I think they are going to split and I have about 8 or ten inches below me cuffs thusly.

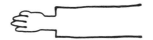

please say I can have them long ones.
                    Your drowned son Ernest Hemingway
                    R.S.V.P. P.D.Q.
PS My shirt buttons all fly off when I take a full breath.

Ernest appeared a different boy when he returned to Oak Park High in September 1914, and it was much more than the addition of long pants. As a freshman he'd been one of the smallest boys in his class. Now, as a sophomore, he was one of the biggest. He still wouldn't wear glasses, but he'd make some new friends.

In general, there were two "types" at Oak Park High from which Ernest could choose. First, there was the "inner circle," students like Gordon Shorney, who participated in almost every school activity except athletics and wore a suit to school almost every day. These boys were particular favorites of the new principal, Marion Ross McDaniel, whose style they imitated. Second, there were the students who, because he wore rubber-soled shoes and appeared noiselessly, called the principal "Gum Shoe McDaniel." These boys played various sports with varying degrees of success and drank a little on weekends in the Mills brothers' barn. They were Lloyd Golder, a German with whom Ernest had a long-running joke about usury; Paul Hasse, who sometimes dated Ernest's sisters; George Madill, whom Ernest, like everyone else, called "Pickles"; Lyman Worthington, a tall blond boy as big as Ernest and a free spirit whose parents were wealthy; Ray Ohlsen, who had the build and face of a lightweight boxer; and Hale Printup, a buck-toothed, boisterous young man who was a male cheerleader and a highly successful seducer of Oak Park girls. Also, Ernest encouraged a quiet, competitive feud with the most popular boy in school, Morris Musselman. When they both tried out for the senior class's production of Clyde Fitch's *Beau Brummell* and Musselman got the lead, Ernest was furious.

At Oak Park High it was compulsory—at least it was thought to be by the people Ernest cared about—for every able-bodied boy to turn out for football. And so, in the fall of 1914, Ernest tried out for the junior varsity. Because he was clumsy and inexperienced, Ernest warmed the bench all that season. But at scrimmages he practiced long and hard. A year later he earned the first-string center position on a team that won seven out of eight games, scored 183 points to its opponents' 53, and was Lightweight Champion of the Suburban League.

Football, Ernest discovered, was good training for life, but not because of the teamwork involved:

> When you played football and had the ball, you were down with your legs spread out and the ball held out in front of you on the ground; you had to listen for the signal, decode it, and make the proper pass. You had to think about it all the time. While your hands were on ball the opposing centre stood in front of you, and when you passed the ball he brought his hand up smash into your face and grabbed you with the other hand under the chin or under your armpit, and tried to pull you forward or shove you

back to make a hole he could go through and break up the play. You
were supposed to charge forward so hard you banged him out of the play
with your body and put you both on the ground. He had all the advantage. It was not what you call fun. When you had the ball he had all the
advantage. The only good thing was that when he had the ball you could
roughhouse him. In this way things evened up and sometimes even a
certain tolerance was achieved.

His senior year, Ernest gave the varsity squad a try. Unfortunately,
team captain Gordon Shepherd ridiculed him for his size-eleven feet, and
in the locker room the boys called him "lead-ass." Although Clarence disliked football and was against Ernest's playing, he said that as a member
of the school board he ought to attend some games. Mindful of his job,
Coach Thistlewaith saw to it that Ernest played enough to earn his varsity letter despite Captain Shepherd's objections.

In his senior year Ernest also earned a place on the varsity swimming
team, but not as a sprint or distance man. Instead, his specialty was the
token event, "plunging": diving from poolside and floating along as far
as possible without coming up for air. He could hold his breath longer
than anyone in the school, Ernest said, and he once ate a banana and
drank a gill of milk underwater to prove it. Besides his sports, Ernest de-
bated in the Burke Club, shot for the Boys' Rifle Club, and played his
cello in the school orchestra. Only Gordon Shorney had a longer list of
"credits."

To his friends and classmates at Oak Park High, Ernest seemed a
happy and successful young man. He was energetic, clever (his picture
line in the 1917 yearbook reads: "None are to be found more clever than
Ernie"), enthusiastic, and always involved. And yet life was not as comfortable for him as it appeared. Lewis Clarahan noticed how, in any
group Ernest always contrived to be the center of attention. He would
tell of incredible adventures in Michigan with the Indians, dare to eat or
drink anything, and take any dare and "laugh it off" when he hurt himself, as he often did. In arguments with classmates, Ernest would back his
opponent up against the wall and deliver a lecture, the main points emphasized with light punches to the other fellow's arm. And he was so at-
tracted to the young ladies at Oak Park High that he opened Marcelline's
mail to "find out what the dames think of me." When Marcelline ridiculed him during their senior year with a nasty little "sonnet"—"He won-
ders if F[rances] Coates is looking his way / He straightens his tie, and
heaves a great sigh / But on how he jumps when sweet FC comes by! /
Nobody likes Ernest, that is straight stuff / And when he writes his stories
we all say Enough"—Ernest had not yet had a date. That past summer he

had written to a friend in Montana what he thought women want in a man and what they do to get it:

Miss Emily Goetsmann   Mailed July 15,
714 Pine Street   8 AM 1916
Helena
Montana
. . . We have been working hard on the farm haying and have got in about 8 tons of alfalfa and clover. I don't know whether you know an awful lot about hay so you are hereby informed that that is quite a lot for a junk of a place like ours.

Marce has been visiting over at Horton's Bay, a summer resort near here. There she met a freshman at Illinois named Horace. The sweet lad's sole interest is Mathematics and he believes fishing is an idle waste of time. Can you conceive such a creature. Yes he wears ambre, tortoise-shell glasses. Yet the more or less same sister of mine spent some time with him and says he is a nice boy. The marvel of the Feminine mind! How are you getting along on the Ranch? I'll bet you are having a stupendous time.

My old Ojibway Pal and woodcraft teacher, Billy Gilbert, was over to see me Sunday. Billy relapsed into a state of matrimony three years ago. The last time I saw him he was a part of the forest, one of the last of the old woods Indians. Now he lives in a cabin and raises vegetables and cuts cord wood.

"My woman," said Billy, "she no like the woods." Do you remember this fragment from Kipling? It seems to apply to Billy (This inserted to clarify.)

> "Through the nights when thou shalt lie
> Prisoner from our mother sky,
>   Hearing us, thy loves, go by
> In the dawn when thou shalt make
>   To the toil thou canst not break
> Heartsick for the Jungle's sake."

The rest of it doesn't matter; that is the part that applies to Bill. You remember that part don't you? It is what the animals say to Mowgli when he leaves the Jungle to be married.

If the lad Horace is what they turn out at Illinois, me for Cornell. Just think how pleased my family would be if they would civilize me and inculcate for Math and a distaste for Fishing.

                                                    Your sincere Friend,
                                                    Ernest Hemingway

Then, too, there was an uncommon persistence (at least for a seventeen-year-old) in Ernest's revenge. A few weeks after the varsity football season ended, Ernest noticed an advertisement in one of the Chicago papers for boxing lessons at a local gym. Well-known boxers—Sammy Langford, Jack

Blackburn, Harry Greb—were named as instructors. The course would run ten Saturdays. The fee was to be paid in advance. Ernest was surprised that Clarence willingly gave him the money to cover both the carfare and the fee.

As things turned out, the boxing lessons Ernest signed up for were actually a confidence game. The student would pay his tuition, arrive for his first lesson, and be knocked out. Naturally, he would not return. Ernest, however, although he too was knocked out in his first lesson (by a local professional called "Young A'Hearn"), arrived the following Saturday right on time. The instructor was reluctant to continue the course, and so Ernest learned his boxing the hard way. One sparring partner, Morty Hellnick, hit him in the pit of the stomach after the bell, and Ernest was sick for a week. The second time they boxed, he fouled Ernest deliberately, and "one ball swelled up nearly as big as a fist." But by the end of the course, Ernest had mastered a few rudimentary skills and had discovered how hard he could hit with his right hand.

For Christmas, 1917, Ernest got a pair of brown leather boxing gloves from Clarence, and soon he was shadow boxing all over the house. His favorite place was in front of the full-length mirror on the landing just below his parents' bedroom. At one time or another that spring, Ernest invited every member of the football team up for an afternoon of boxing in Grace's music room. He beat them all, some quite severely. Grace, who knew what was going on and didn't disapprove, eventually put a stop to these bouts because, as she quipped, " 'the house' objected [to] mopping up the blood." But it was no laughing matter to Ernest; he even knocked out his old friend, Lewis Clarahan.

In his junior year at Oak Park High, Ernest enrolled in Journalism and in a writing course built around the short story. Both were taught by the best teacher in the school, Miss Fannie Biggs.

When Ernest met Fannie Biggs, she was thirty years old, tall, sharp-faced, with thick glasses on rimless gold frames. Unlike the rest of the Oak Park faculty, who dressed in the "prescribed fashion," Miss Biggs wore bright-colored sashes around her waist, opened the neck of her dresses, and kept a very loose topknot in her hair. Walking down the long locker-lined corridors, she had a swinging and, some thought, masculine gait.

Miss Biggs conducted her Journalism course as though the classroom were a newspaper office. A rotating student editor gave out the daily assignments, and there were news stories, features, sports, columns, and advertising. Miss Biggs's criteria for a good article were: "Tell your whole story in the first paragraph; develop details in relation to their importance; leave the least important things till the end. The editor may have to cut your stuff." In addition, she gave exercises in expanding one-sentence news items to fill a column. Possessed of a sharp tongue but a fair and perceptive critic, Fannie Biggs saw to it that her best students always went on to produce, as Ernest and Marcelline did, the high-school weekly *Trapeze*.

Ernest's first article appeared in the *Trapeze* on January 20, 1916, midway through his junior year. Entitled "Concert A Success," it reported on a performance the Chicago Symphony Orchestra had given in Oak Park. Ernest told what was played: "Concerto In G-Major" by Bach, Brahms's "Symphony No. 2 D-Major," and "The Siegfried Idyl" by Wagner. Thanks to the help Grace gave him, he included "professional"-sounding phrases: "very brilliantly played," "very syncopated and spirited," "excellent staccato work," "smoothly flowing motif."

In his next five articles, Ernest covered meetings of the Hanna Club (before which Clarence once did his best to give a rousing speech about adolescent sexuality, called "hygiene" at the time), the doings of the Athletic Association, varsity sports, and the Burke Club Junior Debates, an assignment he felt he'd been set up for. Reporting the words of a "prominent Chicago jurist" who had spoken to club members, Ernest had to write:

> There is also something gratifying in seeing a huge, athletic fellow, who usually emphasizes his remarks by poking his fist under his opponent's nose, be squelched, crushed, and verbally sat upon by a little ninety-eight-pound lad who had hitherto been in abject awe of the rough person with the large mouth.

The pieces with which Ernest distinguished himself on the *Trapeze* staff and by which he made a name for himself at Oak Park High were not, however, his straight reporting but rather his imitations of the popular *Chicago Tribune* journalist—humorist, Ring Lardner. Of the five articles he wrote in the Ring Lardner style—the conceit that the semiliterate are sincere and express themselves humorously—the last is the best. It appeared on May 4, 1916, and took the form of a "letter" to Marcelline:

Ring Lardner Returns

Dear Marce:—They tell me subscriptions and advertising has both fell off something immense since I writ one of these letters last and so as I ain't very busy I might as well try and put some of what Mussy [Morris Musselman] calls good old JAZZ into the publication again.

But do not think I am stuck on myself because that is not so as you must of knew, living right in the same house with me all these years. Is it not so, Marcelline?

Well, there is not much to tell about now because there is not much doing only the Prom and C. Bailey Savage ast me to write on it so I won't. But C. Bailey had charge of the lights and done it in a good manner. (advt.)

Say, Marcelline, did you know that there is 5 pairs of brothers and sisters in school and invariabsolutely it is a strange coincidence that the sister is good looking and the brother is not? Schwabs, Shepherds, Condrons and Krafts and Hemingways. Is it not most peculiar that except in one family the sister is an awful lot better looking than the brother. But we are too modest to say which family is the exception. Huh? Marce?

Now don't get sore and cut that out of the paper because you ain't got no proof I meant our family, and you know what "Blight" Wilcoxen says, "they can't can you if they ain't got nothing on you. . . ."

In her Journalism course, Fannie Biggs emphasized such techniques as how to arrest the reader's attention, how to convey information clearly and quickly, and how to edit. But in her writing course the demands were greater. The clichés and stereotypes that could give journalism a casual and familiar tone now were to be abjured. Posing and mannerisms would not be tolerated, and sentimentality would be mocked. How pleasant it was for Ernest to hear his stories (usually based on incidents he said he'd heard about from the Indians at the bark peelers' camp or from the old lumberjacks who hung around saloons in Boyne City) read aloud in class, and praised in detail, and called an ideal the other students, including Marcelline, should aim for.

Of the three stories he published in the *Tabula*, Oak Park High's literary magazine, Ernest's favorite was "Judgment of Manitou." It rendered friendship betrayed and the ironies of justice of the chief Indian god.

As the story begins, a trapper, Dick Haywood, in northern Michigan, is about to push off in forty-below weather to Loon River to check his and his partner Pierre's trap line. Dick, "as do travellers of the 'silent places,' " talks to himself. He speaks of the hostility of his friend Pierre: "Wonder why Pierre is so grouchy just because he lost that money. Bet he just misplaced it somewhere." But Pierre, convinced that Dick has stolen the money, has set a trap for his friend. "De tief will tink it a blame sight

cooler when he's swingin' by one leg in the air like Wah-boy, the rabbit;
he would steal my money, would he!" Pierre, however, has made a terrible
mistake.

> Back in the cabin Pierre, as he lay in his bunk, was awakened by a gnaw-
> ing sound overhead, and idly looking up at the rafter he saw a red squirrel
> busily gnawing away at the leather of his lost wallet. He thought of the
> trap he had set for Dick, and springing from his bunk he seized his rifle,
> and coatless and gloveless he ran madly out along the trail. After a gasp-
> ing, breathless, choking run he came upon the spruce grove. Two ravens
> left off picking at the shapeless something that had once been Dick Hay-
> wood, and flapped lazily into a neighboring spruce. All over the bloody
> snow were the tracks of My-in-gau, the wolf.
> As he took a step forward, Pierre felt the clanking grip of the toother
> bear trap that Dick had come to tend close on his feet. He fell forward,
> and as he lay on the snow he said, "It is the judgment of Manitou; I will
> save My-in-gau, the wolf, the trouble." And he reached for the rifle.

Ernest also worked hard during his junior year on another piece, a play
he could never bring to final draft. It was based on the Longfellow Festi-
val's presentation of *Hiawatha,* performed annually at Round Lake, near
Petoskey, by Indians who traveled two hundred miles south from Canada
to honor the poet.

"No Worst Than a Bad Cold" is, according to the introduction, an
"Indian Passion Play" given at the town of "Wa ga ga wug in Michigan."
The scene, "which is the only artificial part of the stage" (the rest being
the shore of the lake) is the interior of a tall rock (canvas on a wood
frame). Inside, there is a "big wind turned by hand and a large wooden
beaver." The edge of the rock is over water, and in the back of the scene
there is a lake. Behind the lake is a grandstand with spectators. As the
curtain rises, a voice begins: "By the shores of Gitchy Goomie—By the
shining big sea water—." Richard Boulton, aged sixteen, one of the two
characters in the play, sits astride the wooden beaver. He shakes his head
at someone outside the entrance to the rock, saying, "uh uh No No
not now."

A dialogue then ensues between Boulton and the other character in the
play, an Indian named Albert but called Paw Paw Keewis throughout.
Paw Paw begins by claiming, "Red Man always bitched. Redman on the
bum. Redman don't last long." Boulton asks what's wrong, and Paw Paw
replies, "God damn eskimo died, catch cold. Died just now goddam es-
quimo." It seems that Paw Paw had paid three hundred dollars for the
Eskimo's performance, and now there was no one to play the role. (At
three, Ernest's favorite doll was a "white eskimo" that Clarence had given
him for his fifth birthday at Walloon Lake.)

Then Paw Paw mentions that there is a little girl outside, apparently the voice off-stage to which Dick had earlier responded. Paw Paw asks Dick, "What you do with her?" When Dick says, "Nothing," Paw Paw calls him a "damned fool." Dick protests, "She's a good kid," and maintains that he doesn't want to "get mixed up with her." Paw Paw answers, "Ain't any mixed up with Indians. Fuck um say goodbye, you never seen em again." Still Dick Boulton refuses to "take" the girl, and so Paw Paw says he'll "take her myself." "Like hell you will," Dick says.

Finally, Paw Paw, sensing that Dick is getting angry at him, offers the boy a drink from a pint bottle the Indian takes from his buckskin shirt. "Old Grand-dad-Dollar whisky. Great Spirit all right. Only spirit I ever seen. Great Spirit of the Red Man." Dick has some and tells Paw Paw, "It's damn good." Paw Paw drinks again and says, "Great Spirit all right. Change wooden beaver into real thing. Makes the water run up hill. ~~Brings back all the trees they cut down.~~ [Crossed out by Ernest.] Makes the red man lie down on the railroad track—only train that take him to the happy hunting grounds—Bring back the wild pigeon—if you wake up you find he shit in your mouth in the morning." Dick remarks that he didn't know Indians talked so much, and Paw Paw replies, "Listen, Indians talk alone to themselves all right—Finally every Indian live alone and talk to himself—when he hear enough from himself he go lay down on the railroad *track*."

After they both drink again, Paw Paw encourages Dick to "take" the little Indian girl, and Dick agrees. Then Paw Paw suggests that Dick take the bottle along, but Dick says, "I don't want any bottle." Paw Paw insists, "Just a little bit. That won't hurt you any. That's a good thing for a young man. For me no." Finally, when Paw Paw is about to leave—to go play the "old moccasin game" (masturbation), Dick commiserates with him about the Eskimo. "That's all right," Keewis says. "He wasn't no good. Nobody believed he was a eskimo anyway. All we do was lose money on him."

On the morning of June 13, 1917, graduation day, Ernest and Marcelline stood on the front lawn, and Clarence, as he had four years earlier, took their picture. Marcelline wore a cotton summer dress with long sleeves, a satin bodice, and satin trim. Ernest had on a dark double-breasted jacket and pants that reached halfway down his high-buttoned shoes. While the picture was snapped, Marcelline, her hair fashionably bobbed, smiled at Ernest, who was now more than three inches taller than she. At Grace's insistence they had gone to the senior prom together a few nights before.

During the past winter, while Ernest wrote for the Oak Park High *Trapeze,* he had read *Stories for Boys* by the popular American writer and former war correspondent Richard Harding Davis. The first and longest story in the book was called "The Reporter Who Made Himself King." Davis wrote that his young reporter would crowd "the experiences of the lifetime of the ordinary young business man, doctor, or lawyer, or man about town, into three short years" and learn "to think and act quickly, to be patient and unmoved when everyone else has lost his head, actually or figuratively speaking; to write as fast as another man can talk, and to be able to talk with authority on matters of which other men do not venture even to think until they have read what he has written with a copy-boy at his elbow on the night previous." The young reporter, Albert Gordon, dreams of eventually becoming a war correspondent or a novelist. When Clarence said that Uncle Tyler Hemingway, now living in Kansas City, had some influence at the *Kansas City Star,* Ernest asked that it be used on his behalf. He was pleased when in several days Tyler reported that there was indeed a place for him at the *Star* in October. That meant another summer in Michigan before his "future" got under way.

During the summer of 1917, Ernest spent more time each day working on Longfield Farm than ever before. There was the old tenant farmhouse to be moved off the property, the ice shed to be built and stocked with sawdust for the coming winter's supply, twenty acres of hay to be cut and cured, and the usual tasks in the orchard and the vegetable garden. This year, too, Clarence had hired a rodent-jawed farmer named Warren Sumner, and he always left it up to Ernest to tell Sumner what to do.

After two summers of living in a tent on Longfield Farm, Ernest now began eating his suppers and sleeping at an inn four miles over the ridge in the little town of Horton Bay. The inn, called Pinehurst, was locally famous for its chicken dinners, and Ernest had spent many Sunday afternoons there with his parents over the years. The proprietor and chef was Liz Dilworth, wife of the local blacksmith, Jim.

Like Grace Hemingway, with whom she eventually took up painting, Liz Dilworth was an enthusiast for the arts. She was a regular at lectures, concerts, and courses in "self-betterment" held each summer at an exclusive settlement near Petoskey called Bay View. Her husband Jim, who looked more like a "drummer" with his narrow shoulders and broad handlebar mustache, would often tease Liz about her "cultural interests," and privately he called her friends "change-of-lifers." But since Liz never proselytized and Jim knew that "culture" made her happy, he always let her go to her "events."

Ernest spent most of his evenings the summer of 1917 sitting in the parlor at Pinehurst reading two-day-old newspapers (*The Chicago Tribune, Oak Leaves*) that Clarence sent him or writing letters on the screened-in porch. In a letter to Grace that summer, Ernest joked, "Please don't burn any papers in my room or throw away anything you don't like the looks of and I will do the same for you." In a letter to his former teacher and friend at Oak Park High, Ernest showed off his writing skill:

> Dear Miss Biggs—,
> It is so lonesome up here that if I should see J. Carl Urbaur I would fall on his neck and loan him half a buck instantaneously! If it wasn't for the mosquitos and the fish I would go absolutely bats. Mosquitos are very companionable and I am trying to get a full chorus. I have captured a soprano, two basses, a baritone, and an alto, and if a good tenor can be secured there will be complete harmony in the tent. The fish are running big. Saturday a five pound rainbow succumbed to the back to the land movement. Before making the journey, however, he raised quite a fuss. It was 11:50 p.m. and I was alone and the moon forgot to shine, you oughta been there. But it was a good thing you weren't because all the time I had him on I was just wishing there was somebody there to swear at. . . .

But Fannie Biggs had been much more affected by two poems Ernest had written for her the year before: the first is a fishing idyll, the second a comment on the role of the artist.

The Day

I
You may trout fish all the summer,
You may take the gang of bass
You may catch the muskallonge or sullen pike
But the time you'll remember
When you've put away your rods
The time that you'll remember is The Day.

II
When you started before daybreak,
Mist a-rising from the water;
When your oar strokes sped the row boat past the reeds
When the line trailed out behind you
Then a splash! The bass broke water
He had struck it right beside you
Tell me brother
Was not that The Day?

III
When the three of you departed
To fly-fish a brand new trout stream
Wading three abreast against the icy flow
And when Al hooked a big one
And Jo one that was larger
And you snagged to a mighty one
And there was not a net among you
Tell me brother
Wasn't that The Day?

IV
When the ice has gripped its rivers
And the lakes are frozen fast
And we're living in the city, trying to earn three squares
    a day
And we're getting kind of grumpy
And the world looks pretty glum
When you get in this condition
And you wish that you were fishin
Stop a minute, Brother Sportsman
Just remember of The Day.

The Stoker

Far down in the sweltering guts of the ship
    The stoker swings his scoop
Where the jerking hands of the steam gauge drive
And muscles and tendons and sinews rive;
While it's hotter than hell to a man alive,
    He toils in his sweltering coop.

He is baking and sweating his life away
    In that blasting roar of heat;
But he's fighting a battle with wind and tide,
All to the end that you may ride;
And through it all he is living beside;
    He can work and sleep and eat.

Although Ernest stayed close to Horton Bay during the week, on weekends he frequently packed up his gear and hiked off into the open country between the cove of Little Traverse Bay and Indian River. Travel was
hard in this region; the old logging roads were sometimes so overgrown
he had to stoop to avoid hitting branches. But finally, after crossing a
slashing strewn with dead gray trees rotting amid fireweed and ragweed,
Ernest would come to a stand of virgin forest. The trees, mostly hemlocks, were fifty feet high before their branches, and they rustled in the

wind when it was calm on the forest floor. There was no underbrush here, only brown springy matting, cool underfoot. There were very old Indian fire stones in this forest, and, when Ernest went in far enough, an open meadow sloped to where white birch trees grew along a stream.

Ernest usually set up his camp on the edge of the forest just back from where the meadow met the line of trees. In the clear, fast water of the stream he would catch lively pan-sized brook trout and, in the forest behind him, shoot partridge and ruffed grouse. Ernest carried bacon and cornmeal for the trout, and he fried them quickly, basting and turning them often. When they were done, the trout were crisp outside and cooked well and very tender inside, and Ernest ate them slowly with rye bread dipped in the bacon fat and drank tea with condensed milk. The birds, however, were something to be cleaned and washed in the stream and, with their feathers smoothed, wrapped in ferns, put in a flour sack, and taken to Windemere or to Liz Dilworth's so she could cook them up in her famous fried-chicken style.

On the trips he made alone into open country, the time before sleep on his browse bed of cut hemlock and balsam bows was long enough for Ernest to recall his eighteen summers in Upper Michigan. There was the Indian who gave him a canoe paddle made of ashwood when he was a little boy. That Indian lived alone in a shack on the shore near Windemere, and he drank plenty of painkiller and walked through the woods at night. Coming home from a fourth of July drunk in Petoskey one year, he committed suicide by sleeping on the tracks of the *Pere Marquette*.

Then there were Nick Boulton and Billy Tabashaw, two Indian sawyers. Boulton, who some of the local whites believed was a half-breed, lived with an Indian squaw named Annie and had two children, Eddy and Prudence. One night in town, Boulton drank whiskey with opium and, back at his shack, lay delirious half under the bed. Summoned by neighbor Joe Bacon, Clarence Hemingway had pumped Boulton's stomach out. But the next night Boulton went into Charlevoix, drank the same mixture, and died.

Most of all Ernest remembered the young Indian girls, some hardly into their teens, with whom he discovered the pleasures of adolescent sex. Years later he created a composite of these experiences in a short story and called the girl Trudy, after Prudence, Nick Boulton's daughter:

Could you say she did first what no one has ever done better and mention plump brown legs, flat belly, high little breasts, well holding arms, quick searching tongue, the flat eyes, the good taste of mouth, then uncomfortably, tightly, sweetly, moistly, lovely, tightly, achingly, fully, finally, unendingly, never-endingly, never-too-endingly, suddenly ended, the great bird flown like an owl with the twilight, only in daylight in the woods and hemlock needles stuck against your belly.

Ernest loved only one other girl during those early years in Michigan— his sister Ursula. She had high cheekbones, sparkling brown eyes, and a broad mouth with full lips. Her hair was golden brown, like grain burned in the sun. At night, diving nude off the dock at Windemere, she seemed to him as much a part of the forest as any Indian girl. Once, when Ernest shot a blue heron at the "Crakin" on Mud Lake, Ursula bloodied her hands rowing to tell him "turd-faced Evans," the game warden, was at Windemere harassing Grace.

The impressions life "up North" left with Ernest were vivid and poignant, and he made of them the best short stories he would write. They were what he later called "country": the sweetish smell of Indians and their silent walk, the water-soaked logs called dead heads which broke from logging booms and ended up half-buried on Windemere's beach, the place under the birch log where he always found fishing worms because he always rolled the log back again, the can of Copenhagen snuff he carried his best bait in, the heavy feel of trout on his line, the thrill of "horsing them out" with a willow pole, the sandy bottom of narrow streams against the dark forest floor, the tiny white mushrooms growing up through the pine-needle droppings on the forest floor, a fish hawk circling on a cloudy day, the gray batter of buckwheat cakes bubbling and sizzling over the campfire griddle, the smell of Log Cabin syrup poured from a tin chimney, the white morning fog on the lake, the sound of oars in the distance, his Mackinaw coat, the glow of campfire coals brightening in the wind.

While Ernest spent his time working at Longfield Farm, fishing for trout, or camping in his secret places, Marcelline spent a month of her summer over at Bay View with what she felt was a "wonderful crowd." They were all wealthy college students and resorters who were or had once been professionally involved in the arts. Marcelline played the violin in the Bay View Orchestra (she was thrilled to sit beside a member of the Chicago Symphony Orchestra), and she stayed with the manager of the Bay View Chautauqua that year, Trumbull White. Mr. White was the recently retired editor of *Everybody's Magazine*.

In late August, at Grace's urging, Marcelline invited all her new friends to Windemere for a "pot-luck" picnic. Many came, including Sterling Sanford, a senior at the University of Michigan and Marcelline's future husband. Marcelline decided she would bake her specialty, a "mahogany cake," for the affair. Ernest, who had been recruited to play the host in Clarence's absence, volunteered to take the family's open launch, the *Carol*, to pick up some of his sister's guests at Walloon Village when they arrived by train from Petoskey. On the trip back to Windemere, Ernest kept the bow into the wind and the throttle wide open. The *Carol* was no speedboat, but when Marcelline's guests arrived they looked as if they had been caught in the rain.

During the party that followed, Ernest asked Trumbull White how an unknown could quickly break into print. White told him that he must learn to write by writing and that the best subjects would come from his own experience, two things Ernest had known since his freshman year in Mr. Platt's class at Oak Park High.

Ernest did not return to Oak Park with the rest of his family the first week of September 1917. (Grace had left early with Marcelline, who was about to begin her studies at the Oberlin College Conservatory.) Instead, he fished off the point in Lake Charlevoix at Horton Bay and caught a "mess of perch," none under a quarter-pound. One catch, a seven-pound nine-ounce rainbow, was put on exhibition at Bump and MacCabe's hardware store and won five dollars' worth of fishing tackle for Ernest.

Besides his fishing, Ernest picked apples and dug potatoes, which he sent south in barrels and sacks from Petoskey on the "PM or the GR and I" and with Clarence worried about "three straight nights of frost." Ernest also worried a lot that fall about his chronically sore throat. It had been sensitive since, at five years old, he'd punctured it with a stick. This time Ernest believed he had gotten sick from pulling carrots in stormy fall weather windy enough to put whitecaps on Walloon Lake and cold enough for freezing rain. Ernest was especially afraid because Grace had told him she had once gone blind from a disease that began with a sore throat.

> Petoskey 5:00 P.M.
> Tuesday [undated] 1917

Dear Dad:

 . . . Had a light attack of tonsillitis Thursday and Friday but gargled alcohol and water and peroxide and it cleared up in the throat. I was working all the time shoveling gravel and helping build the road for Wes [Dilworth]. Cutting brush Saturday felt alright but (pain is best helped by working) kept on working with a pretty bad headache. Sunday I felt good but Monday morning had awful headache on top of head in front. (Don't get excited.) Went to bed Monday and head bad all night. Today my head was better, and I came into Petoskey to see Doc Witter. He said that the toxin from the tonsillitis had given me the headache and that my pulse was 120 but no fever. He said my heart was going a lot faster than it ought to and a trifle irregular and gave me some stuff for my headaches

and some gargle for tonsils. He said to take it easy and loaf around for
three or four days, and I would be alright. I was very weak and the pounding in my head was kind of getting my goat, but I will be alright now. I
have written you everything there is so you won't be worried. . . .

Love to all,
Ernie

Ernest kept mostly to himself the summer of 1917, though he did draw
and clean twenty-six spring chickens for a Red Cross benefit Liz Dilworth
ran). But now and then he would walk up the sandy road from Pinehurst,
turn onto the main road through Horton Bay for half a mile, and walk
past the big elm trees and the last cluster of R.F.D. mailboxes at the crossroads. On Pincherry Road through the orchard toward the top of the hill
was the old Stroud cottage with its bare porch, a garage in the back, a
chicken coop, and a second growth of timber "like a hedge against the
woods behind." Two young "summer" people lived in the Stroud cottage.
Bill and Kate Smith.

Bill Smith and his sister Kate lived out on Pincherry Road with their
aunt, Mrs. Joseph Charles. She was the wife of a prominent St. Louis oculist and had raised them both since the death of their mother from tuberculosis in 1899. Mrs. Charles and her husband were considered gentry by
the residents of Horton Bay. When they arrived by train from Chicago
each June, they'd be taken to their cottage by the finest auto in town—
Lester Fox's brass-trimmed Ford.

At twenty-one, Bill Smith was as tall as Ernest but thin, with straight
sandy hair and narrow shoulders. Although a city boy, he walked on his
heels like a farmer. He read widely, considered himself "sophisticated,"
and believed wit meant polysyllabic verbosity.

Kate Smith, at twenty-five, was a bold, emancipated young woman, with
high cheekbones, fine white skin, and "eyes so green they almost made you
think she could see in the dark." Mrs. Charles, who used to shock the
"porch contingent" at the general store by the way she handled her buggy
and whip, was thought to be a fine-looking woman. But Kate reminded
men of Anna Held, the British actress whose likeness was embossed on
cigar-box lids. Kate was dating a friend of Ernest's from Petoskey named
Carl Edgar. He was twenty-eight years old, and during the winter months
he worked in Kansas City for the California Oil Burner Company. Carl
loved Kate very much and wanted to marry her. But she was cool toward
him and, Bill thought, very fond of Ernest.

The last two weeks of September, Ernest spent his days at Longfield
Farm harvesting the large potato crop and picking apples and his nights
at Pinehurst resting a sore back and feet cramped from hours on the lad-

der. Every few days, after supper, he would write a postcard in telegraphic style reporting his progress to Clarence back in Oak Park and mail it with stamps his father had sent. When Clarence asked, "Do you get lonesome for Sunny and 'Dess'?" Ernest wrote, "Sure I miss Sunny and the Biphouse [Leicester] and all the rest of you. But haven't had any home sickness." Ernest always signed himself "EMH" in imitation of the signature Clarence used under "Daddy" or "your old Dad."

On September 25, Ernest sent down from Charlevoix the final shipment of farm produce: three barrels of apples (one crab, one fall, and one winter) and ninety bushels of potatoes (he insisted that the bill-of-lading estimate of sixty-two was ridiculously low). Then, feeling "good and peppy" in the clear, brisk fall weather, Ernest left for home from the Petoskey station, Wednesday night, October 4, 1917.

In the days between his arrival at Oak Park and his departure for Kansas City, Ernest said goodbye to those few high-school friends who were not at college, visited a great-uncle (Julius Hall, a heavy-drinking "remittance man"), and, as hurriedly as he had intended, made the necessary preparations for his trip. Then, on the morning of October 15, 1917, he and Clarence loaded the recently reconditioned Model T with luggage and drove to the LaSalle Street Station in downtown Chicago. Grace, who had seen Marcelline off to Oberlin a few weeks earlier, decided to stay at home.

For some time Dr. Hemingway and Ernest stood quietly on the station platform beside the Kansas City train. Then, just before the conductor picked up the box Ernest would step up on to reach the steps of the day coach, Clarence kissed his son and said, "May the Lord watch between me and thee while we are apart the one from the other." It was the same application of the lines from *Genesis* 31 (with these words Laban is actually warning Jacob against betrayal) Grace herself usually made at farewells.

⌘ 3 ⌘
The Intern in Kansas City

In 1917, more than three hundred thousand people lived in Kansas City, Missouri. There were well-lighted, broad cobblestone streets, "modern" office buildings, some twelve stories high with awning windows, tall four-faced public clocks on most downtown streets, broad high-curbed sidewalks, and ubiquitous streetcars with bold advertisements for clothing, cigarettes, automobiles, pharmaceuticals, and shoes. Besides the famous stockyards on the Missouri River, which had handled the great Texas herds of the 1880s, Kansas City had a growing industrial district, with three flour mills and the largest automobile factory outside Detroit. In the four corners of the city there were neighborhoods of Italian, Irish, Mexican, and German immigrants. A fifth of the population was black.

Kansas City in the early 1900s was run by entrepreneurs like Arthur E. Stillwell, whose railroad to the Gulf of Mexico had "saved the West" from ruinous shipping prices to East Coast ports, and William Rockhill Nelson, a crusading progressive who was a friend of Theodore Roosevelt and Woodrow Wilson and had founded the *Kansas City Star*. Like most western boomtowns (the city had grown from the town of Kansas, population twenty-five hundred in 1850), Kansas City had its share of crooked politicians, prostitutes (12th Street was known as Woodrow Wilson Avenue—where one could get "a piece at any price"—and "Blossom House" flourished on Union Avenue), dope peddling (mostly marijuana and heroin from Mexico), and frequent epidemics of contagious diseases (in the fall of 1917 it was smallpox). The new Union Station in downtown Kansas City had walls like an armory and arched windows like a church. Ernest's train from Chicago arrived there late in the afternoon, October 15, 1917.

Uncle Tyler Hemingway, with his square-shouldered carriage and the handkerchief he always wore in his jacket pocket, met Ernest at the station. They drove down Main Street to Fifth, past the walls of the Union Cemetery, to Warwick Boulevard, number 3629. That night in the small pink dining room of Tyler's three-story rose-colored Victorian house, Ernest was especially pleased with the warm welcome he received from his Aunt Arabella. She was the daughter of the highly successful lumber dealer, J. B. White, whose business Tyler believed he was being groomed for. Ernest admired the way Arabella made pleasant conversation, and, with her plump shoulders and her plump round chin, he thought her quite beautiful, too.

To Ernest, Kansas City was just what he expected it to be—"a fine, clean Western town." At the end of this first day on his own, he could recall only one real disappointment. When the train had crossed the Mississippi River over a long bridge at Hannibal, Missouri, there were desolate hills on the far side and on the near side a flat mudbank. The river moved "like a solid shifting lake, swirling a little where the abutment of the bridge jutted out." Ernest had expected bluffs for the Mississippi shore.

The next morning, as Tyler drove Ernest back downtown, the stench of a great stockyard fire put out the day before still hung over the city. But the weather was clear and bright with the temperature in the mid-fifties. It was just the kind of day Ernest liked. At Nineteenth Street, a three-story building of red brick stretched almost a city block from Grand Avenue to Magee Street. It had two identical wings, with a short tower over the rift. There were bushes and trees and a large fountain at the entrance. To Ernest everything looked fresh and well cared for. It was the *Kansas City Star*. On the elevator ride up to the second floor, Uncle Tyler explained that many Kansans considered this new building (the *Star* had operated at Eighth and Main streets until 1911) a monument to the paper's founder, William Rockhill Nelson. Ernest, on his part, thought it strange the building faced due south, directly away from the center of town.

The city room of the *Kansas City Star* was big and bright and noisy. There were no partitions, and rows of desks ran out to the walls. Amid the sounds of typewriters and ringing phones, white-shirted copy boys scurried about in the smoky air. At the city desk in the center of the room sat the man Ernest was there to see, editor George Longan. Ernest carried the letter of introduction his uncle had typed up the night before in the pocket of his new brown suit.

Because arrangements for the job had already been made by Tyler's friend Harry Haskell, the interview between Ernest and Longan was brief. Longan told Ernest that he'd be working the day shift from eight to five, six days a week with Sundays off. Ernest's salary would be fifteen dollars a week, and he would start the next day.

When Ernest got to work Wednesday morning, October 17, he reported to the assistant editor, C. G. "Pete" Wellington. Wellington, a small, pale man with a poker face, explained to Ernest that the *Star* had a policy of giving each reporter a thirty-day trial period and that there were no exceptions. Then he gave Ernest several galleys clipped together, on which were printed "rules" for good writing the paper's publisher had laid down years before. The clipped galleys were called the *Star*'s "style sheet." Wellington told Ernest to study these rules; he must abide by them in his work. All in all, the style sheet contained little Ernest had not heard at Oak Park High and seen examples of in the writing of Richard Harding Davis: "Use short sentences. Use short first paragraphs. Use vigorous Enlish. Be positive, not negative." But, because it was clear that Wellington himself had made emendations in the details of the text and that he was proud of his work, Ernest listened attentively. Finally, Pete Wellington assigned Ernest to the same desk and typewriter the movie editor used. Would he have to share? Ernest asked. No, Wellington said, the movie editor only worked nights. For the rest of his first day at the *Star,* Ernest answered calls on two rows of telephones of different lines—the "Home" and the "Bell." It was "Mr. Hemingway, Bell Five" and "Mr. Hemingway, Home One."

That night Ernest wrote home. Clarence noted on the envelope that this was the first letter received from Ernest in Kansas City. Ernest claimed it was the second:

Kansas City   October 17, 1917
Wednesday

Dear Folks: I suppose you have got my first letter by now. I had a good trip and got in O.K. Carl Edgar met me the first evening I was here and I am sure glad he is here. He sends his love to all the kids. Aunt Arabell wants me to stay here until the end of the week. Today I had three stories in the star [sic]. It seems like a pretty good paper. They have a very big plant. I start work at 8:00 a.m. and quit at 5:00 p.m. and have the Sabbath off. So far I have all I spent [sic]. Carl and I are going to try and get rooms together as we are both alone here. All the relatives send you their kind regards.

With Love,
Ernie

In a postscript to this letter, Ernest announced that he was moving from his Uncle Tyler's to a boarding house at 3733 Warwick Avenue, two

blocks down the road. It was "very disciplined, very exclusive." Many junior staffers at the *Star* stayed there and said it was just like home.

During Ernest's first months in Kansas City—his "trial" at the *Star*—he
had four bases: the *Star* itself, where he punched in at eight in the morning and picked up his copy of the day's assignment sheet; the Union Station, where he got tips from the railroad police when the famous and the
infamous came to town; the General Hospital, where he got reports on
accidents and violent crimes; his Warwick Street boarding house, a twelve-
block ride south from the *Star* on the Prospect Street streetcar line. Since
the *Star's* management was committed to exposing the hospital administration and the Board of Health for misuse of public funds, Ernest was
ordered to watch for "unsavory conditions." He called his beat the "short
stop run" because of the ground to be covered and the quickness required.

As soon as Ernest became familiar with his "territory," he voluntarily
expanded it, particularly on the west arm from Union Station to the
stockyards and the Missouri River. There, on Wyoming Street and Bellevue and Summit avenues, he covered pool halls, dance halls, and roller-
skating rinks, where prostitutes did business and dope peddling was rampant. Farther north, in the Kansas City railyards, he learned something of
the life of the railroad "bums." Ernest developed a special sympathy for
the prostitutes, who believed semen was a specific against tuberculosis,
and an ear for the patois of railroad-yard homosexuality: "slash is fine but
one eye for mine" and "five-fingered sex with your old mother." Nevertheless, he liked it that his appearance and manner and his press card gained
him admittance to St. Luke's (in the suburbs at Main Street and Forty-
third), Kansas City's hospital for the rich. On nights when Ernest was too
busy or too tired to make it back to Warwick Avenue for supper and bed,
he would stay at the Hotel Muehlebach at Baltimore and Twelfth Street.
It was a second-class hotel where even the regular reporters got only a
seedy room. Ernest slept on bath towels in the press-room tub.

On November 18, 1917, Ernest covered a fire in a barn next-door to his
Uncle Tyler's house. He helped the firemen break down the door of the
barn and carry a hose up onto the roof. In the process, he got his new
brown suit burned full of holes. When he added fifteen dollars to his expense account, Pete Wellington turned him down. But Wellington liked
Ernest's enthusiasm ("He seemed always to want to be where the action
was") and his dedication ("He took great pains even with a one-paragraph
news story"). Ernest thought his boss a harsh and stern critic but a very
just disciplinarian. In late November, Wellington offered Ernest a regular
reporter's job, and Ernest accepted.

With his place at the *Star* secure, Ernest felt free to leave the boarding house on Warwick Avenue (his landlady insisted he would become a "lost soul") and to move into Carl Edgar's bachelor apartment at 3516 Agnes Avenue. On December 6, 1917, Ernest wrote home: "Carl and I have a nice big room with easy chairs and a table, dresser and a sleeping porch with two big double beds for $2.50 apiece per week. And [I] am boarding in restaurants." He omitted that his new room was an attic and the "sleeping porch" was a broad dormer window so cold (1917–18 was the coldest winter in Kansas City in a decade) that he had to wear his Mackinaw to bed.

During the six months Ernest worked at the *Kansas City Star*—from mid-October 1917 to the end of April 1918—he made a few friends. Among them were Russell Crouse, who worked at the sports desk under an editor named MacBride, Harry Van Burst, who worked in the exchange department (a kind of in-house library of clippings from various sources to be used by reporters for research and background material) and lived in the boarding house on Warwick Avenue, and Wilson Hicks, whom Ernest considered the most intelligent man at the paper. Indulging his dexterity in coining nicknames, Ernest called a relentlessly cheerful fellow, H. Merle Smith, "Smith the Beamer"; a young Australian, "the Tasmanian Woodsman"; a nearsighted copy reader named Harry Godfrey, "the Pensive Hebrew"; and one of his better friends, Charles Hopkins, the assignment editor, "Hop" or "Hophead." Hopkins was "a serious though not a heavy man who argued well and was a great coffee drinker and spoke without moving his lips."

On the whole, these young men accepted Ernest's nicknames in the spirit of good fun. But one veteran reporter with whom Ernest covered the police headquarters at Fourth and Main Street did not. Because Bill Moorhead usually lost money when he played poker or shot craps with the bailbondsmen and the policemen on his shift at the station, he would leave the room when Ernest called him "Broken Will."

Besides his boss, Pete Wellington, and his young friends, there were two other employees Ernest paid particular attention to at the *Star:* a young, flamboyant reporter, Lionel Moise and a brusque little office "boy," Leon Korbreen.

When Ernest arrived at the *Star* in the fall of 1917, Lionel Calhoun Moise was twenty-six. He was a loner with a reputation for brawling; he drank a great deal and was a notorious womanizer. For the "literary" members of the *Star's* staff and their gossip, Moise cultivated his image. The boys in the smoking room, Ernest said, considered him "picturesque."

By and large, Moise's stories for the *Star* were written in a style that defied all the rules of the style sheet. They were facile, rhetorical, and ver-

bose. Yet they also had the flash of life that a great ego and an undisciplined talent can give. Ernest pitied Lionel Moise and was appalled by
his drunken violence and his profligate waste of talent. Years later he
wrote a sketch of Moise:

> Lionel Moise was a great rewrite man. He could carry four stories in his
> head and go to the telephone and take a fifth and then write all five at
> full speed to catch an edition. There would be something alive about each
> one. He was always the highest paid man on every paper he worked on.
> If any other man was getting more money he'd quit or have his pay raised.
> He never spoke to the other reporters unless he had been drinking. He
> was tall and thick and had long arms and big hands. He was the fastest
> man on a typewriter I ever knew. He drove a motor car and it was under-
> stood in the office that a woman had given it to him. One night she
> stabbed him in it out on the Lincoln Highway half way to Jefferson City.
> He took the knife away from her and threw it out of the car. Then he did
> something awful to her. She was lying in the back of the car when they
> found them. Moise drove the car all the way into Kansas City with her
> fixed that way.

Ernest found Moise's "toughness" offensive, but he felt differently about
the tenacity of Leo Korbreen. Leo Korbreen was several inches short of
five feet, had broad shoulders and close-cropped hair. He spoke with the
thick accent of an immigrant Russian Jew. Before his job at the *Star*, Leo
had worked for a news vendor on a particular corner in Kansas City, de-
fending his boss's territory from "poachers." He had won many fights on
this job, and this had led to his boxing professionally in the three-round
preliminary bouts at "smokers" in Kansas City clubs. After he and Ernest
became friends, Leo told Ernest that the worst thing about boxing was
breathing in the tobacco smoke that filled the hall. On a good night, he
and his opponent would pick up two and a half dollars satisfied customers
had thrown into the ring.

A sketch written by Ernest appeared in the *Star* on December 16, 1917.
He entitled it "Kerensky, the Fighting Flea" because of the remarkable
facial resemblance Leo had to the "perpetually fleeing Russian states-
man" and "because they both wore standing formal collars." After telling
about Leo's life at the *Star* and as a boxer, Ernest ended the sketch
this way:

> After hard days in old Russia, this life is full of joy for Leo, and who can
> say that he is not making the most of his opportunities? When he talks of
> the past it is of a pogrom. That Christmas season the workmen in a sugar
> refinery near Kiev made a cross of ice and set it up on the frozen river. It
> fell over and they blamed the Jews. Then the workmen rioted, breaking
> into stores and smashing windows. Leo and his family hid on the roof for

three days, and his sister fell ill of pneumonia. One studies to change the subject and asks:
"Leo, do they ever match you with a bigger boy?"
"Oh no," he says, "the crowd wouldn't stand for that. But sometimes I catch one on the street."

On October 24, when he had just "finished [a] week of work yesterday," Ernest wrote his father that his job at the *Star* was "enjoyable," that the *"Star* gets out a morning paper, the *Times,* 4 editions, and the *Evening Star* is 5 editions. Also a weekly on Wednesday and a Sunday paper." The paper had a "very large circulation and is pretty influential, I guess." He wrote the letter on his own typewriter, as he said he did *"everything* else." Then he let Clarence in on how he'd handled some classified information:

I got a scoop on the other papers yesterday about a troop train of soldiers at fort —. I got thru the lines and talked with the Captain and got all the Dope. Nobody was supposed to see him and the troops couldn't leave the train. He told me that officially he couldn't say a thing. Then he went off a ways with me and told me everything. Don't tell this around everywhere. Where they were from, where going, etc. Nobody else had it. I promised him I wouldn't publish it until the train had gone. So it was O.K.

A week later, Ernest sent Clarence a "Thanksgiving letter" in which he thanked his father for the "stamps and postcards," sent along a blank "Miscellaneous Report" form of the "Metropolitan Police Department, Kansas City, Mo.," and assured Clarence that he'd had a nutritious Thanksgiving dinner of "pig" and turkey for five cents at "Woolf's famous place."

In mid-December, Ernest wrote home from the press room of the Hotel Muehlebach on a typewriter that had a ¾ key where the period should have been. It was a self-admitted duty letter: "I owe a lot of people letters and I have been so blame busy and this aft¾ I am going to try and clear some of them up¾" The weather, he said, was very cold: "I have been wearing my Big red sweater under my Mackinaw and it wasn't a bit too hot¾" He expected a raise soon: "All the fellows say there ought to be one coming to me¾" And his "package of Christmas things" for the family would arrive "about a week late as pay day is just one week after Christmas¾" Also, Ernest said he was moved by one particular scene he had recently witnessed: "Last night I saw the negroes that were sentenced to life imprisonment being taken to Fort Leavenworth¾ There were three special cars of them and three guards armed with rifles at each end

of each car¾ They came into the Union Station last night on their way
up from Houston¾"

Perhaps because he knew Clarence fondly remembered their trips to the
ball park in Chicago, Ernest, in mid-March, sent his father a handwritten
letter (all others were typed at work) telling the whole story of his meeting with the Chicago Cubs baseball team and "the world's greatest pitcher"
on their way to spring training in California:

                                                              March 14, 1918

Dear Dad,
        The Oak Leaves and the Trapeze arrived O.K.—much obliged. I en-
joyed them greatly. For the last three or four days it has been hot here
85° in the shade official. Yesterday I was sent down to meet the Chicago
Cubs coming—to California. I had a long talk with manager Mitchel and
a number of the players. I was sent down to see Grover Cleveland Alexander, the world's greatest pitcher [he had had sixteen shut-outs the year
before, a Major League record] who was sold to the Cubs for $75,000 from
Philadelphia. He was holding out for a $10,000 bonus. We met and talked
for half an hour before the special train came in that he was to get on.
While the train was stopped I met a number of the Chicago Cubs Baseball
writers on the *Trib, News, Examiner, Post,* and *Herald* and they gave me
a royal welcome. I met all the players and had a fine time and wrote my
story for the associated and united Press so you ~~probably~~ [crossed out by
Ernest] could read it in Chicago if you wanted or anywhere in the world.
I bought Alex and Pete Kilduff and Claude Hendrix coca colas and they
purchased me a lemon phosphate all of which goes on the expense account. Drinks purchased to get a story are by order of the boss called
"carfare."
        We are having a Laundry Strike here and I am handling the police end.
The violence stories. Wrecking trucks, running them over cliffs, and yesterday they murdered the nonunion guard. For a month I have averaged
a column a day.
        This warm weather is great, just like summer. How is it with you? It
is very busy now but I will write as often as I can.
                                                              Love to all,
                                                              Ernie
Any more Traps or Oak Leaves much appreciated.

To Grace, Ernest wrote about the smallpox epidemic that was raging in
Kansas City and told her that, because of his frequent trips to the General Hospital, he'd gotten vaccinated. A month later he wrote to her that,
just to be on the safe side, he'd gotten vaccinated again. "It itches right
merrily," he said of the second vaccination. "So I guess it is taking good."
Later, he sent Grace word that he couldn't write her as often as he would
like to because he was very busy—so busy, in fact, "I haven't seen a girl

yet in Kansas City and that is a hard predicament for a guy who has been in love with someone ever since he can remember." In October, Ernest commiserated with Grace over the death of her aunt, Emma Hall, and recalled the effect his great-aunt had had on him: "I am sorry the feeble one went and that you are so busy, but better to stoke a liner than look at that face much, Gee it haunts me yet." And several times he wrote with good-humored excess of the sour-milk chocolate cake his mother sent him. It was, in fact, the only good thing Grace could bake.

March 2, 1918

Dear Mither:
    The box came tonight and we just opened it at the Pressroom. The cake was sure great. There were about four of the fellows here and we opened the box and ate the cake. It was a peach. . . . The fellows all agreed that Mother Hemingstein must be some cook. Your praises were sung in loud and stentorian tones. The cake sure fed a multitude of starving and broke newspapermen tonight.

Ernest sometimes wrote to Grace about his work, too. But his references were vague and verbose, mostly adolescent bravado and nothing like the informative and sincere reports he offered to Clarence:

    . . . There is not much doing here now except my hospital fight. Things are going great in that. I was officially barred from entering the institution by the Manager yesterday and the Boss and the big political men are sure raising the merry deuce. We are panning the hide off'n them for fair. But the boss said to disregard the fact that I am barred and sent me out there anyway to get the dope on them. And so we are having all sorts of rows. I have about five conferences with the Managing Ed. per day and am getting along swell. We sure are making them hunt cover. The reason they are trying to keep me out of the joint is because I have enough on them to send them all to the pen, pretty near. Any way they sure hate the great Hemingstein and will do anything they can to frame on him.
    But we fight them high, wide, and handsome. . . .
                                                            Love,
                                                            Ernie

Yet when Grace wrote him a sermon on religion and "ethics" and slandered his friends, Ernest's reply was forceful and specific:

    . . . Don't worry or cry or fret about my not being a good Christian. I am just as much as ever and pray every night and believe just as hard so cheer up! Just because I'm a *cheerful* Christian ought not to bother you.
    The reason I don't go to church on Sunday is because I always have to work

until 1:00 a.m. getting out the Sunday *Star,* and every once in a while, until
3 and 4 a.m. And I never open my eyes Sunday morning until 12:30 noon
anyway. So you see it isn't because I don't want to. You know I don't rave
about religion but am as sincere a Christian as I can be. Sunday is the one
day in the week that I can get my sleep out. Also Aunt Arabell's church
is a very well dressed stylish one with a ~~fat bigoted~~ [crossed out by Ernest]
not to be loved preacher and I feel out of place.

Now, Mother I got awfully angry when I read what you wrote about
Carl [Edgar] and Bill [Smith]. I wanted to write immediately and say
everything I thot [sic]. But I waited until I got cooled off. But never
having met Carl and knowing Bill only superficially you *were* mighty
unjust. Carl is a *Prince* and about the most sincere and real Christian I
have ever known and he has had a better influence on me than anyone I
have ever known. He doesn't drool at the mouth like a Peaslee [a young
female family friend of the Hemingways] with religion but is a deep sincere Christian and a gentleman.

I have never asked Bill what church he goes to because that doesn't
matter. We both believe in God and Jesus Christ and have hopes for a
hereafter and creeds don't matter.

Please don't unjustly criticize my best friends again. Now cheer up because you see I am not drifting like you thought.

With love,
Ernie

Don't read this to anyone and please get back to a cheerful frame of
mind!

To the "Kids," Ernest wrote about how hard he was working—"Harvest
is heavy and the Laborers few"—how poor he was nevertheless, and how
tough they should believe "their large and burly" (sometimes "brutal")
brother to be. Also, he sent them Kansas City streetcar transfers for souvenirs. On the backs of the tickets were drawings of a woman dressed, as
Grace usually was, in the extravagant fashion of the 1880s, demonstrating
the right and wrong way to disembark.

But to his grandmother Adelaide, who despite her arthritis had knitted
him a pair of woolen socks a month before, Ernest wrote on Lincoln's
birthday, 1918:

Dearest Grandmother:
This is a long, long time to wait before writing to you to thank you for
those great socks, but here are the thanks. All that the paper will hold.
They are wonderful and sure saved my life in the 20° below weather we
had for a long time down here.

In the letters Ernest wrote to his parents from Kansas City, he enclosed
clippings of his articles in the *Star.* Sometimes he would send a whole
sheet with his work circled in red. Despite the stories on dope raids, po-

litical corruption, rape, and robbery, Ernest usually implied in his letters that being a reporter in this "beautiful and unsavory city" meant having fun. Had Clarence and Grace been intelligent readers, they would have sensed in the irony of his words that Ernest took in much more than he would say.

Ernest wrote two of his best pieces for the *Star* in January 1918, one before and the second just after his letter to Grace admonishing her for slandering his friends. Coincidentally, both articles were written while Ernest was covering the hospitals and the undertakers. The first article, written on January 8, is a tale of incompetence and callousness leading to death.

Death Beat Slow Doctor

Man Lay Unattended Two Hours After Call
to General Hospital.

The proprietor of the Midland Arcade at Seventh and Walnut Streets found one of his guests, J. C. Duncan of Smithville, Mo., on the roof of his establishment, in a drunken stupor, early today. He was taken to police headquarters.

On examination at 11:30 o'clock this morning, Duncan's condition was found to be so dangerous that the General Hospital ambulance was summoned. The ambulance was out at the time of the call and could not be located. A physician from the municipal hospital was summoned.

At 12:30 o'clock the doctor had failed to arrive and in the interim Duncan died.

Duncan lay in the holdover one hour and fifty minutes after the doctor had been summoned. At that time the undertaking wagon of Quirk and Tobin, undertakers, appeared and carried away the body. The doctor even then had not appeared. Lieut. John Rogers called the General Hospital and informed them that the doctor's services were no longer required. . . .

Two weeks later, a series of sketches Ernest based on what he had seen in two months "At the End of the Ambulance Run" appeared in the *Star*. The three best anticipate, with their powerful imagery, the vignettes of *in our time,* Ernest's small experimental collection published in Paris in 1923.

That night ambulance attendants shuffled down the long, dark corridors at the General Hospital with an inert burden on the stretcher. They turned in at the receiving ward and lifted the unconscious man to the operating table. His hands were calloused and he was unkempt and ragged, a victim of a street brawl near the city market. No one knew who he was, but a receipt bearing the name of George Anderson, for $10.00 paid on a home out in a little Nebraska town, served to identify him.

The surgeon opened the swollen eyelids. The eyes were turned to the left. "A fracture on the left side of the skull," he said to the attendants who stood about the table. "Well George, you're not going to finish paying for that home of yours."

"George" merely lifted a hand as though groping for something. Attendants hurriedly caught hold of him to keep him from rolling from the table. But he scratched his face in a tired, resigned way that seemed almost ridiculous, and placed his hand again at his side. Four hours later he died.

One night they brought in a negro who had been cut with a razor. It is not a mere joke about negroes using the razor—they really do it. The lower end of the man's heart had been cut away and there was not much hope for him. Surgeons informed his relatives of the one chance that remained, and it was a very slim one. They took some stitches in his heart and the next day he had improved sufficiently to be seen by a police sergeant.

"It was just a friend of mine, boss," the negro replied weakly to questioning. The sergeant threatened and cajoled, but the negro would not tell who cut him. "Well, just stay there and die, then," the officer turned away exasperated.

But the negro did not die. He was out in a few weeks, and the police finally learned who his assailant was. He was found dead—his vitals opened by a razor.

"It's razor wounds in the African belt and slugging in the wet block. In Little Italy they prefer the sawed-off shotgun. We can almost tell what part of the city a man is from just by seeing how they did him up," one of the hospital attendants commented. . . .

One day an aged printer, his hand swollen from blood poisoning, came in. Lead from the type metal had entered a small scratch. The surgeon told him they would have to amputate his left thumb.

"Why, Doc? You don't mean it do you? Why? That'd be worse'n sawing the periscope off a submarine! I've just gotta have that thumb. I'm an old-time swift. I could set my six galleys a day in my time—that was before the linotypes came in. Even now, they need my business, for some of the finest work is done by hand. And you go and take that finger away from me and—well, it'd be mighty interesting to know how I'd ever hold a 'stick' in my hand again. Why, Doc!—"

With face drawn, and head bowed, he limped out of the doorway. The French artist who vowed to commit suicide if he lost his right hand in battle, might have understood the struggle the old man had alone in the darkness. Later that night the printer returned. He was very drunk. "Just take the damn works, Doc, take the whole damn works," he wept.

Ernest met many people his first four months in Kansas City, and he went to Aunt Arabella's weekend dinners and moved in with Michigan pal Carl Edgar. But it was not until mid-February that, at the General Hospital, he found a real friend.

On the morning of February 18, 1918, while he was covering the Union Station, Ernest saw a small crowd standing around a man lying unconscious in the middle of the main floor. A policeman who called to Ernest by name was keeping the people back, and he warned Ernest back, too. The man had smallpox; the ambulance had been sent for an hour earlier. Ignoring the policeman's warnings, Ernest picked the sick man up, put him over his shoulder, and carried him out the main entrance to one of the taxis parked on Pershing Road. It was snowing. The cabby thought the man was drunk.

At the General Hospital, Ernest told the cabby to wait and then carried the patient, an insurance agent from Cherrydale, Kansas, into the receiving room. The ambulance surgeon on duty thanked Ernest for his efforts and took over. Ernest admired the doctor's efficient examining technique (performed with what he thought were "gambler's hands") and the way he told the nurse and the attendants what to do. Later, the doctor asked Ernest to help him disinfect the cab.

Although he kept it to himself, Ernest soon began spending much of his free time at the General Hospital. The "municipal" doctor was always willing to talk and to listen. Also, he affected a "certain extravagance of speech" Ernest thought the "utmost of elegance." Ernest grew to respect the doctor's knowledge of life and to appreciate his "eagerness to speak truly."

During one of their conversations in the receiving room, with its smell of "cigarettes, idoform, carbolic, and an overheated radiator," the doctor told Ernest that he had once practiced medicine on the West Coast and had lost his license there for supplying dope to addicts who could get their fixes in no other way. Eventually he asked Ernest to accompany him on midnight trips to the Kansas City jail and to carry the bowl of morphine while he gave the shots. Some of the addicts would be quietly ill when the doctor arrived, while others would say, "Oh, shoot me just once in the gut, Doc. For Pity Doc." If Ernest spilled anything from the bowl, they would get down on the floor and lick it up.

The big news in Kansas City in the fall and winter of 1917–18 was not narcotics, nor was it the smallpox epidemic, nor for that matter was it the political corruption the *Star* was determined to expose. As in every other American city, the big news was the war.

On April 6, 1917, the Congress of the United States had declared war on Germany. In the months that followed, the national anxiety the declaration of war created was amplified first by Germany's resumption of un-restricted submarine warfare and then by a string of allied defeats: a huge French offensive at the Aisne River had broken down with terrible losses; a carefully prepared offensive in the Balkans had been pushed back to Salonika by the Bulgarians, the Germans, and the Austrians; and on the Italian Front the Austrians were building toward their smashing victory at Caporetto. The government, in its rush to mobilize, had set up "boards" and "administrations" that touched every facet of people's lives. The War Industries Board, under Bernard Baruch, could tell manufacturers which materials could and could not be used, what products to make, and which transportation they could have access to. The Food Administration, under Herbert Hoover, controlled the supply and distribution of food, led the fight for conservation (the people were encouraged to plant "war gar-dens" and have "wheatless" and "meatless" days each week), and set a high price on wheat to encourage farmers to expand their acreage.

It was the responsibility of the Emergency Fleet Corporation to see that the U.S. shipyards built ships faster than the German submarines could sink them. The propaganda agency, called the Committee on Public In-formation and run by fomer muckraker George Creel, was charged with building public support for the war. Two of its most successful promo-tions were the Liberty Loan drives (bond sales staged as rallies and enter-tainments most often conducted by celebrities) and its famous poster—beneath the words "Halt the Hun!" an American doughboy, looking very much like a farmer, holds back a rapacious German about to ravish a kneeling, bare-breasted woman holding a naked child. To train the more than two million men the Selective Service Act would supply for the Army, the War Department established thirty-two camps, mostly in the south and west. One was Camp Funstan just north of Kansas City.

From the time Ernest arrived in Kansas City, war news made the front page of almost every edition of the *Star*. Stories of German fanaticism and brutality were juxtaposed with articles on British and French victories or heroism in defeat. On the inside pages there were usually columns on lo-cal boys who had volunteered. Lieutenant Dale L. Schelling, a former re-porter for the *Star* and "an expert on gas engines," was featured with a photograph of him in uniform for duty as mechanic with the Lafayette Escadrille. Other articles scattered throughout the paper announced the participation of civil organizations like the Mothers' Band of Swope Set-tlement and the Kansas Women's Farm and Garden Association in war projects such as planting flowers along sidewalks and the cultivation of several acres of "war gardens" in public parks. A shoe company advertising in the *Star* promised that its "Grand Gripper Shoe . . . would not only prevent but cure fallen arches" (fallen arches would mean rejection for a volunteer). Any able-bodied young man in Kansas City not in uniform at this time risked being called a "slacker." Even Pete Wellington, despite his obvious ill health, tried to enlist.

On November 5, 1917, less than three weeks after he arrived in Kansas City, Ernest joined the Seventh Missouri Infantry of the National Guard. He wrote home proudly that the uniform was "regular army stuff" except for the "Black and Gold hat cord of Missouri State" and the gold "MS" he would wear on the collar. On Tuesday nights there would be drills at Camp Funstan, and on some weekends "mock battles in the woods outside of town."

Despite the uniform, the weekly drills, and the occasional maneuvers, however, Ernest knew that his service in the National Guard was far from the real thing. (He was called to active duty only once, from March 27 to April 3, 1918, when his unit saw riot duty in the Kansas City "Laundry Strike.") Less than two weeks after he joined up, he wrote to Clarence and Grace: "I will plan to work here until spring and then get in one more good summer before enlisting. I couldn't possibly stay out of it any longer than that under any circumstances. It will be hard enough to stay out until then."

In late fall of 1917, Ernest, his roommate Carl Edgar, and Bill Smith, who was visiting from St. Louis, went to hear the famous Chicago evangelist, Billy Sunday, speak about God and patriotism at a rally in Kansas City. Sunday, who had once been a professional baseball player, spoke in his popular "straight from the shoulder" style about the sins of the "Hot Dog Crowd" and the virtue of sympathy for those who fought against them. Now that Congress had declared war on Germany, Sunday said, anyone who "stands off is a traitor." After the talk, Ernest said he would try to enlist in the Marines in the fall unless he could "get into aviation when I am 19 and get a commission." He knew of course that his nearsightedness would keep him out of both services.

Although enlisting in the Marines or in aviation was out of the question, Ernest soon found there was something he'd be considered fit to do. One month after he joined the staff of the *Star,* another young man, Theodore Brumback, was hired as a cub reporter. He was the son of Judge Hermann Brumback of the Jackson County Circuit Court, and he drove to work in a new Ford roadster. In 1913, Ted Brumback had entered Cornell University. But two years later, after a golfing accident cost him an eye (a ball he'd hit ricochetted off a nearby tree), he left school. Dur-

ing the summer of 1917, while Ernest was up in Michigan, Brumback
spent four months driving ambulances for the American Field Service in
France.

On his first day at work, Ted Brumback stood behind a "tall, dark-
haired chap" pounding a typewriter at the next desk and admired his
speed and concentration. He was delighted when, after the fellow had finished his story and called for the copy boy, he turned and said, "My
name's Hemingway, Ernest Hemingway. You're a new man, aren't you?"
Although he was four years older than Ernest and knew something of the
world, Ted Brumback did not mind the sidekick role Ernest cast for him.
Brumback also enjoyed the way Ernest would listen with attention and
appreciation whenever he told the stories of his ambulance service in
France.

As luck would have it, sometime in late February representatives of the
Italian government visited Kansas City to recruit drivers for Red Cross
ambulances in Italy. Only men who were unfit for duty with the U.S.
Army would be accepted. Ernest and Ted were very pleased when they
found the Italians would take a man who was nearsighted and a man
with one eye. In late March they gave Pete Wellington their month's
notice.

While Ernest prepared to join the Italian Red Cross Ambulance Service
(the casual physical exam, plenty of propaganda to read, a patriotic party
at the Italian Club in Kansas City), he wrote home only that he would be
leaving the *Star* by the first of May. In the letter to Clarence, he said that
he was tired from the six months of hard work at the *Star,* that he felt he
had learned enough to be able to take up newspaper work again whenever he wished, and that he wanted to go up to Michigan for a few
months' rest. Grace, to whom Ernest had scarcely written since her letter
criticizing his friends, could not, on this occasion at least, resist opening
Clarence's mail. She wrote immediately of her enthusiastic endorsement
of Ernest's plans:

> April 17, 1918
>
> Dear Old Kid,
>   Your letter to Dad just arrived and as he has gone downtown I have
> just read it. It's a superb setting forth of your position, and I am sure you
> know best about your immediate plans. We, who love you best, don't
> want you to work yourself to death, far from it. You have surely made a
> record for yourself and shown your ability. We shall be royally glad to
> see our "Newspaper Man" home again; and will bid you God speed to
> the country of rest, long nights + wholesome days—"far from the madden-
> ing [sic] crowds." Gee! But I'm glad you can go there and get fit again.
> (Don't bother to write Mother.) I can wait till you get rested up north for

THE INTERN IN KANSAS CITY

my next letter, only just let us know when to expect you on May 2. God
bless you my own precious boy—I think you know how proud I am of you
and how I love you.

Your G.H.H.

On May 2, 1918, Ernest boarded the Chicago train at Union Station.
Traveling with him were Carl Edgar, Charles Hopkins, and Bill Smith.
They would all spend a day in Oak Park and then head for northern
Michigan. Edgar was going to visit his family in Petoskey. Hopkins and
Smith had accepted Ernest's invitation to spend a week fishing with him
on the Fox River near the Canadian Soo. Ted Brumback, whom Ernest
had also invited, decided at the last minute to remain at home in Kansas
City and to meet Ernest in New York for their induction.

The day Ernest and his friends spent in Oak Park, Clarence and Grace
made certain there was good food, friendly conversation, and much picture taking. The young men were asked to dress up in their three-piece
suits (Ernest wore a touring cap with his). That afternoon Clarence spoke
of how he had wanted to serve in the Army Medical Corps in the Spanish
American War but could not because his first daughter had just been
born. Marcelline, who had failed in her first semester at Oberlin, took
many pictures with her new camera. That day, for the first and only time
for a photograph, Ernest embraced Grace. Before going to bed, he told
his mother and father that his Michigan vacation would be much shorter
than they believed.

At the end of the first week in May, a wire arrived in Oak Park to
notify Ernest that he was to report to the headquarters of the Red Cross
in New York on May 13. Clarence immediately wired Ernest at Seney,
Michigan. According to family legend, the Indian runner who worked for
the telegraph office took three days to locate Ernest and his friends. However it was, Ernest returned to Oak Park just in time to pack his things.
Up north he had learned that Prudence Boulton, three months pregnant
by a French-Canadian lumberjack, had committed suicide. Both had
taken strychnine, the Indians said, and their screams had been heard for
hours across Susan Lake.

Before Ernest left for the train station, he danced with his sister Ursula
in the music room. The song on her victrola was "A Pretty Girl Is Like a
Melody."

⋈ 4 ⋈

The Intern in New York

Ernest's train from Chicago to New York took the northern route: around the southern tip of Lake Michigan, across southern Michigan to Detroit, east into Canada at Windsor, along the north shore of Lake Erie to Buffalo, then through larger towns like Batavia and Geneva and smaller ones like Lockport and Seneca Falls. Finally, the train turned south at Albany and followed the Hudson River to New York City. Ernest rode in the second car, at the last window on the left side.

In a novel he began in 1928 but never finished, Ernest wrote about this trip. The train to New York was smooth, steady, and fast. Towns passed quickly, and smoke from many gray stacks billowed as their furnaces flared in the wind. At dusk the lights of small stations shone in puddles on the wet station pavement, and people stood watching as the express train went through. At dinner that night, Ernest was impressed with the politeness and efficiency of the dining-room waiters (they were light-skinned negroes, while the porters were very black), the ice water (which he drank too much of), and the finger bowls on every table. In the wash-room, from which he pilfered a towel and some soap, there were spigots for the ice water and collapsible tube cups. That night he bedded down in the pullman's lower berth because he wanted to look out the window in the early morning, and put his shoes outside the curtain to be shined. He liked it between the sheets with the blanket pulled up and it all dark and the country dark outside and that there was a screen across the lower part of the window and the air came in cold. He liked the green curtain of his berth buttoned tight and how the car swayed but felt very solid and

54

was going very fast. Several times before he went to sleep, Ernest heard the train's whistle blow.

Ernest awakened twice during the night. The first time, the train was going very slowly and crossing the Detroit River, and the lights shone on the river and on the iron framework of the bridge. The second time, the train stopped in a railway yard, and two men came by with torches and stopped somewhere beneath his window and hit on the wheels of the car with hammers.

When he awoke on the morning of the twelfth of May, he saw fine shooting country outside his window. It looked like Michigan to him, except the hills were higher and all the country seemed connected, as if it belonged to somebody. He got dressed inside his berth and then reached under the curtain for his shoes. He walked down the aisle between the rows of buttoned curtains to the front of the car, opened the door, and stood for a moment in the draft and the cindery air.

In the washroom there was a porter asleep in the corner on a leather cushioned seat. He had his cap over his eyes, feet up, mouth open, head tipped back, and hands together in his lap. As the train passed a covey of kildeer plover feeding, Ernest saw three fly up. Then there were blue-jay finches in the air and, higher up, a hawk and his mate hunting over a field. On one curve Ernest saw the engine's wheels going very fast.

When the train finally crossed the Hudson River sometime about noon, it began raining hard. The air smelled good to Ernest, and there were big clouds over the mountains. In the rain the country reminded Ernest of engravings he had seen printed in magazines. As the train drove south along the Hudson, he saw a great stone building on an island. It was gray and built close to the shore of the river. It looked like a castle, and there was a channel between the building and the shore which looked like a moat. Near New York City, the train passed through a long tunnel of cement and painted steel. And finally there was Grand Central Station. As soon as Ernest left the train, he mailed a letter he'd written to Clarence and Grace when the train was "approaching Buffalo":

May 12, 1918

Dear Folks—
    We are having a great trip and the bunch is very good. There are fifteen fellows mostly from New Tier and Evanston and they are a dandy bunch. I hope you saw Ted [Brumback's train stopped in Chicago] and had Hop out to dinner all O.K. The roadbed sure is rocky and we are going fast coming into Buffalo so the writing is a little more rotten than usual. We left Toledo after Breakfast and have been running along Lake Erie all day. We hit Buffalo at about four o'clock and soon will be well into New York. At New York I am going to get a canvas waterproof

duffle bag with a chain and lock to keep all my stuff in. The meals have
been very good so far. Well, goodbye and love to all . . . *Ernie*.

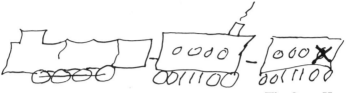

The Great Hemmys

Ernest was quartered by the Red Cross, along with seventy other volunteers from various parts of the country, at the Hotel Earle. It was a
small residential hotel in Washington Square, in the heart of Greenwich Village. From the front door of the hotel, Ernest could see the famous Washington Memorial Arch. It was a reproduction of the Arc de
Triomphe in Paris.

On his first full day in New York—Tuesday, May 13—Ernest reported
to the Life Extension Institute on West Forty-fifth Street for his physical
examination. He learned he was in fine shape, with a blood pressure reading of 128 over 75. However, he got a B rating because of his nearsightedness 'and was advised by the examining physician, Dr. Dunn, to consult
an oculist.

To supplement the regular Army issue—"officers overcoat, 1 rain coat,
1 cocky field service cap, one Dress cap, 4 suits heavy underwear, soft
buckskin driving gloves, 1 pair cordova leather aviators puttees, 2 pair
officers shoes, 1 knitted sweater, six pair heavy woolen socks, two khaki
shirts, 1 woolen shirt, an officer's trunk with his name stenciled on it . . .
$200 worth of equipment"—Ernest used part of the money he had saved
in Kansas City to buy a thirty-dollar pair of cordovan leather boots. He
and Ted Brumback, who had also arrived in New York on May 13,
roomed together at the Hotel Earle and commiserated with each other
over the discomfort the mandatory smallpox injection caused them both.
It was Ernest's third inoculation in seven months.

The next morning—Monday, May 14—Ernest had his uniform fitted.
Then, in the afternoon, he, Ted Brumback, and Howell Jenkins, a five-
foot-four-inch boy with a mouth twisted to one side by "an operation,"
rode the streetcar "down to the Battery and went through the aquarium."
Afterward they went sightseeing up on the "Woolworth Tower where we
could see the camouflaged boats going in and out of the harbor and see
way up the East River to Hell's Gate." The day before, Ernest had gone
by himself "all up and down Riverside Drive and seen N.Y. from the
Harlem River on the north and Grant's Tomb to the Libber of God-
dessty in the south."

Ernest found New York different from Chicago. It was tall and clean, "not sprawled out." The streets in New York, though more crowded than even State Street, were hushed, and many people looked like foreigners. There were more taxis in New York, more barber shops, and more red-capped doormen. And there were no smells. The New York subway, with its tile walls and bright lights, reminded Ernest of a hospital or of public toilets. On the walk he took up Fifth Avenue, Ernest at first thought the famous street not so very wide nor the buildings so high. But as he walked on, this changed, and he was impressed by the Flatiron Building and the policemen directing traffic from towers.

Besides the sightseeing he did his first two days in New York, Ernest attended a few parties given by socialites who, as a patriotic duty, had taken up the entertainment of young officers before they went overseas. Ernest, in the warm spring weather, wore his high-collared, choke-neck shirt, his riding pants, his cordovan boots, and red-enameled Red Cross insignias to ornament his collar and overseas cap.

At one such party, Ernest met Mae Marsh, an actress he had admired ever since he had first seen her in the film *Birth of a Nation* with his grandfather in 1915. In that film she had given a remarkable performance as the teenage Flora, the vital southern heroine who commits suicide to escape the black rapist, Gus, in the South of Reconstruction. Mae was a blue-eyed blonde with a sparkling smile and a wonderful figure. On the seventeenth of May, Ernest wrote to Dale Wilson, a friend at the *Kansas City Star*, about Miss Marsh:

> This is also not for publication but I have been out to see Mae several times and am out there for dinner tomorrow evening. I have spent every damn cent I have too. Miss Marsh no kidding says she loves me. I suggested the little church around the corner but she opined as how ye war widow appealed not to her. So I sank 150 plunks Pop gave me in a ring so I am engaged anyway. Also broke. Dead. . . . Anyway my girl loves me and she believes I am going to be a great newspaperman and says she will wait for me, so what the Hell Bill. Anyway maybe I can win an honest to god commission. Gee she is a wonderful girl, Wilse! Too damn good for me.

Surprisingly, Ernest also told his parents about this affair. On May 14, in a letter to the "Folks," he wrote, "As soon as I don my officer's uniform I have an engagement with the Mrs. and have already investigated the possibility of the Little Church around the corner. I've always planned to get married if I could ever get to be an officer, you know."

Clarence and Grace, who on May 12 and May 15 had written Ernest letters about a misplaced latchkey and a trip to a revival meeting held by Billy Sunday, were thunderstruck by the news. On May 16, the same day

they received Ernest's letter, they replied. Grace, who was writing to
Ernest at the time, broke off in the middle of her first letter and began
again:

> Thursday, May 16, 1918
> 10:00 A.M. Oak Park Home
>
> Dear Son Ernest,
> We are so eager to hear from you. Mrs. Newburg gets a letter from her
> son [Art Newburg, a fellow citizen of Oak Park whom Ernest thought a
> dullard and a prig] every day, she is sorry for me and so shares her news
> with me.
>
> 4:00 P.M.
> After receiving Your
> Letter.
>
> Dear Son,
> Your Father and I are greatly troubled; I must have been a very poor
> success as a Mother, that you refused to give me your confidence when I
> asked you about the girls. You have never mentioned any girl to me, and
> now you speak of engagement. I do trust you will think hard before
> making such a mistake as to marry at 18, and without any income or
> visible means of support. I fear you do not realize what a laughing stock
> you would make of yourself. Marriage is a beautiful and wonderful thing;
> but it is sacred in proportion to the prayerfulness with which it is entered
> into. You may come home disfigured and crippled; would this girl love
> you then? A marriage ceremony should be followed by constant com-
> panionship, a little love nest, a bit of heaven roofed over + walled in, for
> just two loving souls. —Such marriage as you suggest, would be unnatural
> and apt to bring great sorrow and misunderstanding.
> God help you, dear boy; I cannot; I can only keep on loving you and
> praying that you will use your best judgement and ask God's guidance.
>
> Your devoted
> Mother

Clarence followed her lead in the telegram he sent:

> May 16 P.M.
>
> Ernest M. Hemingway
> Care Hotel Earle
> 272 Wash Square, New York, N.Y.
> Your New York letter received. Stop. Happy such excellent equipment.
> Stop. May great success follow. Stop. Please consider most seriously any
> adventure that might tempt you. Stop. Much love. Stop.
>
> Dr. C. E. Hemingway

Then Grace herself wrote again:

> May 18, 1918
>
> My Darling Boy,
> Little Leicester came in this morning with a fist full of dandelions and

that wonderful smile, for Mother. If I were an artist I would paint a picture entitled "That Dandelion Smile." It reminded me so of you Ernest.
It was only yesterday that you were Mother's little yellow headed laddie,
and used to hug me tight and call me "Silkey Sockey." Don't forget,
Darling, that any girl who is worthwhile is worth waiting for and working
for; and if she really loves you she will be willing to wait till you are a
man, and able to take care of her. Oh! How I long to help you at this
time, but tho' I cannot, God will, for He stands ready to guide your life
ship.

Always your loving
Mother

On May 19, however, Clarence and Grace were relieved by a telegram
from Ernest which read:

Dr. Hemingway 600 N. Kenilworth Ave.
    Cheer up. Stop. Am not engaged married or divorced. Stop. This is
authentic. Stop. Just joking. Stop. Here till Wednesday. Stop.

Ernie

And by a letter he sent the same day:

Sunday, May 19, 1918

Dear Dad—
    I got your good letter and telegram O.K. Cheer up ye old Pop for no-
body gets my insurance save yourself. Also the matrimonial status is negative and will be for some years. Sound ye loud timbrels. Everybody knows
it so I guess it won't hurt if you don't tell anyone what I told you. So we
sail Wednesday via France. Landing at Bordeaux. Go to Paris and then to
Milan. . . . I am going to Trumbull White's tonight. Try and see Bruce
Barton tomorrow. [Barton, who would become a highly successful advertising executive and a famous writer of enthusiastic religious histories—
The Man Nobody Knows; The Book Nobody Knows—had met and be-
friended Clarence in Oak Park.]
    Don't worry about me whatever you do and trust my good judgement.
I'll write before I go. Arthur Newburg is a nice enough fellow but not in
our bunch. We have a great bunch of rare birds. Thanks for sending the
ten to Carl very much. I may have you send the proceeds of my Lib Bond
to me in Milan.

Much Love,
Ernie

As soon as he received Ernest's telegram, Clarence wrote his goodbye
letter to his son.

May 19, 1918

Sunday 2:00 P.M.
My dear Ernest,—
    Your wire explaining the "joke" which has taken five nights sleep from

your mother + father received about half-hour ago. —So glad to receive it,
hope you have written your dear mother, she was broken hearted. —No
one knows what mother + I know. And never will. —God bless + keep
you dear boy, we have prayed so earnestly for you + now I know prayers
are answered. —Wire us a good long nightletter before you leave and
write as often as possible. —I will take this to the Post Office now so it
will be sure to reach you before you leave. —Let us know your *unit* + how
to address mail to you. —May great success always follow you + keep you
pure and a hundred percent a Christian gentleman, willing to fight for
the Right. We are great Red Cross Boosters + Y.M.C.A. too. You do the
same. Good Bye + love from your Daddy. C̶E̶H̶

But in her farewell letter the next day, Grace was skeptical about
Ernest's denial:

My Precious Boy,
    Your telegram yesterday was such a relief. Your Father and I slept last
night and this morning. We are so rejoiced to get your good letter telling
about donning the uniform + drilling on the roof [of the Hotel Earle].
Dear Boy, no one knows of your "church around the corner" idea but
your Father + I and we shall not let it get out. If you are really engaged,
won't you let us know to whom? I want to learn to love the girl who will
be as dear to me as my own daughters, but if you are only joking, please
tell the truth to your mother, who loves you so dearly.
    This is my good-bye letter to you, so again "Mizpah" which means—
The Lord watch between me + thee while we are absent, one from the
other.
                                                              Your loving
                                                              Mother Gracie

Grace's suspicion, however, was unfounded. After he left New York,
Ernest never saw Mae Marsh again.

There was, of course, much more to his time in New York than Ernest
could write home about to Clarence and Grace. There was the girl he'd
taken particular notice of on his trip to the Battery. She was "just as clean
looking as a Madonna," but there were "thirty-seven dollars in one dollar
bills in her stocking from that many sailors and she was the most beautiful girl I ever saw. Black hair parted in the center and drawn back off
her forehead, high cheek bones, lovely creamy skin, and a beautiful
mouth. You never saw a finer built girl. She'd play the flute and swallow
the wad alright. You've got a wonderful chin for a pair of balls, lady."

Then there were the derelicts he'd met at Grant's Tomb: "The fleet lay
there in the river opposite Grant's Tomb and there was a bunch of them
you'd find there near Grant's Tomb that raised beards. You could piss
in their beards for seventy-five cents. They did a good business when the

fleet was in. There was another fellow you could take him in a vacant lot and shit on his bare chest for $5. I swear to god."

And there was " 'Big Jack,' the manager of a theatre." "He took on twenty-two sailors one night in Brooklyn . . . he took on twenty-two and he was ready for more. He gave them a dollar apiece. Somebody on board ship said they were going to beat the shit out of Big Jack. But the next morning he came aboard and Big Jack had almost killed him. Big Jack told him 'I have to do that. Nobody has to do it with me that don't want to. But you come over here just looking for trouble. Alright. You got it.' "

Finally, there was a young "Mr. Lennox," with a Harvard accent, who seemed like such a "nice, clean, straight, innocent American boy." Mr. Lennox said he preferred going to the aquarium instead of whoring. But, in the ride in the cab with Ernest, he wanted a kiss.

In his farewell letter to Clarence and Grace, sent two days before he left on the French Line's *Chicago*, Ernest wrote:

May 20, 1918

Dear Folks—:

All day today we have been out getting our passports, visas, and war passes. A big lot of the fellows' passports have not come and so they have to go on the next boat.

Our sailing has been delayed one day so that gives us a little more time. There are a few awful mutts in the unit but the majority are a swell bunch and we are having ye grand time. Anything you want to know about N. Yawk ask me. I may take everything with me as I haven't any extra clothes to send really and I may need that old brown suit back of the lines. I don't know yet I may send it along. We are certainly well out-fitted alright. The biggest bore is the constant returning salutes. If you go up town at night it is awful because there are hundreds of soldiers in town. Captain Utarsi went over with the Harvard bunch that left last week.

We are under a bird named Mosina. Ted and I will be together and we'll be driving partners. Latest dope is that we drive from Paris to Milan. Maybe we do, I'm sure I don't know nor does anyone else. I was up along Riverside Drive this afternoon and saw the big French warships in the Hudson River. There are three French Cruisers and a U.S. Dreadnaught. The transports are going in and out all the time. The society girls are very nice to the officers here. One took three of us in her big car for a long drive this aft. They make us have as much fun as possible. It may be cheering news to you the U. Boats have not sunk a ship between the U.S. and France since the last of March. They are pretty jolly well bottled up.

Much love
Ernie

On the envelope in which this letter arrived in Oak Park, Clarence wrote, "Last Recv'd before he sailed."

≥ 5 ≤
War Is Kind

On Tuesday evening, May 21, Ernest and the other volunteers left the
Hotel Earle on Red Cross buses for the mile drive to the French Line
terminal on West Fifteenth Street. It was a warm evening in New York,
the sky clear, the moon almost full. The *Chicago*, an old tramp steamer
of American registry but leased to France for the duration, was berthed
at the end of the French Line pier. In the moonlight, she looked to Ernest
"a rotten old tub" with a slight starboard list. That night, for the first
time since his Nantucket trip with Grace, he breathed the strong salt smell
of the sea.

On the morning tide, the *Chicago* steamed down the Hudson River,
past Battery Park, and into New York Bay. To minimize the danger from
German submarines, the captain avoided the customary route across the
North Atlantic and turned south instead in a zigzag course toward Ber-
muda and the Sargasso Sea. The first day out, Ernest made two new
friends: Leon Chocianowicz, from Buffalo, who was on his way to France
to join the Polish ambulance unit forming there; and Bill Horne, a
quick-witted Princeton alumnus, class of 1913. Ernest and Bill both admired Leon's soft, peaked cap and the Sam Browne belt he wore.

There was, surprisingly, a young female passenger on board the *Chicago*. Her name was Gaby, and she was rumored to be the daughter of an
official of the French Line. Ernest found Gaby had a loud laugh and a
bad odor of some sort. And she would spend a half-hour in a lifeboat
with almost anyone. At first, Ernest believed Gaby was committing incest
with the older man who brought her aboard. Eventually he discovered
that wasn't true. "But I swear to Christ," he told Bill Horne, "it gave me
a hell of a feeling when I first knew he was fucking her."

Because the *Chicago* made a southern crossing, the trip to Bordeaux took ten days. The first two days out, the weather was clear, the sea an oily calm, and the sky red at dawn. On the third day; a great storm began which lasted forty-eight hours. The old *Chicago,* Ernest wrote to the "Folks," "pitched, rolled, stood on her ear and swung in wide legubrious [sic] circles, and I heaved but four times." He didn't mention that, with his nose against the brass handle of a screwed-tight porthole and vomit in his mouth, he thought he had smelled death.

Soon after the ship left New York, the young Red Cross volunteers took up the usual diversions: they shot craps (Howell Jenkins became "Fever" Jenkins), played poker in a perpetual game in the bar, and drank many bottles of very good and very cheap French wine. For a while, some of the young men kept an unofficial watch for submarines, and others listened to the few good storytellers among those who had already driven ambulances in France. But soon the highlight of the day became the two meals—breakfast, Ernest wrote, "wasn't worth getting up for"—cooked by the French Line chefs. In the evenings the YMCA men aboard tried to organize "entertainments," but the young men preferred friendly conversation and a few songs on a well-played mandolin.

On the nights Ernest couldn't sleep, he would go into the bar and drink glasses of different wines and talk to the barman, Girard, who spoke English with a cockney accent and disdained lifeboat drills. Sometimes, too, Ernest and the tall Pole, Leon, climbed out over the davits into a lifeboat (Ernest afraid because he walked in his sleep), made themselves comfortable against the thwarts, clinked their bottles in the dark, and agreed they had something special that wouldn't let them be killed. Despite the sickness she had caused him, Ernest affectionately called the sea an old whore, giving what she used to sell, and being scorned.

Oily Weather

The sea desires deep hulls—
It swells and rolls.
The screw churns a throb—
Driving, throbbing, progressing.
The sea rolls with love,
Surging, caressing,
Undulating its great loving belly.
The sea is big and old—
Throbbing ships scorn it.

The *Chicago* docked at Bordeaux early on Saturday morning, June 1, 1918. The city, with its tan brick townhouses and cobblestone streets, looked antique in the sunlight, and beyond it the rolling vineyards were covered with mist. On their twelve-hour leave, Ernest and his comrades enjoyed some sightseeing, some excellent food, and a great deal of the splendid wine. In the lovely and slow-paced Bordeaux, it was easy to forget France was a country at war. But at the Gare du Nord in Paris the next morning, the young Americans were saluted emphatically by French captains and colonels. Under General Pershing, the second and third AEF divisions and a contingent of Marines had just stopped the Germans fifty miles from Paris at Château Thierry.

In Paris, Ernest was billeted at the Hotel Florida on the Boulevard Malesherbes. It was a small and, by French standards, a Spartan hotel run by the British, Australian, and New Zealand YMCA's. Throughout his week in Paris, Ernest heard the rumbling explosions of German long-range artillery shells randomly lobbed into the city to break French morale. Writing home to Clarence on Red Cross stationery, Ernest reported that there was virtually no effect on the French by the Hun long-range artillery. "The people accept the shells as a matter of course and hardly show interest in their arrival. We heard our first shell arriving soon after breakfast. Nothing but a dull boom. We had no means of knowing where it hit, but it was a long ways away. There were several more during the day but no one evinced any alarm or even interest. However, about four o'clock (3:05) BOOM came one that seemed about 100 yards away. We looked to see where it had fallen but an English artillery officer told us it alighted at least a mile away."

Then Ernest continued about how much he had already seen in Paris and what a linguist he was becoming. (Certain of Ernest's words are illegible due to erratic penmanship and to the deterioration of the paper.)

This afternoon Ted and Jenks who you met at the train, Dad, went all through the hotel [illegible] Napoleon's tomb. They have a wonderful exhibit of captured enemy artillery and aeroplanes there. It covers several acres. We have been all over the city in the [illegible] two cylinder buses that pass for one's access. You can ride for about one franc.

Have seen all the sights, the Champs Elysees, the Tuileries and the Arc de Triumph [sic] and so on. Our hotel is right on the [illegible] where the guillotine [illegible] where Marie Antoinette and Sidney Carton [illegible]. Paris is a great city but is not as quaint and interesting as Bordeaux. If the war ever ends I intend to bum all through this country.

I picked up a lot of French and can sling it pretty fast. I don't know what it looks like and can't write it, but can speak fairly well and read easily. On the boat all the garçons and femmes dechamps [sic] and everyone spoke nothing but French and it was a case of learn or starve.

Ted and Jenks and I are haveing [sic] La grand time. Tonight we went to the Folies Bergere [illegible] ye straight and narrow for me. I got my

Kaiki cap and Sam Browne belt today and look like the proverbial million
dollars. We leave for Milan tomorrow. Thursday night. First class all the
way. Tis ye gay life. Write me at Milan. Much love to all and everyone.

> Your old kid,
> Ernie

As he had in New York, Ernest wrote home only about what his parents
were able to hear. But Paris in 1918 offered much more to see than war
museums and the Folies Bergere:

> It was the first day of my leave. I was walking along the Boulevard Male-
> sherbes. A car passed me and a beautiful woman leaned out. She called
> to me and I came. She took me to a house, a mansion rather, in a distant
> part of Paris, and there a very beautiful thing happened to me. Afterwards
> someone took me out a different door than I had come in by. The beau-
> tiful woman had told me that she would never, that she could never, see
> me again. I tried to get the number of the mansion but it was one of a
> block of mansions all looking the same.
>
> From then on all through my leave I tried to see that beautiful lady.
> Once I thought I saw her in the theatre. It wasn't her. Another time I
> caught a glimpse of what I thought was her in a passing taxi and leaped
> into another taxi and followed. I lost the taxi. I was desperate. Finally on
> the next to the last night of my leave I was so desperate and dull that I
> went with one of those guides that guarantee to show you all of Paris. We
> started out and visited various places. "Is this all you've got?" I asked
> the guide.
>
> "There is a real place, but it's very expensive," the guide said. We com-
> promised on a price finally, and the guide took me. It was an old mansion.
> You looked through a slit in the wall. All around the wall were people
> looking through slits. There, looking through slits could be seen the uni-
> forms of men of all the Allied countries, and many handsome South
> Americans in evening dress. I looked through a slit myself. For a while
> nothing happened. Then a beautiful woman came into the room with a
> young British officer. She took off her long fur coat and her hat and threw
> them into a chair. The officer was taking off his Sam Browne belt. I recog-
> nized her. It was the lady whom I had been with when the beautiful
> thing happened to me.

On June 6, Ernest and the other Red Cross volunteers boarded the
Paris Lyon Mediterranée train at the Gare de Lyon for the overnight trip
to Milan. Passing through central and southern France at night, the
young men missed some of the loveliest pastoral landscape in Europe. But
when they awoke the next morning they were compensated for their loss.
As the PLM express labored through the French Alps (passage through
neutral Switzerland was forbidden), the sky was the bluest, the snow-
capped mountains the highest, the meadows at the edge of woods the most
verdant, the valleys still in shadows the deepest Ernest had ever seen.

Later, under clouds blown in from the Ligurian Sea, came the sculptured hills and large estates of Lombardy. At midday, the train entered the great railyards of the Garibaldi Station in Milan.

According to Red Cross scheduling, the Americans were to spend some thirty-six hours in Milan before departing for their ambulance posts near the front lines. During this time they would be billeted at the Hotel Vittoria, a first-class hotel in the heart of the city, and, should they choose, be taken to see such celebrated landmarks as the Milan Cathedral with its three thousand statues of white marble, the Galleria Vittoria Emanuele, and La Scala Opera House. At Red Cross headquarters on 10 Via Manzoni, Ernest, Howell Jenkins, and Bill Horne learned that, along with twenty-two others, they had been assigned to Section IV at Schio, near Lake Garda, one hundred fifty kilometers east of Milan.

Before Ernest had time to unpack, however, an official of the Italian Red Cross came to the rooms at the Hotel Vittoria. He reported that a munitions plant twenty-five kilometers from Milan had blown up. He asked for volunteers. For the next twelve hours Ernest, at eighteen, endured a "body detail." Years later he called the experience "A Natural History of the Dead":

> We drove to the scene of the disaster in trucks along poplar-shaded roads, bordered with ditches containing much minute animal life, which I could not clearly observe because of the great clouds of dust raised by the trucks. Arriving where the munition plant had been, some of us were put to patrolling about those large stocks of munitions which for some reason had not exploded, while others were put at extinguishing a fire which had gotten into the grass of an adjacent field; which tasks being concluded, we were ordered to search the immediate vicinity and surrounding fields for bodies. We found and carried to an improvised mortuary a good number of these and, I must admit, frankly, the shock of it was to find that these dead were women rather than men. In those days women had not yet commenced to wear their hair cut short, as they did later for several years in Europe and America, and the most disturbing thing, perhaps because it was the most unaccustomed, was the presence and, even more disturbing, the occasional absence of this long hair. I remember that after we had searched quite thoroughly for the complete dead we collected fragments. Many of these were detached from a heavy, barbed-wire fence which had surrounded the position of the factory and from the still existent portions of which we picked many of these detached bits which illustrated only too well the tremendous energy of high explosive. Many fragments we found a considerable distance away in the fields, they being carried farther by their own weight.

Early Sunday morning, June 9, 1918, Ernest and the other men of Section IV straggled through the main porticoes, topped by two winged lions, of the Garibaldi Station in Milan and entrained for Vicenza, one hundred forty kilometers east across the Lombardy plain. The final twenty-four kilometers northwest to Schio, they rode as passengers in six of the ambulances they had come to drive. To Ernest, the gray, top-heavy, blunt-nosed Fiats that met the men in Vicenza looked like moving vans. As they climbed the thousand feet into the foothills of the Dolomites over steep, pebbly roads, there were harsh vibrations and the deep whine of the heavy Fiat gears.

At the end of the two-hour ride from Vicenza, the convoy rolled down a narrow cobblestone street and into the paved courtyard of a factory building, its limestone walls white in the moonlight. Under Lieutenant Charles Griffin's orders, the men shouldered their footlockers and were herded up to a long narrow room on the second floor. There were two rows of cots (a dozen or so occupied), open casement windows, and under bare rafters one large gaslight before an American flag. The mattress on the wroughtiron cot felt thinner to Ernest than his bedroll in Michigan. But neither that nor the unmistakable odor of sheep kept him awake.

When Ernest arrived at Schio in early June 1918, the Italian front stretched across a third of northern Italy, from Lake Garda and the Cornelle Pass on the west to the delta of the Lower Piave beyond Venice on the east. Italy's principal allies, Great Britain and France, considered it a stable line, of secondary importance to the Western Front. In Italian newspapers it was called picturesque. But to Italy's government, its military, and its people, the front line from Garda to the Adriatic was a constant reminder of a national disgrace.

Eight months earlier, on the stormy morning of October 25, 1917, German and Austrian troops under the command of General Otto von Below had begun an assault on the Italian line at Caporetto, a small mountain town in northeastern Italy. Within two weeks, despite the heroism of certain Italian corps d'élite—the Alpini on Mount Nero held out for three days and died almost to a man, and the cavalry regiments (the Novaro Lancers and the Genoa Dragoons) made suicidal charges—von Below drove the Italian army back seventy miles, across the Tagliamento to the shores of the Piave River. Indeed, if heavy rains had not flooded the Piave just after the Italian Third Army crossed it, Venice would have fallen and with it the whole of Italy's industrial plain.

In his published report to the Italian people, General Luigi Cadorna, Italy's commander-in-chief, made the usual excuses for his defeat: poor communications, lack of reserves, bad weather, bad luck. But in lines censored from his communique, he fixed the blame where everyone knew it belonged—on incompetent officers and cowardly troops.

At the Council of Rapallo, which convened even before the Caporetto retreat was completed, Lloyd George of England and Clemenceau of France decided that six divisiòns of Allied troops (three French, three British) should be sent immediately to bolster the new Italian lines, and Italy's newly appointed prime minister, Vittorio Orlando, publicly expressed his country's deep gratitude. There were many ceremonies and much flag-waving. But to the Italian people it was the few hundred American Red Cross volunteers—within a month of Caporetto there were five ARC sections on the front line—who symbolized the Allies' faith in their country and embodied the Allied spirit.

At Section IV, at Schio, Lieutenant Griffin soon established a simple and efficient routine for his newly enlarged unit. Every other day, each new recruit would accompany a veteran driver on the ten-mile trip through Posina to the front on 7000-ft. Mt. Pasubio, overlooking the Barcole Pass. At the emergency dressing stations, they would pick up the sick and wounded, haul them back to the clearing stations (called *smistamento*), and then distribute them to the hospitals according to their papers. For the most part, the patients from the lower altitudes suffered from jaundice, gonorrhea, self-inflicted wounds, and pneumonia. Now and then there would be a wounding by rock fragments. But from higher up on the mountain, where the narrow roads were bordered by drapes of camouflage cloth to keep the drivers from panic and wayside shrines remembered victims of accidents there, the Schio ambulance drivers would take down a member of an Alpini regiment, wounded by an Austrian sniper, blood collecting in his raw woolen mountain coat.

Before each trip, the new recruit was responsible for checking his ambulance's tires for cuts and stone bruises and for making sure the ventilation slots in the box of the Fiat were open in good weather and closed in the rain. On the way back from Mount Pasubio, he was to see to it that the awkward system of slings that supported the stretchers was carefully adjusted and, should there be a seriously wounded passenger aboard, that the heavy curtain was drawn around him.

On days off together, Ernest, Bill Horne, and Howell Jenkins took advantage of a privilege granted to all the drivers and used one of the half-dozen small Ford ambulances (which usually sat idle in the courtyard because their planetary gears and weak brakes made them suspect on mountain roads) to explore the lovely countryside around Schio. Driving south, they would pass through rolling hills covered with vineyards and crowned by houses with many windows and high chimneys at either end. To the north the houses were smaller, with stone piles in the front yards, stubby chimneys, and long roofs slanted toward the path of the winter sun. On one clear evening, while driving west to Lake Garda, the young men stopped to watch the light gray Dolomites turn red, then purple, then a light luminous blue.

The mess at the Schio barracks (the former Cazzola woolen mill) was on the first floor beneath the sleeping quarters. Every evening, prompt and friendly Italian waiters served the young men large helpings of spaghetti (to be eaten very quickly and seriously), game stews (usually rabbit), dark bread, and sausage. One morning a week, as a gesture to the American palate, they served fried eggs. On each of the long, narrow, thick-legged tables, the waiters at every meal placed several pots of apricot jam and two wicker-covered gallon flasks of wine in metal cradles. A driver need only pull down the neck of the flask with his forefinger to fill his large tumbler held in the same hand.

When Ernest and his friends were bored with the fare at the barracks, they would walk into the center of Schio to the Due Spadi ("Two Swords") and enjoy the house specialty, its antipasto, and the priority service accorded Americans. Later, they would drink warm beer at cool marble-topped tables in the trattoria across the square from the church.

Although Ernest refused to take part in a head shaving some of the new drivers thought would make them look more "military," he did once reconnoiter the "official" officer's whorehouse, where the girls "climbed all over you and put your cap on backwards as a sign of affection between their trips upstairs with brother officers."

The veterans of Section IV printed a monthly newspaper they called *CIAO,* and there was a degree of celebrity for anyone whose work appeared in it. Shortly after Ernest arrived in Schio, L. Fisher, the editor, posted a note on the bulletin board in the barracks. It read, "We hope the new men will contribute largely to *CIAO*. We know that there is talent among them. . . . Make a name for yourself by writing for *CIAO*."

In response, Ernest wrote a carefully crafted thousand-word "letter" in his high-school "Ring Lardner" style:

Al Receives Another Letter

Dear Al:

Well Al we are here in this old Italy and now that I am here I am not going to leave it. Not at all if any. And that is no New Years revolution Al but the truth. Well Al I am now an officer and if you would meet me you would have to salute me. What I am is a provisional acting second lieutenant without a commission but the trouble is that all the other fellows are too. There ain't no privates in our army Al and the Captain is called a chef. But it don't look to me as though he could cook a damn bit. . . .

It is a very soft life for you back in the States Al because at least you always have plenty to eat and a place to sleep and a wife. But this Trench life is hell Al. I would tell you about our hardships Al but we mustn't reveal no military secrets even to those that are nearest and dearest to us. But I can tell you we have been in two battles Al. The Battle of Milan and the Battle of Paris. That is a joke Al and maybe you can't understand it but it will show you anyway I am the same old joker Huh Al . . . ?

Ernest signed the article "Your Old Pal Steve now known as the second Gerry Baldy."

Bill Horne, on one of their nights at the trattoria, told Ernest that Schio seemed to him like a fraternity, or like one of the eating clubs at Princeton. Ernest, although he had never experienced a fraternity, agreed.

In the harmonious life the young men enjoyed at Schio, there was, however, one discordant note. It was sounded by the dozen or so veterans who had been there for six months and before that had driven for the Norton-Harjes Ambulance Corps in France. Years later, one of these veterans, Emmett Shaw, characterized the mood at Schio in June 1918 this way:

> At Schio all the new arrivals were uncomfortable, not only Hemingway. With the exception of Bill Horne, who was a real gentleman, they never mixed really with our group. And Hemingway, we didn't like him and he didn't like us. Many of us veteran drivers had already served with the French on the Western Front. We felt that at Schio we were doing good work and we hoped that we would be able to continue it. Of course we also liked to relax. We liked to swim. We liked to sun bathe. But not him. He wanted action. He wanted to "participate in the struggle." He thought we were a bunch of do-nothings. On our part we thought he was an impulsively presumptuous child come to endanger our nice life at Schio.

But to Ernest and many of the other newcomers, the veterans' fast one-handed driving, their hotly contested baseball games in the orchard across the road, their cynical and cryptic conversation at mess, and their running joke about hemorrhoidal wounds from the hard-riding Fiats and the pasta diet were in the worst sort of taste.

At the end of his first week at Schio, it seemed to Ernest that the antagonistic mood at the "Country Club," as the men now called their barracks, was deeply entrenched. But suddenly, on the night of June 15, 1918, something happened that started a dramatic change. At three in the morning, the barracks at Schio awakened to what sounded like rolling thunder east toward Bassano and looked like lightning against the heavily overcast sky. The next day the newspapers trucked in from Vicenza reported the start of a new Austrian offensive against the Italian line from Mount Grappa to the Lower Piave.

As in their successful attack against the Italian lines on the Isonzo eight months before, the Austrians opened their June offensive with four hours of intense heavy artillery fire (the thunder and lightning that had awakened Schio). Then, at seven in the morning, their infantry made two rapid and sharp-edged thrusts: the first between Mount Grappa and Mount Corno on the Asiago Plateau; the second between Montello and San Dona on the Lower Piave. To create disorder, the Austrians lobbed hundreds of gas shells toward the massed Italian reserves a half-dozen miles or more behind the lines. By afternoon the Italians had retreated up to a mile at places along the mountain front and in the delta. Then, incredibly, by nightfall of the fifteenth, the Alpini broke the Austrians at Asiago. After two days of heavy fighting it was clear the mountain assault would fail.

On the Lower Piave, however, the Austrians did have some success establishing small beachheads on the western bank at Saletto and Fagore and between Fossalta and Capo Sile. But by Tuesday the eighteenth, the Italian Third Army broke through the Austrian center between Candelo and Fagore and occupied the riverbank at Saletto, at Zensone, and established itself along the Fossalta Canal.

In their success the Italians were blessed (as they had been at the Tagliamento eight months before) by the weather. Just as the Austrian general Boroevitch was preparing to attack the flank of the new Italian commander Diaz, heavy rains fell in the mountains, and the piles of trees Italian woodcutters had amassed there to be floated down the Piave to market broke loose from their booms and battered away the Austrians' supply bridges fifty miles downstream.

Although this "defensive victory," as it was quickly called in the papers, was hardly sufficient to erase the stigma of Caporetto or to satisfy the country's longing for revenge, it did resuscitate the patriotic spirit in the Italian people and in their press. Suddenly articles began appearing in *L'Astico, Il Savoia,* and *La Tradotta* (all of which were read by a number of the veterans at Schio) praising the Italian foot soldier for his courage and durability, the Italian officer for his coolness under fire, and extolling the virtue of a "new fraternity of arms."

The Battle of the Piave also had a surprising effect at Schio on both the veteran ambulance drivers and the new recruits. Suddenly they found they shared a fresh enthusiasm, a spirit of camaraderie, and a renewed sense of the value of the job they had come to do.

On June 28, Lieutenant Griffin brought the men at Schio some welcome news. The Red Cross, he said, intended to establish eight rolling canteens in the midst of the battle zone on the Lower Piave, and at each an officer was needed. It would be the duty of the canteen officer to help sustain the morale of the Italian troops by distributing small amenities—cigarettes, chocolate, writing paper, clean water, magazines—and by "showing the uniform." The work would be dangerous, Lieutenant Griffin warned, because there was much Austrian "infiltration," and casualties from snipers and artillery bombardment were very high. When he asked for volunteers, the entire unit stepped forward.

Early on July 1, 1918, the eight men Lieutenant Griffin selected to man the Red Cross stations—among them Bill Horne and Ernest, Emmet Shaw, Dick Baume, Howell Jenkins, and Warren Pease—left Schio in two of the Fiat ambulances for the fifty-mile trip to Mestre, across the Venetian plain. That night at Mestre, they were transferred to the command of Captain James Gamble, introduced to them as "Inspector of Rolling Canteens." The next morning, Captain Gamble had two new Buick trucks, just arrived from America, take the men the last dozen miles to the Italian lines on the Lower Piave.

As Ernest rode along in the softer-sprung Buicks through the mud and the mosquito swarms that sifted into the truck box like clouds of dust, he had a good look at the residue left when the tide of battle had receded east toward the Piave and crossed it the week before.

Just beyond Mestre, where the built-up road seemed a levee between the sunken fields, there were small mud-brick farmhouses (all deserted), lines of woven fences ripped by shell blasts, and defoliated, barkless trees. Closer to the front there were bodies scattered in the fields and then clusters of bodies all uniformed and twisted into bizarre postures. Once, near the road, the trucks passed an Austrian machine-gun nest, the fifty-caliber gun's fluted nozzle stuffed with mud, the cooling hoses twisted, the legs of dead soldiers swelling against their leather puttees. Later there was a German biplane, the pilot a week dead in the cockpit, on the fuselage an Iron Cross, the Mercedes tristar on the tail. The stench of the Kansas City stockyard fire seemed like nothing, here. Close enough to the front to hear the leaden thunking of machine guns, Ernest saw a crater, as wide as a farmhouse, shoulder-deep, half-filled with water, a wall of dirt raised around its rim. Captain Gamble said that that kind of shell, an Austrian Minenwerfer, had killed his friend Edward McKey, the Red Cross man at Fossalta, almost a month before.

When the Buicks reached the front at San Dona, they turned north, passing through close-lying villages along the Piave, and Captain Gamble allowed the men to drop off where they wished. Bill Horne and Warren Pease chose a heavily shelled two-story farmhouse at San Pedro Novello. Ernest chose a four-room farmhouse, one of the few buildings still standing at Fossalta di Piave. Just beyond Fossalta, in a severe L-shaped bend, the Piave River moved between reed-congested banks, a muddy blue.

Although Ernest thought Fossalta the most "miserable, gloomy" place he had ever seen, he was happy with his duties there. Each morning and afternoon he would load up his haversack with cigarettes and chocolate, take his helmet and gas mask, and, on the bicycle lent him by the commander of a Bersaglieri cycle battalion—an Italian corps d'élite composed of young aristocrats who rode to battle under the blare of their own trumpeters—rode the mile and a quarter to the trenches along the river. Among the Italian infantry, veterans of a month's continuous fighting, Ernest was at first called "giovanni Americano" and greeted with much back slapping and attempts at American slang. Later the men called him Ernesto, showed him family snapshots, and taught him a few "Villa Rosa" (whorehouse) songs.

On the fourth of July, Ernest left off his rounds in the trenches and, wearing his Sam Browne belt, his Bersaglieri helmet, and his leather puttees, he slung a borrowed Italian carbine on the frame of his bicycle and rode over the few miles of rock-strewn road to San Pedro Novello to celebrate the holiday with Bill Horne. To his surprise, however, he found Bill and Warren Pease bored and frustrated. They hadn't been to the trenches yet, they told him. For the last two days they had sat at the post waiting for supplies.

That night, while Warren Pease (who would one day be an admiral in the U.S. Navy) slept soundly, Bill and Ernest lay awake talking of their families (Bill's father held a Columbia University Ph.D. in chemistry and taught at Rutgers), their ambitions (Bill too hoped to become a writer), and girls. Bill felt that marriage was the best cure for insomnia; Ernest was not so sure. When Bill admitted to Ernest he had spent the five years since Princeton drifting from job to job and had lost many opportunities, Ernest in turn confessed to Bill that because he was lonesome at Fossalta he had just written a letter to a hometown girl implying that he'd already been under heavy fire and that his post was only a stone's throw from the Austrian lines.

During the first days of July, the troops on the Lower Piave felt that the Austrians' June offensive was over and a period of quiescence, such as had followed Caporetto, had begun. Despite a smattering of small-arms fire and brief machine-gun duels, the war was now a sniper's game in which the wounded sharpshooter, grasping branches, fell slowly from his post in the tree.

When Ernest rode to the trenches on Sunday, July 7, a day so hot his tunic stuck to his skin, he found a striking change. Instead of thanking him with their customary enthusiasm for the toscani, a highly prized Italian cigar Ernest had made a habit of acquiring, the troops were preoccupied and subdued. Ernest learned from the officers that an attack on the Austrian positions north and south of Fossalta was imminent. They said they expected heavy shelling all along the line.

That night, in heat only a little diminished since the afternoon, Ernest rode his bicycle to the front lines again. It was new moon, and the terrain along the river lay in darkness. The troops, all helmeted now, moved quietly in the trenches or stood watch over a river they could only smell and hear flowing through the reeds. Close to midnight, Ernest asked permission to move out to an advanced listening post, a hole in the ground a hundred and fifty yards closer to the Piave and the Austrian lines. Two sharp-eyed enlisted men manned the post, and over the last yards they guided him with the radium dials on their watches.

A half-hour past midnight on July 8, the troops all along the line at Fossalta heard the first rush of battle: an Italian 350 shell, sounding like a railway train, arced over the river. Then, as if on signal, the crack of rifles, the staccato of machine guns, and the boom of field pieces—75s or 149s—began. Overhead, the white burning phosphorus of Austrian star shells crackled and left trails of silver smoke.

As Ernest and the two soldiers lay hunched against the rim of their hole, they heard across the river a "cough," then a "chuh, chuh, chuh, chuh," then a long descending roar. "Then there was a flash, as when a blast furnace door is swung open, and a roar that started white and went red and on and on in the rushing wind." Ernest "tried hard to breathe but my breath would not come and I felt myself rush bodily out of myself and out and out and out all the time bodily in the wind. I went out swiftly, all of myself, and I knew I was dead and that it had all been a mistake to think you just died. Then I floated and instead of going on I felt myself slide back. I breathed and I was back."

Conscious again, Ernest saw that one of the soldiers beside him had had his legs blown off. The stumps still twitched, but the man was dead. The other soldier had taken shrapnel in the chest but was still alive. Ernest hoisted up the wounded Italian in a fireman's carry, and, with his own legs full of shrapnel and feeling as if he "had rubber boots full of water on," he started back toward the trenches. Suddenly, in the blaze of an Austrian searchlight, Ernest was pitched forward by machine-gun slugs tearing into his right foot and the side of his right knee. Then he was "on his knees, hot-sweet choking, coughing it onto the rock." Somehow he hoisted his wounded a second time and staggered to the trenches, fifty yards away.

For the next two hours, Ernest moved in and out of shock, and all that happened to him passed with the logic and continuity of a dream. There was the Italian captain in the dugout who, taking the blood on Ernest's tunic as evidence of a mortal wound, stood by reverent and inert; there were the stretcher bearers who seemed maddeningly insistent on leaving the road and crossing lots, and laying Ernest down roughly, sometimes with his head so low his eyes felt like weighted doll's eyes, sometimes with his legs placed so they hurt as if "devils were driving nails into the raw"; there was the roofless stable where Ernest lay alone with the deep stomach cold of reflex fear each time the big shells arced overhead. But on the ride in the ambulance to Fornaci, three kilometers behind the front lines, the pain in his legs became hard and permanent, and his mind cleared.

At the dressing station in Fornaci, many casualties from the front lay on the ground outside the operating tent. The wounded, distinguished in the dark by their bandages and the sounds they made, were on one side. On the other side were the dead. Every few minutes the flap of the operating tent opened wide for a stretcher. In the kerosene light, Ernest saw the surgeons, their sleeves rolled up to the shoulders and their arms red as butchers. There was low keening, the rush and splatter of vomit, the roar of oaths he had learned in the trenches. Once, on orders from a surgeon who came to the entrance and pointed, a bandaged soldier was carried moaning over to the side of the dead.

As Ernest lay with the wounded, feeling the night chill, he heard a voice he remembered. It was his C.O., Captain James Gamble, talking to a medical sergeant in fluent Italian. As soon as Captain Gamble finished with the sergeant, he came over to Ernest and crouched by his side. He had noticed him first, Gamble said, when Ernest chose the post at Fossalta, the former post of his friend, Edward McKey. After asking about the wounds, Gamble went into the operating tent. Then the stretcher bearers came out and carried Ernest inside.

Amid the harsh smell of antiseptic and the sweet smell of blood, two burly orderlies lifted Ernest onto the operating table. The Italian surgeon, working quickly and efficiently, cleaned the wounds and removed the larger pieces of shrapnel. He described everything he found to Ernest in Italian, but Ernest judged the size and weight of the extractions by the sound they made dropping into the basin. The pain was sharp, and

Ernest's stomach fluttered each time the flesh was cut. Finally, the surgeon stroked Ernest's head, gave him brandy and a shot of antitetanus, and told the stretcher bearers to carry him outside carefully. After a rough ride from Fornaci—the slings that held his stretcher in the Fiat ambulance allowed for swaying, and that and the morning heat made him vomit on the floor—Ernest arrived at the field hospital in Treviso, ten miles due east of Fossalta.

For the next five days, the doctors in Treviso watched for infection (which they did not expect, since the projectiles had all been sterilized by the heat of the blast) and, as a result of damage to an artery, for gangrene. The orderly tried to keep Ernest as comfortable as possible by pouring mineral water over the bandages to stop the itching and to keep the bedding cool, by scratching Ernest's feet on demand, and by making a swatter of shredded newspaper for the flies. For Ernest, the worst times came when a screen was put up around a patient's bed, and only the puttees of the doctors and the men nurses showed below the screen, and there was whispering; and during the hours in the dressing room each day, when out of the windows he could see graves, some freshly dug, in the garden. The best time was the evening, when, because of the blackout, the dark came after dusk and remained, and he felt very young.

With Bill Horne back at Schio—he and Warren Pease had left San Pedro Novello the day after Ernest's visit—and Howell Jenkins on the front at Portogrande, Ernest had but one regular visitor at the field hospital: Captain James Gamble.

In 1918, James Gamble was thirty-six years old. He was handsome, well educated (Yale, 1904), and cosmopolitan (he could speak familiarly of Paris, Monte Carlo, and Madrid). A Philadelphia blue-blood, he had been a favorite of Main Line debutantes for years. In 1914, after a long affair with a wealthy divorcee, he settled in Florence. As soon as America declared war on the Central Powers in 1917, he volunteered for duty with the Red Cross.

Partly because Ernest listened with great attention and partly because Jim Gamble could speak easily of many things, the captain's visits soon grew from polite inquiries about Ernest's condition and the delivery of convenience gifts—mosquito netting, brandy and vermouth, English newspapers from British officers at the front—to long and sometimes intimate conversations. Jim Gamble spoke of the artists he most admired (Giotto for his powerful simplicity and Masaccio, who he said was Giotto born again a hundred years later); of his grandfather, the railroad president who had spent his life with trains and died early one morning as a passing freight blew its whistle; and of his family's summer estate, Altamont, at Eagles Mere in the Allegheny mountains near Williamsport. There was a lake there, Gamble said, surrounded by great patches of laurel and rhododendron, a grass tennis court, a long rising lawn, and a great house with a front-door portico supported by four fieldstone pillars. In the main room were two bronze plaques: one, a lion rampant; the other, St. George killing the dragon.

Ernest, on his part, was very pleased when Jim Gamble seemed delighted by the stories he told of rustic life in Upper Michigan (Ernest confessed he hoped to be a good writer someday) and by what he had seen in Kansas City while he worked for the *Star*.

On Friday, July 12, the major in charge of the ward told Ernest that his wounds had healed enough for safe travel and that his legs should now be x-rayed at a new American hospital in Milan. He asked Ernest if he felt strong enough to leave. Ernest said yes and asked in turn to have two notes cabled immediately, one to his parents, the other to Ted Brumback in Milan. The major said they would ship him out early the next morning, before it got too hot.

That afternoon, when Jim Gamble came through the visitors' entrance beside the dressing-room door, Ernest was especially happy to see him again. As soon as Jim was seated, Ernest gave him the news. Jim said he had just spoken to the doctor himself, and, should Ernest wish, he would accompany him on the forty-eight-hour train ride to Milan. Jim told Ernest they would pass through the most famous Italian cities in English literature: Verona and Padua. Ernest was quietly proud that he knew Jim alluded to *Romeo and Juliet* and *The Taming of the Shrew*.

In the early morning of July 15, the train from Mestre pulled slowly through the freightyards of Milan and stopped at a large red-brick building. There was a fountain with benches out front, a flower garden on one side, and the sounds of American ragtime coming from a gramophone within. It was Milan's Red Cross Station Canteen, the largest in Italy.

As soon as the services of two stretcher bearers could be obtained, Gamble shepherded Ernest—along with his footlocker heavy with hardware battle souvenirs, his uniform bags, and two half-filled bottles of cognac used as anesthetic on the trip—through the swarms of troops and into the canteen lounge. While Ernest drank coffee from a condensed milk can, Gamble arranged transportation to 3 Via Bacheto, the site of the new American Red Cross hospital. When the ambulance was ready to leave, Jim said that he would return to his command on the Lower Piave. Ernest thanked his friend, and they said goodbye through the lyrics of "Alexander's Ragtime Band."

After a short stop-and-go ride through morning traffic across the center

of Milan, Ernest was lifted out of the Fiat's box in front of an old mansion, four stories high, with gray stucco walls, empty flower boxes along
the balustrade, and many windows with white, newly painted trim. The
stretcher bearers had a quick conference with much gesticulating and
then carted Ernest inside to a small elevator in the rear. The stretcher,
however, would not fit in the elevator's cage, and the men had to hold
Ernest up under his arms and under his bent knees. The hospital porter,
a small man with a gray mustache and a doorman's cap, pushed the button for the fourth floor.

On the fourth floor, Ernest met the nurse on duty. Her name was Anne
Scanlon, and she squinted nearsightedly at him. She told the porter that
the hospital had just opened, that they were not expecting any patients,
and that all the linen was locked up. As the porter stood, cap in hand,
looking at her, Ernest felt the pain going in and out of the bone. Finally,
he ordered the stretcher bearers to take him into any room.

The room the stretcher bearers chose for Ernest, since all the rooms
were indeed empty, was down at the end of a long hallway. The blinds
were drawn, the furniture newly varnished, and the walls calcimined a
soft cherry tint. There was a small brass bed against one wall and a big
wardrobe with a mirror against the other. The nurse, who had followed
the men down the hallway and had come into the room after them,
closed the door. Ernest tipped the stretcher bearers five lire apiece and
asked one of them to give his papers to Miss Scanlon. There were three
folded sheets describing, in Italian, Ernest's wounds and the treatment
already given. The stretcher bearers saluted Ernest and left, and Ernest
told Miss Scanlon she could leave too.

Soon after Ernest awoke from a short, restless sleep (he had lain very
still, hoping to sleep again), Miss Scanlon came in and announced a
visitor. It was Ted Brumback, and he had the letter in hand Ernest had
requested he write to Clarence and Grace. While Brumback looked on
with delight, Ernest smiled at how the bloody details of his wounds were
cautiously replaced by assurances he would be decorated for his bravery
"with a very high medal indeed." Because Ernest could not write the
kind of letter his parents needed at this time, he asked Ted to include a
logical excuse: "He has not written himself because of one or two splin-
ters lodged in his fingers." But Ernest did add a postscript:

> I am all OK and include much love to ye parents. I'm not so much of a
> Hell raiser as Brummy makes me out. Lots of love.
>
> Ernie
>
> S.H. Don't worry Pop!

When Ted Brumback, with a volley of promises to visit often, finally left, a nurse Ernest had not seen before came in. She was heavy and short, and despite her bobbed hair she looked forty. But, introducing herself as Elsie MacDonald lately from New York, she had a nice voice, Ernest thought, and a friendly grin.

While Ernest answered Miss MacDonald's questions about his wounding and about what he had eaten so far and now wanted for supper, she undressed him and washed him very gently and smoothly. Then, after she took his temperature, she went out and came back with Miss Scanlon, and together they made the bed with Ernest in it. For supper that night, Miss MacDonald brought Ernest an eggnog and, to his surprise, a strong martini with what Ernest recognized as Cinzano vermouth. Instead of an olive, however, he found a glob of castor oil in the dregs.

In the heat of late July, Ernest adjusted to the tedium of his convalescence by anticipating the several "events" of his day. Each morning at eight, he was served a "genuine American breakfast" of Italian sausage, fried eggs and potatoes, bitter Italian coffee, and hard rolls. It was all prepared, the porter assured him, in an immaculate kitchen in the nurses' quarters on the floor below. Ernest ate his breakfast slowly and, as Dr. Hemingway had always encouraged him to do, chewed his food carefully and well. At the end of the meal, Ernest smoked a Macedonia, a loosely rolled mild cigarette, until, in order to avoid the frustration and embarrassment of the bedpan, he made the painful trip on crutches to the toilet down the hall.

Usually Ernest spent his mornings alone. But because he was thought to be the first American wounded on the Italian Front, he enjoyed a brisk celebrity in the afternoons. Among his frequent visitors were two buxom American matrons, Mrs. Stucke and Mrs. Spiegel, who called Ernest their "dear boy" and brought him cakes, marsala, and candy (Mrs. Stucke also brought along her daughter); an affectionate Englishman, Mr. Engelfield, who claimed he had "adopted" Ernest and brought him everything from the London papers to eau de cologne; a Catholic missionary priest from India with whom Ernest loved to talk; and a "Tenente" Brundi, a well-known Milanese artist who insisted on painting a souvenir portrait of Ernest. One day the Pathé news service made a film of Ernest in uniform, in a wheelchair, with a blanket across his knees.

During these visits, Ernest was loquacious and very polite, though he did pepper his speech with Italian army slang he'd picked up in the trenches along the Piave. But later, when he was alone again, he listened for the voices of nurses coming off duty and for the victrola and the piano in what the nurses called their music room. After supper, Ernest watched the small light come over the city and, over the quiet street, listened for the voices of troops manning antiaircraft batteries on nearby roofs. Sometimes the searchlights came on and directed their shafts toward the sound of airplane engines, and the antiaircraft batteries came alive. But then these sounds subsided, the searchlights went off, and Ernest saw bats outside his windows darting like morning larks and heard mosquitos in his room as loud as any he'd heard in Michigan.

On July 21, his nineteenth birthday, Ernest wrote his first letter home. The salutation was "Dear Folks," but the letter was especially intended for Clarence. Besides describing his wounding in sanitized details and telling of "photographs of the Piave and many other interesting pictures" and his "wonderful lot of souvenirs"—"Austrian carbines and ammunition, German and Austrian medals, officers' automatic pistols, Bosch helmets, about a dozen bayonets, star shell pistols and knives, and almost everything you can think of"—Ernest wrote that "one of the best surgeons in Milan" had decided on the most conservative treatment for his wounds:

> The surgeon, very wisely, is, after consultation, going to wait for the wound in my right knee to become healed before operating. The bullet will then be rather encysted and he will make a clean cut and go in under the side of the knee cap. By allowing it to be completely healed first he thus avoids any danger of infection and stiff knee. That is wise, don't you think, Dad?

Years later, Ernest wrote again of this consultation in *A Farewell to Arms,* but this time without allowance for his father's anxiety or point of view:

> "Only one thing I can say," the first captain with the beard said, "It is a question of time. Three months, six months probably."
> "Certainly the cynovial fluid must reform."
> "Certainly. It is a question of time. I could not conscientiously open a knee like that before the projectile was encysted."
> "I agree with you, doctor."
> "Six months for what?" I asked.
> "Six months for the projectile to encyst before the knee can be opened safely."
> "I don't believe it," I said.
> "Do you want to keep your knee, young man?"
> "No," I said.
> "What?"
> "I want it cut off," I said, "so I can wear a hook on it."
> "What do you mean? A hook?"
> "He's joking," the house doctor said.

❧ 6 ❧
His Lady Fair

During the first week of August, the Red Cross hospital at 3 Via Bacheto began crowding up as men wounded or sick checked in from the field hospitals or from the six sectional units along the Eastern Front. One of the new arrivals was Henry Villard, an ambulance driver from Section I at Bassano, who had dysentery and jaundice and got the room next to Ernest's. With his tall frame and narrow shoulders and his habit of looking away when he spoke, he reminded Ernest of Harold Sampson. He asked to be called Harry and took to calling Ernest "Hem."

A patient Ernest was happy to see arrived with Henry Villard. It was Bill Horne, and like Ernest he came in on a stretcher. (Bill had contracted malaria at San Pedro Novello.) When his fever subsided, Bill spent most of his time in Ernest's room. At first they spoke of Schio—there was nothing much doing at the old "Country Club," Bill said, and the men were getting fat and dull on pasta and too much frascati—and of Ernest's experience on the Lower Piave. Eventually their talk turned to their chief mutual interest: writing. Newspaper work, Ernest said, had been good for self-discipline, teaching him to write every day with or without "inspiration" and forcing him to bring into focus quickly and smoothly the essentials of a story. Yet Ernest told Bill that newspaper work was as far from real literature as a snowman is from the Pietà and that he would only return to it after the war if his serious writing didn't sell and he had to get a job.

On their afternoons together, smoking Macedonias and sipping Martell Cognac (Bill noticed the empties piling up in the armoire), Ernest asked Bill many questions about his life at Princeton and about the English courses Bill had taken there. Ernest said he often regretted not having gone to college, mostly because his decision had deeply disappointed his father. Bill told Ernest that, at Princeton, literature had been read as history or as biography but hardly ever as art and that the academic style the professors encouraged would hardly do for *The Saturday Evening Post.*

In mid-August, a get-well letter came for Ernest from Schio (Howell Jenkins had addressed the envelope), and Ernest and Bill were amused by the conventional sentiments and assumptions: "Dear ol Hemingstein, ye massive woodsman, Hope he's better and back soon, Jenks; Hello there old fish monger, 'Corps'; Dear Hemmy, Feder; Dear old Gashhound, Jerome Flaherty."

There was, however, a side to Ernest Bill Horne discovered at the hospital that he hadn't anticipated. Although with Bill Ernest listened more than he spoke, endured the discomfort and pain without showing his endurance, recalled his days on the Piave with irony and self-deprecation, and smiled in a shy, hesitant way, he usually greeted the nurses with an eruption of wit and a broad, confident grin. For the buxom, maternal Elsie MacDonald, for the timid Loretta Cavanaugh, for the hospital flirt, Ruth Brooks, even for the pinch-lipped superintendent of nurses, Catherine de Long, Ernest would whistle through his pain, make cryptic allusions to his experience at the Front, show off small fragments of shrapnel he had dug out of his leg with a penknife, and call the women by the nicknames he had given them. Nurse MacDonald was "The Spanish Mac," Loretta Cavanaugh was "Sis Cavie," and Nurse de Long, whose authoritative posing he mocked behind her back, was "Gumshoe Casey." The nurses in turn massaged, combed, washed, fed, and petted Ernest more than any other patient on the floor. And yet, despite this mutual familiarity and affection, Bill noted that Ernest never flirted with these women nor they with him.

Bill Horne usually remained in Ernest's room when Elsie MacDonald or Sis Cavanaugh or Ruth Brooks came in, in part because Ernest seemed to prefer he stay. But there was one nurse whose visits made the exception. She was a tall, gray-eyed young woman, with short chestnut hair, a cameo neck, and, half concealed by the folds of her long, loose-fitting nurse's garment, the smallest waist Bill had ever seen. Ernest introduced this nurse to Bill with formality as Agnes von Kurowsky, from Germantown, Pennsylvania. And Bill saw clearly that Ernest was in love with her.

In the summer of 1918, Agnes Kurowsky was twenty-six years old. She was the daughter of a Polish aristocrat who, with the loss of the family fortune, had emigrated to the United States, and the granddaughter of a Polish brigadier general. In lieu of public high school, Agnes had spent two years at Fairmont Seminary in Washington, D.C. After five years at home, she had entered the School of Nursing at Bellevue Hospital in New York and had graduated on July 17, 1917, one month after Ernest left Oak Park High. Shortly after her graduation, Agnes applied for overseas duty with the Red Cross, and, on June 15, 1918, while Ernest was at Schio, she sailed for Europe aboard the French Line steamer *La Lorraine*. In New York, Agnes left behind a doctor to whom she had been engaged for some time but who had frequently put off their wedding.

Ernest met Agnes Kurowsky one morning his second week at the hospital. When he awoke, she was standing before the French windows in his room with a clipboard in her hand. After putting a thermometer into his mouth and cautioning him to keep his lips tightly shut, Agnes took Ernest's pulse (in two half-minute segments for accuracy), recorded the results, and then—while distracting him with small talk—counted Ernest's respiration. When Agnes removed the thermometer, Ernest asked her about his temperature—it was normal, she said, but he wasn't supposed to know—and about his respiration. Agnes laughed and said his respiration was normal, too, and that breakfast was on its way. Ernest told her that he could hold his breath for three minutes if he wished.

Later on that morning, after Agnes Kurowsky had bathed Ernest, using a bath blanket and tactfully allowing him to wash his genitals himself, and had given him a vigorous back rub, Ernest decided she was the most skillful and efficient, the most capable, and the loveliest girl he had ever seen. For the rest of July, the quality of Ernest's day was determined by how often it would be Agnes who answered when he pulled the cord on the nurses' call.

In early August, 1918, Agnes volunteered for night duty, and, since it was the least popular shift with the other girls, Miss de Long was glad to let her have it. Ernest, because he hadn't slept well for many years and had acquired true insomnia since his wounding, was of course very happy too. As he lay awake waiting for the first light of dawn, when for an hour or two he would sleep, Ernest saw the slant of light in the hallway outside his open door and imagined Agnes sitting under the green-shaded lamp at the white-painted desk by the white nurses' closet. Throughout the night Ernest waited for the end of each hour, when he would hear the doors of the rooms opening and closing and sometimes a muted conversation, knowing that Agnes was moving closer to his room and to such a conversation with him.

After a while, Agnes sat by Ernest's bed in one of the hard-backed chairs and left his room only to make her hourly rounds. When the August nights were especially hot, she moistened a towel for Ernest's forehead,

wiped his neck and chest with cool water, and, to alleviate the itching beneath his bandages, scratched the soles of his feet. To Ernest, Agnes's
voice was soft and low, and, at his request, she sang amusing little songs
for him she had learned at boarding school.

By late August, Ernest in his crisp Spagnioli uniform and Agnes in her
Bellevue cap and cape went sightseeing around Milan in a carriage that
called for them each afternoon. Agnes, who Ernest knew had been study-
ing *Hugo's Italian* in her free time, translated Ernest's directions to the
driver, and the driver, turning from his perch above the low carriage seat,
always said, "Si, si!" and then took the couple where he wished. At the
end of each excursion, however, Ernest always asked to be driven to the
public gardens, and, when the heavy bandages of his leg were replaced by
thinner wrappings and covered with a loose puttee and his crutches were
replaced by a stout Italian cane, Ernest and Agnes walked arm in arm
down the narrow, dusty paths while the driver waited for them.

Back at the hospital, Ernest always paid the carriage fare, and then he
and Agnes rode upstairs in the elevator together. Agnes got off on the
third floor, and Ernest went on up and down the hall to his room. Sometimes he undressed and got into bed, and sometimes he sat out on the
balcony with his leg up on another chair and waited for Agnes.

When Agnes came on duty at eight o'clock, Ernest went along the hall
with her, carrying the basins and waited outside the doors or went in
with her, depending on whether the patients were friends of theirs or not.
When Agnes finished her rounds, they sat out on the balcony outside Ernest's room. Afterwards Ernest went to bed, and when the patients were
all asleep and Agnes was sure they would not call, she came in.

Although by now Ernest was deeply in love with Agnes and believed
she was in love with him, he did resent a certain callousness in her (Bill
Horne had seen it, too) which made him feel anxious and insecure. During one of their afternoon rides, she had shown him carefully posed photographs of herself surrounded by admiring troops on board the *La Lorraine*. When Ernest had his twice-delayed operation on August 10, he was
attended by Elsie MacDonald. Later he discovered Agnes had dined that
night at the "Lorenzo and Lucia" with a glib Italian physician who wore
a patch over his right eye.

All during August and September, while Ernest and Agnes began their
romance, Grace and Clarence Hemingway wrote letters to their son filled
with expressions of affection, encouragement, and family pride. Clarence,
in his dozen letters (some with "From His Father" written in place of a
return address), reminded Ernest of their summers at the lake and of the
fish that were waiting for them next year, spoke of Ernest's "miraculous

deliverance" and "the great work that God surely has in store for you," and cautioned Ernest about "trying to get around too soon." Clarence usually opened his letters with "Dear Old Scout" or "Master Woodsman," and he once sent Ernest a snapshot of a trout.

Grace, who called Ernest "My darling boy" and "My lamb" and signed herself "Your old girl" and "Your loving Motherkins, G.H.H.," wrote half as often. She assured Ernest that "Everybody loves you," sent him clippings of war propaganda from local newspapers, exhorted him to "hold the banner high," remarked how "wonderful" Corningsby Dawson's new book *Carry On* was, and asked "When are you going to write me a nice long letter all for myself?" At one point she bestowed upon Ernest her highest commendation:

> You are surely a lucky boy. But you deserve it all for you are brave and noble and every inch a man. I thank God for you every day. You are like your Grandfather, Ernest Hall, *Clean clear* thru. God Bless you my laddie.
>
> Your Old Pal + Mother

During these months Ernest did not write to his parents as often as they wished or indeed as often as he felt he should. Yet when he did write he had his facts and sentiments well rehearsed, and he charitably appeared as the character each wanted him to be.

August 29, 1918

Dear Mom:

I haven't written before for quite a while because I ain't got no pep. The old limbs are coming along fine. My left leg is all healed up and I can bend it finally and I now get around my room and this floor of the hospital on crutches but I can go only a little bit at a time because I'm awfully weak yet. My right leg was taken out of the cast a couple of days ago and it's still as stiff as a board and awfully sore from so much carving around the knee joint and foot. But the surgeon whose name is Sammarelli—he is the best in Milan and knows Beck of New York, now dead, and one of the Mayos—says that eventually it will be allright. The joint gets better every day and I'll be moving it soon. I'm enclosing a picture of me in bed. It looks like my left leg is a stump, but it really isn't. Just bent so it looks that way. . . .

Now Mom you may not believe it but I can speak Italian like a born Veronese. You see up in the trenches I had to talk it, there being nothing else spoken, so I learned an awful lot and talked with the officers by the hour in Italian. I suppose I'm shy on grammar but I'm long on vocabulary. Lots of times I've acted as interpreter for the hospital. Somebody comes in and they can't understand what they want and the nurse brings 'em to my bed and I straighten it all out. All the nurses are Americans.

This war makes us a bit less fools than we were. For instance, Poles and Italians. I think the officers of these two nations are the finest men I've ever known. There isn't going to be any such thing as "foreigners" for me after the war is won. Just because your pals speak another language shouldn't make any difference. The thing is to learn that language. I've gotten Italian pretty well. And I've picked up quite a lot of Polish and my French is improving a lot. It's better than 10 years of college. I know more French and Italian now than if I had studied 8 years in college and you want to be prepared for a lot of visitors after the war now because I've got a lot of pals coming to see me in Chicago. That's the best thing about this awfulness, the friends that you make, and when you are looking at death all the time you get to know your friends too. I don't know when I'll be back. Maybe for Christmas. Probably not. I can't get in the army or navy and they won't take me in the draft if I go home. One bum lamp and two shaky legs. So I might as well stay over here and play around the old conflict for a while.

Also Ma, I'm in love again. Now don't get the wind up and start worrying about me getting married for I'm not. As I told you once before, raise My right hand and promise, so don't get up in the air and cable and write me. I'm not even going to get engaged. Loud Cheers. So don't write any "God Bless U, My Children": Not for about 10 years. You're a dear old kid, and you're still my best girl. Kiss me. Very good. Now good-bye and God bless you and write me often. . . . So long old dear. I love you.

Ernie.

To his father, Ernest wrote:

I'm in bed today and probably won't leave the hospital for about three weeks more. My legs are coming on wonderfully and will both eventually be O.K. absolutely. The left one is allright now. The right is still stiff but massage and sun cure and passive movements are loosening up the knee. My surgeon Captain Sammarelli, one of the best surgeons in Italy, is always asking me whether I think that you will be entirely satisfied with the operation. He says that his work must be inspected by the great Surgeon Hemingway of Chicago and he wants it to be perfect. And it is too. There is a scar about eight inches long on the bottom of my foot and a neat little puncture on top. That's what copper jacketed bullets do when they "key hole" in you. My knee is a beauty also. I'll never be able to wear kilts Pop. My left leg, thigh and side, look like some old horse that has been branded and rebranded by about fifty owners. They will all make good identification marks.

I can get around now on the streets for a little while with a cane or crutch, but can't put a shoe on my right foot yet. Oh yes! I have been commissioned a first Lieutenant and now wear the two gold stripes on each of my sleeves. It was a surprise to me as I hadn't expected anything of the sort. So now you can address my mail either first Lieut. or Tenente as I hold the rank in both the A.R.C. and the Italian Army. I guess I'm the youngest first Lieut. in the Army. Anyway I feel all dolled up with my insignia and a shoulder strap on my Sam Browne Belt. I also heard that

my Silver Medaglia Valore is on the way and I will probably get it as soon
as I'm out of the hospital. Also they brought back word from the Front
that I was proposed for the War Cross before I was wounded because of
general foolish conduct in the trenches, I guess. So maybe I'll be decorated with both medals at once. That would not be bad.

P.S. If it isn't too much trouble I wish you'd subscribe to the Sat. Eve.
Post for me and have it sent to my address here. They will forward it to
me wherever I am. You need American reading an awful lot when you're
at the Front.

Thanks.   Ernie

. . . I got a long letter the other day from every fellow in the section. I
would like to go back to the ambulance but I won't be much use driving
for about six months. I will probably take command of some first line post
up in the mountains. Anyway don't worry about me because it has been
conclusively proved that I can't be killed and I will always go where I
can do the most good you know and that's what we're here for. Well,
So Long Old Scout,

Your loving son,
Ernie

About a week before Ernest wrote the letter to his mother, Grace, a
young man arrived at the Red Cross hospital in whom Ernest was inter-
ested even before they met. Like Ernest, he had volunteered for ambulance service, had crossed on the *Chicago,* had been wounded on the
Piave, and was to receive the Silver Medal for Valor for his courage under fire. Ruth Brooks introduced him to Ernest as John W. Miller, Jr. He
was the son of a wealthy Minnesota restaurateur.

During the next several weeks (Bill Horne, cured of his jaundice, had
returned to Schio), Ernest got to like Johnny Miller's dry wit (he called
himself a "worn out Ford" ruined by the war) and to respect his serious
interest in art (he intended to work hard, he said, to become a good sculp-
tor). Also, Ernest discovered that he and his new friend shared a delightfully distressing situation. Johnny Miller had fallen in love with his
nurse, too. When Superintendent de Long reluctantly notified Ernest (she
had lately discovered bottles of vermouth and cognac in his armoire and
was furious) that he had been granted a ten-day convalescent leave, Ernest surprised Agnes by deciding to spend it with Johnny Miller at Stresa
on Lake Maggiore, thirty-five miles northwest of Milan.

By late September, the summer season at Stresa was over and most of
the wealthy vacationers had returned to Genoa and Milan. The largest
and best hotel, the Grand-Hotel des Isles Borromées, had shut off wings
of rooms, and several of the smaller hotels, which clustered about it like
cottages about the manor of an estate, had closed down altogether. But

the Grand-Hotel still sent porters and carriages to meet incoming trains. On the hotel's concrete piazza, tables were stacked in a corner, some turned upside down. Along the lake, white dinghies and sailing skiffs were canvased over and moored in rows at white, narrow quays. Ernest and Johnny Miller took a room with a good view of the lake.

Perhaps because of the crisp fall air and the sense of vacancy at the hotel, the young men quickly ordered their days and nights with simple, pleasant routines. At about eleven o'clock each morning, Ernest and Johnny Miller, dressed in their finely tailored uniforms with the silver-on-black wound stripes on the sleeves, walked down the long, empty hall and took the elevator to the bar downstairs. There, along with several other guests whom they soon recognized and nodded to, they sat on high stools, leaned over the mahogany bar with brass fixtures, and ate salted almonds, potato chips, and olives, and drank light Italian martinis. At noon they ordered sandwiches and moved to small tables with comfortable leather chairs along the wall. After lunch, Ernest and Johnny Miller played billiards (Ernest had learned the rudiments of the game in bars and pool halls on the north side of Kansas City) or read foreign papers and smoked.

The barman, who reminded Johnny Miller of Girard on the *Chicago,* was especially friendly to the young men because they were Americans and had been wounded. To Ernest, he seemed wordly and cynical yet cheerful in his cynicism. After listening to Ernest tell his friend about the wonderful fishing back home in Upper Michigan, the barman arranged for the use of a hotel skiff, and Ernest and Johnny Miller went trolling for lake trout almost every afternoon. Ernest, his right leg set rigid against the thwart, usually insisted on rowing out, sometimes all the way to Isola Bella, where a little fisherman's cafe stood close to the shore. On the way back, Johnny Miller amused Ernest with his rowing, and they laughed together when, in the choppy water, he missed the stroke and Ernest said he had "caught crabs."

Partly from pain but partly because their wounding had ignited something in them that would not go out until dawn, Ernest and Johnny Miller agreed, "I am of those who like to stay late at the cafe . . . with all those who do not want to go to bed. With all those who need a light for the night," and, with the dispensation of the barman, they sat for hours and talked about women and art and the war. There was, they decided, a great difference between the girls back home and their nurses, Agnes Kurowsky and Ruth Brooks. These girls were serious and capable, listened much more than they talked, didn't giggle or gossip, and had seen and done a lot. Both Ernest and Johnny Miller, however, eventually admitted that Agnes and Ruth did seem distressingly familiar and self-assured

around men. Ernest said it made him as silly jealous as a high-school
kid, and Johnny Miller said it was something that Ernest, as an artist,
should try to outgrow.

Back in their rooms, finally, with the windows open to the fall scent of
the lake and the trees, Ernest and Johnny Miller talked about the war on
the Piave and about their wounding. Each said that he felt good about
himself because he had behaved like a man when it counted. But Ernest
said that when the Minenwerfer hit and he felt himself drawn out of himself like a handkerchief from a breast pocket, he had discovered it was a
mistake to think you just died. Johnny Miller, who insisted you died
when your time was up and that was that, said such an experience might
be explained in many ways and was not much to build a faith on.

While the fall guests at the Grand-Hotel shared the privilege of aristocratic leisure, by common consent they shared little else. In general, Ernest and Johnny Miller thought this was fine. But there was one guest
whom Ernest was anxious to know: a ninety-four-year-old contemporary
of Metternich who had served in the diplomatic corps of both Italy and
Austria. His name was Count Greppi, and his birthday parties were the
social event of the season in Milan.

Ernest first saw Count Greppi as the Count practiced his strokes at a
corner table in the hotel's billiard room. Under the bright, low-hanging
lamps, the old man's practiced fingers easily formed a closed bridge, and
his stroke was quick and fluent. Between shots, he moved slowly beyond
the rim of light and studied the angles with great care. At the count's invitation, Ernest and he played billiards several times for small wagers and
drank iced champagne. Count Greppi liked Ernest because he played billiards seriously, listened well, and did not talk too much about the war.
Ernest liked the count because he said that after passing through years of
certitude he was again unsure of many things. The count pleased Ernest
too by saying he was still fond of life and valued most someone he loved.

On the morning of October 5, Ernest walked off the elevator on the
fourth floor of the Red Cross hospital. Pietro, the lame elevator "boy,"
held open the cage for him. Ernest gave Agnes, who was starting her
rounds, a broad grin. He was limping, but he did not use his cane.

That night, Ernest took Agnes to dinner at the Grand-Italia, the finest
restaurant in Milan. There, under the glass dome of the galleria, in the
soft gaslight, they ate the supper ordered by a waiter friend, drank white
Capri wine iced in a bucket, and watched the well-dressed patrons at tables around them. After dinner, Ernest and Agnes walked through the
galleria, past the other restaurants and shops with their steel shutters
down, and stopped at a little place to get sandwiches made of very tiny

brown glazed rolls to eat that night. During the walk back to the hospital, Agnes told Ernest that Superintendent de Long had had her transferred temporarily to the American Hospital for Italian Wounded in
Florence to help with an outbreak of the "floo." Ernest said that he feared
she would forget to love him and that he suspected she had volunteered.
Agnes replied she might be gone a month or more, but she had a three-
day furlough before she had to leave. Ernest could choose where they
would spend it.

On the evening of October 15, Ernest and Agnes took a carriage from
the Red Cross hospital to the Garibaldi Station, and Agnes boarded the
night train for Florence. It was raining, and the restless driver allowed
them little time for their goodbye. Before she left, Ernest promised Agnes
that he would avoid trouble with Superintendent de Long, would visit
the Ospedale Maggiore every afternoon to have his rigid knee rearticu-
lated by the clumsy experimental machines, and would not think of her
except at night, when he would write her long letters. Agnes in turn
promised to be strictly faithful to Ernest, to write letters telling him not
what she did but how she felt and why, and to give the "floo" a miss by
eating well and getting plenty of sleep and by following Dr. Hemingway's
prescription: Gargle with alcohol and water several times each day. Agnes
was sure that in six weeks, or less if they were lucky, Ernest would be
there to meet her when she returned to Milan. And that was fine because
now they were engaged.

In mid-Octobr 1918, as Agnes traveled to Florence, the war in Europe
was coming to an end. Each day on the front page of the Milanese papers,
names made infamous in defeat four years before—the Marne, Ypres,
Amiens, the Somme—now reappeared with long stories detailing Allied
victories. In America, President Wilson called for Germany's uncondi-
tional surrender. In Italy, the people believed that after one more great
battle the war would end with the year.

With apocalyptic tension in the air, the irony of Agnes's departure did
not escape Ernest. Contrary to the wartime myth, the "girl" was leaving
her "hero" at home. On the eighteenth, three days after Agnes had left,
Ernest wrote of patriotism and self-sacrifice in an elegiac letter to the
"Dear Folks" in Oak Park:

> I would like to come home and see you all, of course, but I can't until
> after the war is finished, and that isn't going to be such an awful length
> of time. There is nothing for you to worry about, because it has been
> fairly conclusively proved that I can't be bumped off. And wounds don't
> matter. I wouldn't mind being wounded again so much because I know
> just what it is like. And you can only suffer so much, you know, and it

does give you an awfully satisfactory feeling to be wounded. It's getting
beaten up in a good cause. There are no heroes in this war. We all
offer our bodies and only a few are chosen, but it shouldn't reflect any
special credit on those that are chosen. They are just the lucky ones. I am
very proud and happy that mine was chosen, but it shouldn't give me any
extra credit. Think of the thousands of other boys that offered. All the
heroes are dead. And all the real heroes are the parents. Dying is a very
simple thing. I've looked at death and I really know. If I should have
died it would have been very easy for me. Quite the easiest thing I ever
did. But the people at home do not realize that. They suffer a thousand
times more. When a mother brings a son into the world she must know
that someday the son will die, and the mother of a man that has died
for his country should be the proudest woman in the world, and the
happiest. . . .

Does all that sound like the crazy, wild kid you sent out to learn about
the world a year ago? It is a great old world, though, and I've always had
a good time and the odds are all in favor of coming back to the old place.
But I thought I'd tell you how I felt about it. Now I'll write you a nice,
cheery, bulky letter in about a week, so don't get low over this one. I
love you all.

Ernie

On the nineteenth of October, without orders, Ernest left for Schio to re-
join Section IV.

When Ernest had volunteered for active duty on the Lower Piave in
early July, things happened in his favor. He had traveled to the front
with friends, served under a fine commanding officer, and enjoyed his duties. He had been severely wounded. But, under fire, he'd behaved as he
always hoped he would. When Ernest returned to the front the second time, however, circumstances were against him, and everything went
wrong.

First, after a grueling day-long trip to Schio, Ernest found that Bill
Horne had driven over to Section I at Bassano and only malingerers hung
on at Section IV. Ernest stayed overnight on his old cot in the woolen
mill, Cazzola, and on the morning of October 20 he returned to Milan.
He packed his first-lieutenant stripes in his footlocker, said goodbye to
Johnny Miller, and, at an armorer's in the galleria, bought a pistol with
a strong, smooth action for fifty lire. Then, in the rain, he took the east-
bound train to Bassano.

Ernest got to Bassano on the morning of October 23, the day before the
Italian offensive, the Vittoria Veneto, was to begin. After some trouble
with papers, he arranged for quarters at an old villa on the east bank of
the Brenta, up beyond a covered bridge. It was a big marble house with
cypress trees along the drive and statues on either side.

That night, Ernest found Bill Horne, and together they got purposively drunk and spent several hours with an Ardito, one of the shock troops who would lead the assault the next day. While Ernest leaned forward to catch every word, the Italian, dressed in a gray open-collared shirt with big black flames along the side of the neck, baggy gray trousers, black rolled puttees, and a black fez hat with the tassel set back, told of how the men chosen for the corps had to charge two hundred yards under breast-high machine-gun fire, how in training they pulled the pins of four-second grenades they called signorinas and threw them on the ground in front of them before they threw them away, and how platoon commanders shot AWOLs through the head with automatic pistols. The Ardito said they all drank rum and ether before going over, usually with a chaser of opium, or, in an emergency, they drank Grappa. "A thimble full and you're equal to a platoon," he said. "A regular snort and you wonder why the Austrians don't have any troops worth fighting." Later, after Ernest and Bill had tried some rum and ether, had been sick, and had attempted to wash the taste of ether out of their mouths with bottles of Orvito, they talked about Agnes, agreed she was wonderful, and decided that Bill should be Ernest's best man.

The next morning, however, when Bill called on Ernest at four o'clock to start the trip to the Advance Surgical Post a half-mile from the front lines on Mount Grappa, he found his friend too sick to move. At first they thought that the abdominal pain was simple gastritis. But Ernest had a fever, too, and in the night, he told Bill, there were severe cramps and profuse bloody diarrhea.

For the next three days, while the battle on Mount Grappa raged and subsided and the main thrust on the Piave began, Ernest fought the dysentery. Then, on October 27, a rainy Sunday morning, he returned to Milan. Because he was yellow with jaundice, a squabble with Superintendent de Long ensued (she assumed the jaundice had been caused by his drinking), and Ernest felt he was dying by the time he got to bed.

For the next two days, Ernest left the pile of Agnes's letters unopened on his bureau, and he told Johnny Miller he was too sick to talk. But when Ernest could read, he found the letters all he'd hoped they would be. Agnes said he was the "Light of my existence," "Why Girls leave Home," "Old Master," "More precious than Gold in Wartime," "My Dearest and Best," "Old Kid of Mine," and "My Furnace." Also, Agnes tried to write "creatively" for him: "You know your favorite song 'Elegy'? That expresses my feelings very well these days, for in spite of the sunshine I am lost without you and I thought it was the dismal rain that made me miss you so." And in another: "old Luna a big yellowish one amid thick dark clouds over a few twinkling lights of the city and the rain just dripping enough to make a soothing sound." And she fondly recalled their lovemaking: "When I saw that couple on the train yesterday I just wished I had you along side of me so I could put my face in that nice place, you know, the hollow place for my face, and go to sleep with your arm around me." She promised, "I love you more and more and know what I'm going to bring you when I come home." Even Ernest's desire for some jealousy in Agnes to balance the jealousy he felt about her doctor in New York was satisfied, albeit in a peculiar way: "As you said, you couldn't stand seeing me around all day as you did for three days, and so if you come up to Florence you should come up with a pal." And yet, when news came on November 2 of the Italian victory at Vittoria Veneto, and Johnny Miller (who had recently lost Ruth Brooks to another lieutenant) smuggled up to his room "a blond[e] who had come up from a spree in Sorrento and knew only two words in Italian and used them persistently," Ernest took part in the celebration.

For nine days after the party in Johnny Miller's room, Ernest did nothing but follow doctor's orders (no alcohol, castor oil every night, milk and oatmeal for dinner) and read long letters from Agnes, sometimes two or three a day. She wrote that she "dreamed of you every night," saw "some attractive Italian boys" at the hospital but "none as attractive as my boy," and was reading a "romantic novel," *The Golden Triangle* by Maurice Blain, in which she found appropriate quotations: " 'It must have been beautiful to have begun life like that,' she said. 'Yes,' he said, 'at least we had our spring.' 'To be together,' said the lady, 'and so beautifully poor.' " Surprised at Ernest's effect on her, Agnes wrote:

> I really never thought I could write what I feel so plainly and openly. Writing has always made me draw into a shell. It seems so irrevocable. Once written you can't take back what you've said. I guess if Dr. S. ever saw a letter like this from me he'd think I've gone mad. He never saw much of the inner me. You've seen so much. I'd hate to be opening my heart like this on paper if I thought you were not responding in yours. . . . I never imagined anyone could be so dear and necessary to me.

But when, under the stress of tedium and pain, Ernest wrote that he'd been upset at finding a plain silver spoon inscribed "A.V.K." in Henry Villard's room and that his trip to Bassano might be considered AWOL, Agnes was unsympathetic. She wrote only they'd "talk it over when I get home."

On the night of November 11, the date the Armistice took effect and World War I came to an end, Ernest waited at the hospital for Agnes. No need to meet her, she had written. The train from Florence would arrive at midnight. She would come up to their room as soon as she signed in. "I miss you so, dear, and I love you so much," Agnes continued. "I was picturing you the other night, the way you looked when you got off the elevator coming back from Stresa. I can remember every detail of your expression. I wonder if you will look like that when I come back only maybe more so." Fortunately, a surprise visit from Jim Gamble that morning (bringing news of Ernest's Italian "War Cross") had made him feel wonderful, and he was determined to get the look Agnes wanted just right.

Since his return from Bassano, Ernest did not feel at home at the hospital, and he insisted that Agnes leave with him as often as she could. On her few hours off each day (she had patients critically ill with Spanish influenza—one was Johnny Miller), they walked the cold streets of Milan, past game hanging outside the shops, alongside the dark gray, slow-moving canals, over a bridge where an old woman sold roasted chestnuts. Once they went to the beautiful old hospital where Ernest had taken machine treatments for his legs, but a funeral was starting in the courtyard. One day they drove out through the park over muddy roads, past villas with iron fences, to the San Siro racetrack, the most notorious in Europe. Back in Milan, at the Arcade, they had their silhouettes cut by a talkative old man. Then something happened which made Ernest uncomfortable with Agnes no matter where they went.

At one o'clock one morning, Agnes asked Ernest to help her with an influenza patient who appeared to be dying. Ernest, limping with his leg stiff from hours in bed, followed her to a room just down the hall. In a brass bed against the wall, a young man sat bolt upright, soaked with sweat, straining to breathe. There was a small lamp covered by a towel; two girls knelt at the bedside praying; the odor of camphor filled the room. Because the hospital doctor was out of town, Agnes intended to try something desperate with rubber tubes herself. Ernest was to assist. But before she could start, the patient choked and dropped back limp on his pillows. In death, his bowels released and filled the sheets with one final yellow cataract that flowed and dribbled on. After praying with the others, Ernest went back to his room alone, washed his hands and face, and gargled with alcohol and water. When Agnes finally came in, he would not kiss her until she had gargled too.

By the time Ernest got Bill Horne's letter of November 14 announcing the breakup of Section IV, he had recovered from his dysentery and was spending some of his afternoons at the Anglo-American Club in Milan. It was a posh Victorian-style retreat with deep, leather-cushioned chairs and a well-stocked bar. The house drink was a splendid martini, enjoyed with English magazines.

One day, after Ernest had gotten to know the barmaid, Maria, by name, he called for service at the same time as a soft-spoken British officer. Eric Dorman-Smith was a twenty-three-year-old lieutenant in the Northumberland Fusiliers, and, like Ernest, he had just recovered from dysentery.

On that and several other afternoons in November, Ernest and "Chink," as he asked to be called, lunched together at the club, drank at the Cova (Chink always ordered German ale), dined at Biffie's (a fashionable restaurant in the Galleria), and "dropped in," as Chink liked to put it, at the Teatro Scala. During their hours together, Dorman-Smith talked about his wounding, his "being mentioned in three dispatches" (one time for his bravery in Belgium, at Mons), and his ancestral estate in Scotland. To Ernest, Dorman-Smith seemed erudite and wise until, one day, he quoted a passage from *Henry IV, Part 2*—"By my troth, I care not; a man can die but once; we owe God a death . . . he that dies this year is quit for the next"—spoken in the play by Frances Feeble, a feckless recruit "as valiant as a wrathful dove or most magnanimous mouse." Chink implied it was the core of his philosophy of life.

Four years later, in one of the vignettes he collected as *in our time*, Ernest mocked the clipped British fashion of speaking and the hollow affectation of control:

> We were in the garden at Mons. Young Buckley came in with his patrol from across the river. The first German I saw climbed up over the garden wall. We waited till he got one leg over and then potted him. He had so much equipment on and looked awfully surprised and fell down into the garden. Then three more came over further down the wall. We shot them. They all came just like that.

On November 22, after only eleven days at "home," Agnes left Milan again on "a special assignment." This time she had volunteered for duty at a large district hospital crowded with Italians wounded at the Vittoria Veneto. For the next few months she would be north of Treviso, on the Venetian plain.

Shortly after Agnes left, Ernest wrote two stories he would never publish on Red Cross Headquarters stationery. The first told of a young soldier so severely wounded in battle that his arm and leg had to be replaced by metal limbs. While lying in the hospital listening to the Italians cheering "Viva Wilson," the soldier surreptitiously drinks a bottle of bichloride (a poisonous antiseptic in common use in 1918) to "make right the double-cross of God": "I had a rendesvous [sic] with Death—but Death broke the date and now it's all over. God double-crossed me." In the second story, the closing dialogue suggests the subtle difference between fear and cowardice:

"Don't you love me," the girl said. "Why didn't you kiss me then?"

"Didn't I kiss you?"

"No," she said. "You know you didn't."

"I will."

"Kiss me now."

"I don't want to now."

"What's the matter?"

"Nothing."

"It's all right about Connors."

"Oh, hell," I said. "It's not that."

"You don't love me," she said. "If you loved me you'd want to kiss."

"I'm afraid."

"Of what."

"Of getting the floo."

She was quiet sitting there on the bed and what I had said was coming between us solidly.

"You're too afraid to kiss me?"

"Yes."

She was quiet again. Then she said, "I'd have sucked it all out with a tube if it would have done any good."

"You can do that for me."

"You'll get it if you're afraid."

"I'm afraid all right. I never saw anybody die like that."

"Nobody dies very nicely."

"They don't all die like that."

"All pneumonia patients do."

"But this is worse because it is so sudden. There isn't any time to wear the body out and yet, the violence isn't from outside."

"There are plenty of hard ways to die. What about the crushing pain heart patients endure."

"Tell me some more. You know such cheerful things."

"There's nothing wrong with your heart."

"No."

"Why should you worry about that?"

"I don't," I said. "Only about the floo."

She got up from the bed, and I could see her in the light from the corridor as she opened the door.

"Where are you going?"

"Out to gargle," she said. "To please you."

"Then will you come back?"

"Oh, yes."

When she came back I kissed her but we were never as close again as we had been (something was over between us and we never got it back). It was better never than late.

With Agnes in Treviso, the holidays of 1918 were lonely for Ernest, and the morning mail (sorted with a maddening hesitancy by the elevator "boy," Pietro) became the highlight of his day. First to be read and answered were the letters from his mother and father.

Grace, in long letters often written over several days, was playfully jealous ("Give HER my best, I always love all the nice girls"), solicitous ("a boy with Valor medals turning yellow! Oh! Ho! Poor Kiddo, I'm really sorry for oo. Mama kiss it and make it well?"), and proud ("Please send a good photograph with all your medals on"). Nevertheless, she did not hesitate to remind Ernest of what she expected of him: "You will never be satisfied to come home and just live and work for Ernie Hemingway after living on the high mount of Sacrifice. You will not be happy to descend to the low plain of commonplace selfish living."

Clarence, no less fervent than his wife but usually more subdued, tried to be a useful source of homefront news. On his professional stationery, Clarence wrote of family sorrow (Uncle Leicester's wife had died of influenza in California, and Leicester himself was missing in action in France); of local events, with enclosures of *Oak Leaves* and the *Chicago Tribune;* with quaint medical opinions (there was heavy fall rain in Oak Park and "the dust and the influenza will settle"), and, on one occasion at least; with some sharp criticism of Grace's callousness. Clarence was especially disturbed that Leicester, discovered alive in a German prisoner-of-war camp and returned home, found waiting for him at his debarkation port on Long Island a telegram from Grace announcing his wife's death.

Ernest, on his part, wrote long letters to his parents, full of the sort of details that would make them feel he was close to home. For his father, Ernest told of his "awful throat" that "Dad can experiment on," of a bullet he'd found "in the back of my lap" that he would leave for "Dad to take out," of his "old Mackinaw . . . which at the front they thought was a camouflage coat for sniping," and of his drinking "real chocolate frappes" and reading *Field and Stream* at the Anglo-American Club. Next spring he would make a trip to the Abruzzi, Ernest said, with an Italian officer, Nick Neroni, for pheasant and rabbit shooting and fishing in "good trout rivers." But "by Gosh," he wrote, "I'm going fishing in Michigan all next summer and make the fur fly in the fall."

To Grace, Ernest wrote he was attending opera regularly (to see *Aïda, The Barber of Seville, Mephistopheles* with Toscanini conducting, though he wished for something more interesting such as *Carmen* or *La Bohème,* and of his "Silver Medal for Valor, which he drew for her with the ribbon and star. He vowed that once back home he would "commence the real war again, the war to make the world safe for Ernie Hemingway, and I plan to knock 'em for a loop and I will be a busy man for several years.

By that time my pension will have accumulated a couple of thousand lire and I'll bring my children over to view the battlefields."

Unfortunately, the girl Ernest hoped would bear those children was two hundred miles away, and each day he read her letters with growing concern. Agnes wrote that she "began to hunger for you" in a town filled with Arditi, that she had "lost my sickest boy [died of influenza] and felt so badly as he was a dear and I worked so hard over him for days," and that she had, quite unexpectedly, received a letter from "my Dr. in New York." On Saturday, December 7, Ernest requested a three-day pass from Superintendent de Long and headed east to Treviso.

Because of the influenza epidemic, Ernest decided not to risk the day-long trip to Treviso on a crowded train. Instead, he hitched rides in camions and staff cars to Verona, stopped overnight, and then continued on to Padua. Just beyond Padua, at Tornacello, Ernest called on two British artillery officers he had met at the Anglo-American Club in Milan: Lieutenant Hay, an engineer, and Captain Shepherd, an artist for *Punch*. On Monday morning, after being compelled to join in a "ride to the hounds" on the captain's horse, Ernest and Lieutenant Hay (who was in love with one of Agnes's colleagues, a Miss Smith) drove the company's Vauxhall the fifty miles north to Treviso.

That evening, Ernest and Agnes, Lieutenant Hay and Miss Smith went up to look at the Austrian trench network around Tremiglia, walked across the pontoon bridge at Cremona, and saw the ruined houses at Negressa by moonlight. Toward midnight, they returned to the hospital and cooked themselves a "breakfast," and sometime after one o'clock Ernest and Lieutenant Hay started back to Tornacello. By the time he left Treviso, Ernest had told Agnes he would return home immediately and work toward earning a steady two hundred dollars per month. When he did, they agreed, she would come home and marry him.

It was cold and rainy in Milan when Ernest arrived on December 11, and, before going to the hospital, he stopped at a wine shop for a glass of coffee and a piece of bread. Because his plans were changed now, there were several things he had to do. First, there was the chore of informing his parents of his imminent return and the need for a plausible excuse. In a letter he wrote that afternoon, Ernest made his decision appear the act of a "maturing" young man:

> I'd like to stay here and live a while as I may not get a chance for a long while. But I really feel as though I ought to get back and see you all a spell and then get to work. For a while I was going to go down to Madeira with Captain Gamble, but I realize that if I blow down there and bum I will never get home. This climate and this country get you

and the Lord ordained differently for me, and I was made to be one of those beastly writing chaps, you know. You know I was born to enjoy life but the Lord neglected to have me born with money. So I've got to make it and the sooner the better.

> So long and good luck,
> Ernie

Also, there was the problem of securing passage for the United States on one of the Italian steamers crowded with returning American personnel. To his chagrin, Ernest discovered he would have to wait until January 6 and then travel to Naples for a place on the *Giuseppe Verdi* bound for New York. Finally, Ernest needed to confide in someone, if only through implication. And so, on the thirteenth, he wrote to Bill Horne, back home in New York. (The crossed-out lines were obliterated by Ernest himself.)

> Bill, I have ever poured out to you. (Kidding to one side.) I mean you know me pretty well. So pass judgement on this. Oh hell no. I'll tell you some other time. I was going to give some items of my Tedeschi named wife's [illegible] but you know her so why [twelve lines crossed out]. Thank God I got shot and you know the rest. That is you don't know the rest and never will but you know the results [six lines crossed out]. And so I am coming back and starting the battle for buns or the skirmish for stew or the tussle for turnovers as soon as I can. Have to see the family first. They love me dearly now I am crocked and reflect much credit. . . . If you know when the *Giuseppe Verdi* comes in sailing from here the 6th I may see you. I would admire to do so. . . . All the damn luck in the world.
>
> Hemingstein

On December 16, however, Ernest was surprised by a letter from Agnes. She would not be coming to Milan for the holidays, she said, and she offered Ernest some advice: "Be nice now and don't get rash when you hear I'm not coming to Milan—I'm afraid it looks that way. By this I mean don't lap up all the fluids at the Galleria. But I don't really believe it is necessary for me to give that little advice. You're learning fast and soon will be caught up with me in years of experience and wisdom."

Fortunately, Ernest received another letter that day, from Jim Gamble inviting him to the lovely seaside resort, Taormina, in Sicily. Jim said that he had rented "for a few months a little house and garden belonging to an English artist. . . . Now the only thing lacking is company + I only hope you will take care of that. There is plenty of room in the house, two studios, lots of atmosphere, and I should think plenty about which to write."

In fact, Ernest wrote nothing at all during his two weeks at Jim Gamble's villa in Taormina. But with the morning walks he and Jim took through the narrow winding streets and alleys of the town, with the company they had each afternoon (Colonel Bartlett, a short, fat comrade with a walrus mustache Jim had known in Florence and who had also served on the Piave, "Bartie's" pretty wife Louise, two English artists, Woods and Kisten, a charming, generous aristocrat introduced as the "Duke of Bronte"), with the warm nights Ernest spent watching Aetna fuming away in the moonlight, he didn't care.

When Ernest returned to Milan just after the New Year, he told a credulous Chink Dorman-Smith that he had spent the past two weeks in the custody of the lascivious wife of an Italian war hero and had narrowly escaped death in a duel with her husband. In his farewell letter to Agnes, Ernest said only that he missed her very much and was anxious to sail for home.

↯ 7 ↯
Unwelcome News

When Ernest, wearing a cock-feathered Bersaglieri hat, a knee-length officer's cape lined with red satin, and a British tunic decorated with ribbons of the Valor Medal and the War Cross, limped off the *Giuseppe Verdi*, two young men waited to welcome him home. One was a reporter for the *New York Sun*, there to get the homecoming sentiments of the "first American wounded on the Italian Front." The other was Bill Horne.

While Bill stood to one side, amused and happy with the impression Ernest made, the reporter asked his questions and took notes on a small leather pad. Getting much of his information wrong ("Hemingway joined the Red Cross in France" and "was transferred to the Italian front last July"), the reporter nevertheless understood that Ernest wanted "a job on any New York newspaper that wants a man that is not afraid to work." Bill was proud, too, when Ernest said that his life had been saved by heroic Italian stretcher bearers, rather than recounting the details of how he had saved the life of an Italian soldier on his own.

On the springlike January afternoon, with a southwest breeze coming in over the harbor, Ernest and Bill strolled from the Battery to the east side of Central Park. At the Plaza Hotel they met Bill's current inamorata, a small, dark-haired beauty, Miss Ann Sage. The young lady, whom Bill introduced as a relative of the notorious financier Hetty Green, liked Ernest very much and asked him many of the questions about the war she had already asked Bill. That night at the Horne residence, 175 Park Avenue, Ernest apologized for missing Bill when the men from Section IV passed through Milan after the Armistice on their way home. The "Demon [gin] had overthrown" him, Ernest said, and caused him to miss the train.

For the next three days, Ernest and Bill worked at demobilizing in New York. They dined at Churchill's and enjoyed the "beauty, talent, and diversion" of the 1919 Revue, stocked up at the pre-Prohibition liquor sale at Park and Tilford, and chose Al Jolson at the Winter Garden over Rachmaninoff at Carnegie Hall. Then, after a farewell supper with Bill's parents (Dr. Horne shared Ernest's taste for good cognac, and the two talked deep into the night), the young men hurried down to Grand Central Station on foot, and Ernest boarded the *Chicago Special* for the long trip home. At eight o'clock Saturday night, January 25, the cross-country train pulled into the La Salle Street Station, and Ernest stepped onto the same platform he had left nine months before.

Marcelline Hemingway, the only member of the family to accompany Clarence to the station that night, remembered the homecoming this way:

> Daddy picked me up at my school downtown and took me with him to the Station. It was a cold, snowy January night, and when we got to the La Salle Street Station Daddy asked me to stay up at the head of the stairs in the trainshed and wait for Ernest there while he went down to the main platform. He wanted to meet Ernest alone. Mother, of course, was waiting in Oak Park with the other children. . . . Ernie had on an overseas cap. He was wearing a British-type khaki-colored uniform, partly covered by a long black broadcloth cape flung over his shoulders. The cape was fastened at the neck with a double silver buckle. He was wearing knee-high brown leather boots, and he was limping a little and leaning on a cane. He climbed up the stairway slowly toward me, one step at a time. Dad was trying to get Ernest to hold on to him. . . . Dad was moving about nervously. He was excited and eager to help Ernest get out to the car.
>
> "Here, boy!—Here, lean on me!" Dad urged, as we started out of the station down another long flight of steps toward the waiting Ford.
>
> "Now, Dad," said Ernie, "I've managed all right by myself all the way from Milano. I think I can make it OK now." Ernie gestured toward Dad. "You and Marce go ahead to the car. I'll follow down the steps at my own pace. I'm pretty good with this old stick." He was. But we both waited and walked slowly with him to the car.

On the ride home, eight miles from Chicago to Oak Park, Ernest could see in the dusting of snow well beyond the weak lanterns of Clarence's Model T. The streets were as broad as he remembered; the oak trees as thick and tall; the houses, most half-darkened, still as forbidding. Then suddenly along the avenue, one after another of snow-whitened Fords and Dodges, Pierce-Arrows and Chryslers, Cadillacs and Lincolns lined the curb. The "old homestead," with lights on in every room, looked to Ernest like a theater on opening night. Brother Leicester, not quite four at the time, many years later recalled the scene:

> The night that Ernie came home from the war was a moment in our family history. Our two younger sisters were allowed to stay up. And at about nine o'clock I was even awakened on purpose—an action unthinkable except in case of a disaster and maybe not then. All the lights in the house were on. Out in the dining room hot chocolate was served and nobody said a word about holding off on the marshmellows. Ernest stood around being kissed and back-slapped. . . . I was hoisted up on his shoulders and Carol, the next youngest, insisted on being lifted up too. It was pretty glorious stuff being kid brother to the guy who had personally helped make the world safe for democracy. And I was not the only one who saw him in that light.

For a week, Ernest willingly played the part his family and community insisted upon. (The only real fun was demonstrating for seven-year-old Carol his now independently articulated toes.) But by early February he had had enough. On the ninth, in dramatic fashion, he wrote to Bill Horne in New York:

> Dear Bill:
> It's hell, oh, Gosh, but it's hell. For Gosh sakes at once—give me Jenks [Howell Jenkins] address so I can relieve it. Barney [Larry Barnett] is at Wisconsin University. Jerry [Jerome Flaherty] can't be located. Spiegel [Fred Spiegel] is working and I can't find Jenks. Jenks can save me, perhaps. Or how 'bout yourself? Any chance of you coming out? Try and convalesce with 6,000,000,000 females, mostly single and elderly, and 8,000,000,000,000 males, mostly fat and exempt, crying out for second hand thrills to be got from the Front. These people that want to be vicariously horrified have captured the sheep of the X-mounted. God but I'm sick of this country. Ag writes from Torro de Mosta [sic] beyond Sandava de Piave that she and Cavie are going to be there all winter. I gave her your love. Bill I am so damn lonesome for her I don't know what to do. All Chicago femmes look like a shot of Karo Corn Syrup compared to—83 Burgundy. I'll send you that picture as soon as I get stamps. The family raises much sentimental hell over my advent. In the two-and-a-half years since I'd lamped them, much has changed. Dad now chuckles at my tales of cognac and Asti. Indeed much has changed. I miss the old battles. Father has lost his fighting face. What hath Mars wrought? Edgar Rice Burroughs, who perpetuated *Tarzan and the Apes,* is trying to induce me to write a book. If I do I'll send you one. You'll have to buy it 'cause the sales will need it. I'll write you more shortly. And Bill, I want to thank you for everything you done for me. CIAO

Despite all he said, there was a certain value to being a war hero, and Ernest was quick to perceive it. Signing up with a Chicago agency that supplied speakers to all the suburban towns, Ernest cleverly gave the single and elderly and the fat and exempt the vicarious thrills they sought, all in the guise of a historical education. His "Reminiscences" earned him from five to fifteen dollars each, and in less than two months, he wrote Jim Gamble, he'd amassed "$172 and bought a fifty buck Liberty Bond."

Besides the quick money, these speaking engagements gave Ernest something that seemed the key to a writing career. As audience after audience delighted in the persona he created—the plucky, paradoxical American youth, ingenuously shrewd, loyally cynical, practically idealistic, knowingly tender and tough—Ernest was convinced he had found a salable public voice. Hoping for immediate success in the *Saturday Evening Post,* he ascended to the smallest room in his mother's house—third-floor garret with slanted roof and a gabled window overlooking Clarence's garden—tacked a map of the Italian Front on the wall above his green-painted iron bed, and, on a battered typewriter presented to him the day he had left the *Star,* wrote the first serious stories of his career. The best of the lot he entitled "The Mercenaries." It was rejected by *Redbook* and the *Saturday Evening Post* and was never submitted for publication again.

🖾 🖾 🖾 🖾 🖾

The Mercenaries—
A Story

If you are honestly curious about pearl fishing conditions in the Marquesas, the possibility of employment on the projected Trans Gobi Desert Railway, or the potentialities of any of the hot tamale republics, go to the Cafe Cambrinus on Wabash Avenue, Chicago. There at the rear of the dining room where the neo-bohemians struggle nightly with their spaghetti and ravioli is a small smoke-filled room that is a clearinghouse for the camp followers of fortune. When you enter the room, and you will have no more chance than the zoological entrant in the famous camel-needle's eye gymkana of entering the room unless you are approved by Cambrinus, there will be a sudden silence. Then a varying number of eyes will look you over with that detached intensity that comes of a periodic contemplation of death. This inspection is not mere boorishness. If you're recognized favourably, all right; if you are unknown, all right; Cambrinus has passed on you. After a time the talk picks up again. But one time the door was pushed open, men looked up, glances of recognition shot across the room, a man half rose from one of the card tables, his hand behind him, two men ducked to the floor, there was a roar from the doorway, and what had had its genesis in the Malay Archipelago terminated in the back room of the Cambrinus. But that's not this.

I came out of the wind scoured nakedness of Wabash Avenue in January into the cosy bar of the Cambrinus and, armed with a smile from Cambrinus himself, passed through the dining room where the waiters were clearing away the debris of the table d'hotes and sweeping out into the little back room. The two men I had seen in the café before were seated at one of the three tables with half empty bottles of an unlabeled beverage known to the initiates as "Kentucky Brew" before them. They nodded and I joined them.

"Smoke?" asked the taller of the two, a gaunt man with a face the color of half-tanned leather, shoving a package of cheap cigarettes across the table.

"It is possible the gentleman would prefer one of these," smiled the other with a flash of white teeth under a carefully pointed mustache, and pushed a monogrammed cigarette box across to me with a small, well-manicured hand.

"Shouldn't wonder," grunted the big man, his adam's apple rising and falling above his flannel shirt collar. "Can't taste em myself." He took one of his own cigarettes and rolled the end between thumb and forefinger until a tiny mound of tobacco piled up on the table before him, then carefully picked up the stringy wad and tucked it under his tongue, lighting the half-cigarette that remained.

"It is droll, that manner of smoking a cigarette, is it not?" smiled the dark little man as he held a match for me. I noted a crossed-cannon monogram on his box as I handed it back to him.

"Artigliere français?" I questioned.

"Mais oui, Monsieur; le soixante-quinze!" he smiled again, his whole face lighting up.

"Say," broke in the gaunt man, eyeing me thoughtfully; "Artill'ry ain't your trade, is it?"

"No, takes too much brains," I said.

"That's too darn bad. It don't," the leather-faced man replied to my answer and observation.

"Why?" said I.

"There's a good job now." He rolled the tobacco under his tongue and drew a deep inhalation on his cigarette butt. "For gunners. Peru verstus and against Chile. Two hundred dollars a month—"

"In gold," smiled the Frenchman, twisting his mustache.

"In gold," continued the leather-face. "We got the dope from Cambrinus. Artillery officers they want. We saw the consul. He's fat and important and oily. 'War with Chile? Reediculous!' he says. I talked spiggotty to him for awhile and we come to terms. Napoleon here—"

The Frenchman bowed, "Lieutenant Denis Ricaud."

"Napoleon here—," continued leather-face unmoved, "and me are officers in the Royal Republican Peruvian Army with tickets to New York." He tapped his coat pocket. "There we see the Peruvian consul and present papers," he tapped his pocket again, "and are shipped to Peru via way of the Isthmus. Let's have a drink."

He pushed the button under the table and Antonino the squat Sardinian waiter poked his head in the door.

"If you haven't had one, perhaps you'd try a cognac-benedictine?" asked the leather-faced man. I nodded, thinking. "Tre martell-benedictine, Nino. It's all right with Cambrinus."

Antonino nodded and vanished. Ricaud flashed his smile at me, "And you will hear people denounce the absinthe as an evil beverage!"

I was puzzling over the drink leather-face had ordered, for there is only one place in the world where people drink that smooth, insidious, brain-rotting mixture. And I was still puzzling when Antonino returned with the drinks, not in liqueur glasses, but in big full cock-tail containers.

"These are mine altogether in toto," said the leather-face, pulling out a roll of bills. "Me and Napoleon are now being emolumated at the rate of two hundred dollars per month—"

"Gold!" smiled Ricaud.

"Gold!" calmly finished leather-face. "Say, my name is Graves, Perry Graves." He looked across the table at me.

"Mine's Rinaldi. Rinaldi Renaldo," I said.

"Wop?" asked Graves, lifting his eyebrows and his adam's apple simultaneously.

"Grandfather was Italian," I replied.

"Wop, eh," said Graves unhearingly, then lifted his glass. "Napoleon, and you, Signor Resolvo, I'd like to propose a toast. You say 'A bas Chile!' Napoleon. You say 'Delenda Chile!' Risotto. I drink 'To Hell with Chile!' " We all sipped our glasses.

"Down with Chile," said Graves meditatively, then in an argumentative tone, "They're not a bad lot, those Chillies!"

"Ever been there?" I asked.

"Nope," said Graves, "a rotten bad lot those dirty Chillies."

"Capitain Graves is a propagandiste to himself," smiled Ricaud, and lit a cigarette.

"We'll rally round the doughnut. The Peruvian doughnut," mused Graves, disembowelling another cigarette. "Follow the doughnut, my boys, my brave boys. Vive la doughnut. Up with the Peruvian doughnut and down with the chile concarne. A dirty rotten lot those Chillies!"

"What is the doughnut, mon cher Graves?" asked Ricaud, puzzled.

"Make the world safe for the doughnut, the grand old Peruvian doughnut. Don't give up the doughnut. Remember the doughnut. Peru expects every doughnut to do his duty," Graves was chanting in a monotone. "Wrap me in the doughnut, my brave boys. No, it doesn't sound right. It ain't got something a slogum ought to have. But those Chillies are a rotten lot!"

"The Capitain is très patriotic, n'est-ce pas? The doughnut is the national symbol of Peru, I take it?" asked Ricaud.

"Never been there. But we'll show those dirty Chillies they can't trample on the grand old Peruvian doughnut though, Napoleon!" said Graves, fiercely banging his fist on the table.

"Really, we should know more of the country at whose disposal we have placed our swords," murmured Ricaud, apologetically. "What I wonder is the flag of Peru?"

"Can't use the sword myself," said Graves dourly, raising his glass. "That reminds me of something. Say, you ever been to Italy?"

"Three years," I replied.

"During the war?" Graves shot a look at me.

"Durante la guerra," I said.

"Good boy! Ever hear of Il Lupo?"

Who in Italy has not heard of Il Lupo, the Wolf? The Italian ace of aces and second only to the dead Baracca. Any school boy can tell the number of his victories and the story of his combat with Baron Von Hauser, the great Austrian pilot. How he brought Von Hauser back alive to the Italian lines, his gun jammed, his observer dead in the cockpit.

"Is he a brave man?" asked Graves, his face tightening up.

"Of course!" I said.

"Certainment!" said Ricaud, who knew the story as well as I did.

"He is not," said Graves, quietly the leather mask of his face crinkled into a smile. "I'll leave it to you Napoleon, and to you, Signor Riposso, if he is a brave man. The war is over—"

"I seem to have heard as much somewheres," murmured Ricaud.

"The war is over," calmly proceeded Graves. "Before it, I was a top kicker of field artillery. At the end I was a captain of field artillery, acting pro tempor for the time being. After awhile, they demoted us all to our pre-war rank and I took a discharge. It's a long tumble from captain to sergeant. You see, I was an officer, but not a gentleman. I could command a battery, but I've got a rotten taste in cigarettes. But I wasn't no worse off than lots of other old non-coms. Some were majors even and lieutenant colonels. Now they're all non-coms again or out. Napoleon here is a gentleman. You can tell it to look at him. But I ain't. That ain't the point of this, and I ain't kicking if that's the way they want to run their army." He raised his glass.

"Down with the Chillies!

"After the Armistice I rated some leave and got an order of movement good for Italy, and went down through Genoa and Pisa and hit Rome, and a fella said it was good weather in Sicily. That's where I learned to drink this." He noted his glass was empty and pushed the button under the table. "Too much of this ain't good for a man."

I nodded.

"You go across from a place called Villa San Giovani on a ferry to Messina, where you can get a train. One way it goes to Palermo. The other way to Catania. It was just which and together with me which way to go. There was quite a crowd of us standing there where the two trains were waiting, and a woman came up to me and smiled and said, 'You are the American captain, Forbes, going to Taormina?'

"I wasn't, of course, and a gentleman like Napoleon here would have said how sorry he was but that he was not Captain Forbes, but I don't know. I saluted and when I looked at her I admitted that I was that captain enroute on the way to nowheres by Taormina, wherever it should be. She was so pleased, but said that she had not expected me for three or four days, and how was dear Dyonisia?

"I'd been out at the Corso Cavalli in Rome and had won money on a dog named Dyonisia that came from behind in the stretch and won the prettiest race you ever saw, so I said without lying any that Dyonisia was never better in her life. And Bianca, how was she, dear girl? Bianca, so far as I knew, was enjoying the best of health. So all this time we were getting into a first class compartment and the Signora, whose name I hadn't caught, was exclaiming what a funny and lucky thing it was that we had met up. She had known me instantly from Dyonisia's description. And wasn't it fine that the war was over and we could all get a little pleasure again, and what a fine part we Americans had played. That was while some of the Europeans still admitted that the United States had been in the war.

"It's all lemon orchards and orange groves along the right-hand side of the railway, and so pretty that it hurts to look at it. Hills terraced and yellow fruit shining through the green leaves and darker green of olive trees on the hills, and streams with wide dry pebbly beds cutting down to the sea and old stone houses, and everything all color. And over on the left-hand side you've got the sea, lots bluer than the Bay of Naples, and the coast of Calabria over across is purple like no other place there is. Well, the Signora was just as good to look at as the scenery. Only she was different. Blue-black hair and a face colored like old ivory and eyes like inkwells and full red lips and one of those smiles, you know what they're like, Signor Riscossa."

"But what has this most pleasant adventure to do with the valor of the Wolf, Capitain?" asked Ricaud, who had his own ideas about the points of women.

"A whole lot, Napoleon," continued Graves. "She had those red lips, you know—"

"To the loup! Curse her red lips!" exclaimed Ricaud, impatiently.

"God bless her red lips, Napoleon. And after awhile the little train stopped at a station called Jardini, and she said that this was our getting off place, and that Taormina was the town up on the hill. There was a carriage waiting, and we got in and drove up the pipe elbow road to the little town way up above. I was very gallant and dignified. I'd like to have had you see me, Napoleon.

"That evening we had dinner together, and I'm telling you it wasn't no short order chow. First a martell-benedictine and then an antipasto di magro of all kind of funny things you couldn't figure out but that ate great. Then a soup, clear, and after, these little flat fish like baby flounders cooked like those soft-shelled crabs you get at Rousseau's in New Orleans. Roast young turkey with a funny dressing and the Bronte wine that's like melted up rubies. They grow the grapes on Aetna and they're not allowed to ship it out of the country, off the island, you know. For dessert we had these funny crumpily things they call *pasticerria* and black turkish coffee, with a liqueur called cointreau.

"After the meal, we sat out in the garden under the orange trees, jasmine matted on the walls, and the moon making all the shadows blue-black and her hair dusky and her lips red. Away off you could see the moon on the sea and the snow up on the shoulder of Aetna mountain. Everything white as plaster in the moonlight or purple like the Calabria coast, and away down below the lights of Jardini blinking yellow. It seemed she and her husband didn't get along so well. He was a flyer up in Istery of Hystery or somewheres, I didn't care much, with the Wop army of preoccupation, and she was pleased and happy that I had come to cheer her up for a few days. And I was too.

"Well, the next morning we were eating breakfast, or what they call breakfast, rolls, coffee, and oranges, with the sun shining in through the big swinging-door windows, when the door opens, and in rushed—an Eyetalian can't come into a room without rushing, excuse me, Signor Disolvo—a good-looking fellow with a scar across his cheek and a beautiful blue theatrical-looking cape and shining black boots and a sword, crying 'Carissima!'

"Then he saw me sitting at the breakfast table, and his 'Carissima!' ended in a sort of gurgle. His face got white, all except that scar that stood out like a bright red welt.

" 'What is this?' he said in Eyetalian, and whipped out his sword. Then I placed him. I seen that good-looking, scarred face on the covers of lots of the illustrated magazines. It was the Lupo. The Signora was crying among the breakfast dishes, and she was scared. But the Lupo was magnificent. He was doing the dramatic, and he was doing it great. He had anything I ever seen beat.

" 'Who are you, you son of a dog?' he said to me. Funny how that expression is international, ain't it, among all countries?

" 'Captain Perry Graves, at your service,' I said. It was a funny situation, the dashing, handsome, knock em dead Wolf full of righteous wrath, and opposite him old Perry Graves, as homely as you see him now. I didn't look like the side of a triangle, but there was something about me she liked, I guess.

" 'Will you give me the satisfaction of a gentleman?' he snapped out.

" 'Certainly,' I said, bowing.

" 'Here and now?' he said.

" 'Surely,' I said, and bowed again.

" 'You have a sword?' he asked, in a sweet tone.

" 'Excuse me a minute,' I said, and went and got my bag and my belt and gun.

" 'You have a sword?' he asked, when I came back.

" 'No,' said I.

" 'I will get you one,' says he, in his best Lupo manner.

" 'I don't wish a sword,' I said.

" 'You won't fight me? You dirty dog, I'll cut you down!' "

Graves's face was as hard as his voice was soft.

" 'I will fight you here and now,' I said to him. 'You have a pistol, so have I. We will stand facing each other across the table with our left hands touching.' The table wasn't four feet across. 'The Signora will count one, two, three. We will start firing at the count of three. Firing across the table.' "

Then the control of the situation shifted from the handsome Lupo to

Perry Graves. " 'Cause just as sure as it was that he would kill me with a sword was the fact that if he killed me at that three foot range with his gun I would take him with me. He knew it too, and he started to sweat. That was the only sign. Big drops of sweat on his forehead. He unbuckled his cape and took out his gun. It was one of those little 7.65 mm. pretty ugly, short little gats.

"We faced across the table and rested our hands on the board, I remember my fingers were in a coffee cup, our right hands with the pistols were below the edge. My big forty-five made a big handful. The Signora was still crying. The Lupo said to her, 'Count, you slut!' She was sobbing hysterically.

" 'Emeglio!' called the Lupo. A servant came to the door, his face scared and white. 'Stand at the end of the table,' commanded the Wolf, 'and count slowly and clearly, Una-Dua-Tre!'

"The servant stood at the end of the table. I didn't watch the Wolf's eyes like he did mine. I looked at his wrist where his hand disappeared under the table.

" 'Una!' said the waiter. I watched the Lupo's hand.

" 'Dua!' and his hand shot up. He'd broken under the strain and was going to fire and try and get me before the signal. My old gat belched out and a big forty-five bullet tore his out of his hand as it went off. You see, he hadn't never heard of shooting from the hip.

"The Signora jumped up, screaming, and threw her arms around him. His face was burning red with shame, and his hand was quivering from the sting of the smash. I shoved my gun into the holster and got my musette bag and started for the door, but stopped at the table and drank my coffee standing. It was cold, but I like my coffee in the morning. There wasn't another word said. She was clinging to his neck and crying, and he was standing there, red and ashamed. I walked to the door and opened it, and looked back, and her eye flickered at me over his shoulder. Maybe it was a wink, maybe not. I shut the door and walked out of the courtyard down the road to Jardini. Wolf, hell no, he was a coyote. A coyote, Napoleon, is a wolf that is not a wolf. Now do you think he was a brave man, Signor Disporto?"

I said nothing. I was thinking of how this leather-faced old adventurer had matched his courage against admittedly one of the most fearless men in Europe.

"It is a question of standards," said Ricaud, as the fresh glasses arrived. "Lupo is brave, of course. The adventure of Von Hauser is proof. Also, mon capitain, he is Latin. That you cannot understand, for you have courage without imagination. It is a gift from God, monsieur." Ricaud smiled, shaking his head sadly. "I wish I have it. I have died a thousand times, and I am not a coward. I will die many more before I am buried, but it is, what you call it, Graves, my trade. We go now to a little war. Perhaps a joke war, eh? But one dies as dead in Chile as on Montfaucon. I envy you, Graves, you are American.

"Signor Rinaldi, I like you to drink with me to Capitain Perry Graves, who is so brave he makes the bravest flyer in your country look like a coward!" He laughed, and raised his glass.

"Aw, say, Napoleon!" broke in Graves, embarrassedly, "Let's change that to 'Vive la doughnut!' "

☙ ☙ ☙ ☙ ☙

As Ernest assaulted the popular magazines with stories he hoped they would "buy in self-defense," there were suddenly a number of distressing letters from Torro di Mosta, letters which left him desperate and confused. On February 3, Agnes wrote:

> The future is a puzzle to me and I'm sure I don't know how to solve it. Whether to go home, or to apply for more foreign service is a question just now. Of course you understand this is all for the near future, as you will help me plan the next period, I guess. Cavie has been very cruel to me lately, accusing me of being a flirt, which is putting me in the Ruth Brooks's class. You know I don't do anything like that, don't you?

On the fifth, Agnes went a little further:

> I'm getting fonder every day of life in furrin parts. Every time Miss Conway tells my fortune, she tells me I'm going to travel a lot. How do you like the idea? Goodnight, old dear,
>
> Your weary but cheerful,
> Aggie

Then, on March 1, she went as far as a hint could go:

> Oh, I'm going to the dogs rapidly, and getting more spoiled every day. I know one thing. I'm not the perfect being you think I am. But as I am and always was, only it's just beginning to creep out. I'm feeling very *cattiva* tonight. So good night, Kid, and don't do anything rash, but have a good time.
>
> Afft. Aggie

Actually, just after Ernest left for the States to begin work on their nest egg and to bring Agnes home, Agnes herself had begun to pursue a new romance. He was not the trim, athletic hero Ernest feared she would find among the Arditi, but rather a tall, broad-hipped, narrow-shouldered young man who did not carry a gun and who wrote his mother every day. Nevertheless, Dominico Caraccialo, or Nicky as Agnes called him, was a genuine aristocrat, a Neapolitan duke.

On the morning of March 13, 1919, Marcelline Hemingway saw her brother eagerly snatch his letter from the marble-topped mail table and bound up to his third-floor room. But, instead of the customary hour-long, closed-door silence, within a few minutes she heard Ernest vomit in the second-floor bathroom just at the head of the stairs. Agnes, now quite certain of her future with the duke, had written that she had fallen in love with an Italian major, that theirs had been only a boy-and-girl affair, and that she was sorry and knew he would probably not understand but might someday forgive her and be grateful to her. She said that she expected absolutely unexpectedly, to be married in the spring. She said she believed in him absolutely and knew it was for the best.

That afternoon, Ernest wrote to Bill Horne at the Universtiy Club, Bridgeport, Connecticut.

Dear Bill:
    It's kind of hard to write it Bill, especially since I've just heard from you about how happy you are so I'll put it off a bit. I can't write it, honest to god. It has hit me so sudden, so I'll tell you everything I know first.
    Pease was in town. Or maybe it should be Pease were in town. Jenks saw him. Spiegel is going strong. Jenks is still bartering securities. I'm . . . but I'll write it later. I haven't the guts to now. Oh, yes. A letter came from Yak. Written from Fort Worth. Think what the bird is doing there. You couldn't. But after you think of Yak it becomes possible. He went to war at 55 or so. That is nothing. He is in Forth Worth getting a divorce from Mrs. Yak. Can you feature it? He also bemoans the approaching aridity of the nation. He has been married twenty-four years according to his own testimony. What can you make of that, my dear Watson, if anything?
    Now having failed miserably at being facetious I'll tell you the sad truth which I have been suspecting for some time, since I've been back, and which culminated with a letter from Ag this morning.
    She doesn't love me, Bill. She takes it all back. A "mistake." One of those little mistakes, you know. Oh, Bill, I can't kid about it, and I can't be bitter because I'm just smashed by it. And the devil of it is that it wouldn't have happened if I hadn't left Italy. For Christ sakes, never leave your girl until you marry her. I know you can't "learn about wimmen from me" just as I can't learn from anyone else. But you, meaning the world in general, teach a girl—no, I won't put it that way—that is you make love to a girl and then you go away. She needs somebody to make love to her. If the right person turns up, you're out of luck. That's the way it

goes. You won't believe me, just as I wouldn't. But Bill, I've loved Ag. She's been my ideal, and Bill, I forgot all about religion and everything else because I had Ag to worship.

Well, the crash of smashing ideals was never merry music to anyone's ears. But she doesn't love me now, Bill, and she is going to marry some-one—name not given—who she has met since, marry him very soon, and she hopes that after I have forgiven her, I will start and have a wonderful career and everything. But Bill, I don't want a wonderful career and everything. That isn't really fair. She didn't write "and everything." All I wanted was Ag. And happiness and now the bottom has dropped out of the whole world. And I'm writing this with a dry mouth and a lump in the old throat, and Bill I wish you were here to talk to. The dear Kid. I hope he's the best man in the world. Aw, Bill, I can't write about it cause I do love her so damn much. And the perfectest hell of it is that money, which was the only thing that kept us from being married in Italy, is coming in at such an ungodly rate now. If I work full-time I can average about seventy a week, and I'd already saved nearly three hundred. Come on out, and we'll blow it in. I don't want the damn stuff now. I've got to stop before I begin feeling better. I'm not going to do that because I love Ag too much. Write me, kid.

                                                              Ernie

The next morning, before dawn, Ernest took the Lake Street train into Chicago, and at eight o'clock he boarded the steamer *State of Ohio* for Upper Michigan. All day, the broad-beamed boat plowed north in heavy rain, through gray, white-capped swells. From Harbor Springs on Little Traverse Bay, Ernest trudged the nine miles down Washout Road to Resort Pike Road and then on through scrub brush and second-growth pine to Windemere. Jake McConnell, a year-round resident at Walloon Lake, remembered "seeing a limping man walking along the road . . . [on] a cold blustery night in March. We asked him if he wanted a ride, and he said 'No, thank you.' I recognized Ernie and asked him what he was doing up here at this time of year. He said he was going down to their cottage and stay there. I told him that it was all boarded up, but he guessed as how he would have to break in then." When Ernest finally got back to Oak Park, three weeks later, Bill Horne's answer was waiting. It moved him to tears:

April 3, 1919

                                                   Locomobile Co. of America
                                                   Bridgeport, Conn.

Dear Old Kid—

    I just haven't got the words to tell you how terribly sorry I am and how much I sympathize with you. I wish to God, Ernie, that there was some-thing I could do to help you, but I know that this is a one-man fight. So all I can do is pat you on the back and tell you that I'm always with you. That won't help much, I know Kid, but that's all I can do. I can't even come out and do it in person—but Oin I'm just as sorrowful and just as hurt as if it had happened to me.

Kid, you've just got to stick it out. Your letter is full of guts of the highest and bravest kind—and you simply must stick to that spirit. Old man, I know a little of what it is to have everything in the world that is good and holy and beautiful and worth living for knocked plumb out of existence. A fool doctor told me once that I would be blind within three years, and for years I lived under that. He discovered later that he had made a crazy mistake—but in the meanwhile I lived in hell. You're getting it now, Man, but a thousand times worse. But you've got to remember that even the person we love most in all the world is only a symbol of our ideals of good and beauty. Even though she may pass, the truths that she represents cannot. They are forever. We may turn our backs on them—and then our life is worthless—but they are there, nevertheless. You've just got to fight on toward them, Ernie, without any reward in sight. And then perhaps you'll find someday, that you have found a new meaning in life and a new reward for your patience and suffering.

I've got hold of some big idea there, old man. I can't express it. My little weak words make it sound like silly rot. But it isn't. It's true. I believe it, and you've got to. It calls for guts without end, and blind faith. You're young and strong and brave enough to make the fight, Ern. And you've started right. Stick to your ideals, man. And work like hell.

Kid, I'm damn weak reed to lean on in your trouble, but I'm with you, and I believe in you, and I love you like a brother. If there's the littlest bit of comfort in that I'm gladder than I can tell. . . .

Sempre avanti, Amico!
Bill

Ernest had one other "amico" during those dark days that April. Coming home late from drunks with his Italo-American friends in Chicago, he always found his seventeen-year-old sister Ursula waiting for him, sleeping on the third-floor landing just below his room. She wanted to be awakened when he came in, she said, because she knew he had liquor in his room, and that it was bad for a man to drink alone. She would drink something light with Ernest until he went to sleep, and then she would sleep with him so he would not be lonely in the night. Ernest and Ursula always slept with the light on, except she would sometimes turn it off if she saw he was asleep, and then she would stay awake and turn it on if she knew he were waking. Years later Ernest would write: "A broken heart means that never can you remember and not to be able to remember is very different from forgetting."

During the first week of April 1919, the wind in Oak Park shifted from off Lake Michigan to blow southwest from the Mississippi basin; the last patches of shaded snow finally melted; and the broad lawns along Kensington Avenue began to smell like grass again. In the Hemingway household, the arrival of spring caused a kind of seasonal change, too. Clarence, overworked for months by the Spanish influenza, took time off to start his vegetable garden. Grace, now rid of her Red Cross Mothers duties but still suffering through a difficult change-of-life, started to take the long afternoon walks her husband prescribed. (She said she found Ernest's initials on far too many trees.) And Marcelline, depressed since her failure at Oberlin, began a romance with one Freeman Jones. For Ernest, however, the spring brought no such revival, and, though he wrote to unimaginative friends of a broken heart "cauterized by women and booze," life seemed unwilling to begin without his "country."

On April 16, Ernest got a cheerful twelve-page letter from Captain James Gamble, now staying at the Racquet Club in Philadelphia. Jim thanked Ernest for his "bully letter" of March 3, commiserated with him on what they'd lost by leaving Italy, and reminisced about their week together in Taormina. Then he offered Ernest a proposition:

I can't stand this city stuff [either] so am planning to go to Eagles Mere, our place in the mountains, the early part of next month. Here's a proposition. Won't you join me? It's not Taormina but pretty fine at that time of year. I expect to open one of our little cottages. We'll get the others ready for our other summer tenants, work in the garden, enjoy the beauties of Springtime nature in its budding glory + paint. It is truly fine at that time, practically nobody there + plenty of time for thought and good work. Think it over. What joy it would be to have you. There would be no Monge Uova ["Eat Eggs," a nickname Ernest and Jim had for their Sicilian cook] but I being an optimist am sure we will get a hold of someone to fill the bill. I won't take "No" for an answer. You must come. It will do you good. Bring your typewriter along. I have two or three stories to suggest to you. Let me hear from you soon. Address letters here or c/o H. C. Voorhees, Elkins Park, Pa. . . .

Yours,
Jim G.

Before he left his room that morning, Ernest began a long, appreciative reply:

Dear Jim,
Man it was good to hear from you! I'd been wanting to write you here in the states but couldn't but feel that you might be in Madiera [sic]. Why Chief, I feel any amount more kindly toward this country now that you're in it. It isn't such a bad place now with the exception of the approaching aridity. But Taormina is not dry. I'm so darn glad to hear from you, that I don't know what to write. The occasion is not one for writing but for grasping of the hand, greetings, and perhaps the proposal of a toast. It is

the time for the having of another. I'm writing this at my desk in my room. Having hopped out of bed as soon as I'd read your letter a couple of times. On the left is a well-filled bookcase containing Strega, Cinzano Vermouth, kummel, and martell cognac. All these were gotten after an exhaustive search of Chicago's resources. If it were not nine o'clock in the morning, I would suggest the compounding of a Gambler's Delight. Cinquante—martell. There is a good deal of news which should be retailed, tho. First I am now a free man. All entangling alliances ceased about a month ago and I know now I am most damnably lucky—though of course I couldn't see it at the time. Anyway everything is finished and the less said about it, as always with the unfair sex, the better. I did love the girl, though I know now that the paucity of Americans doubtless had a great deal to do with it. And now it's over I'm glad, but I'm not sorry it happened 'cause, Jim, I figure it does you good to love anyone. Through good fortune I escaped matrimony so why should I grumble? Not being philosophical though, it was a devil of a jolt because I'd given up everything for her, most especially Taormina. And as soon as the Definite Object was removed, quelque kicks were implanted on the w.k. [well-kicked] ass for my ever leaving Italy. The first time you're jilted though is supposed to be the hardest. At any rate I'm now free to do whatever I want. Go wherever I want, and have all the time in the world to develop into some kind of writer. And I can fall in love with anyone I wish which is a great and priceless privilege. Here are a few bits of gossip of the old gang. Jenks is here in Chicago and we foregather every so often. Art Thomson writes from Buffalo and is working at his old job. I stopped a couple of days with Bill Horne in Yonkers and he is engaged to some girl there. Bill alleges that she is the most wonderful, etc. His remarks had a faintly familiar sound. Bill is a peach tho and an idealist which makes him too good for any woman to marry. Idealists lead a rough life in this world Jim. But like hermit crabs they acquire shells that they cover their ideals with and that they can retreat into and protect the ideals with. But sometimes something comes along with a heavy enough tread to crush the shell and the ideals and all. Anyway, to return to the gang: I had a letter from Yak Harris and he is down in Ft. Worth, Texas doing guess what? Getting a divorce from Mrs. Yak. There is a bit of real news. After twenty-four years. Yak says, "I'm off all that stuff for life—at least I think I am." I think that "I think I am," is the best thing I ever heard. While separated from his family, Yak made the address care of Goldberg's Cigar Store, Yakima, Washington.

Ernest paused here, but the next day he took up the letter again:

Sunday, April 27th

Dear Jim:
    Before I had a chance to finish this they took me off to the hospital and perpetuated another bit of carving. Throat this time. I'm now at home and darned sorry I didn't get this finished before I went to the hospital.

It was awfully good of you to ask me to Eagle Mere and I know that we would have a great time, but this is the situation at present. A good pal, whom you'd like immensely. Good scout, wonderful sense of humor, and perfect pal is coming to town Wednesday next to stay for a week or so. Bill Smith. Then he is going up north where we go in the summer and open his place up. I'm coming up about the middle of May and we've planned to bum and fish around together. I don't know just when my folks will be going up and as we're not doing anything to the farm this summer, I think it is all rented out, there is nothing for me to do but go over and help them open up the shack on the other side of the lake. They won't be coming up until the latter part of June or first of July anyway and I doubt if I will stay with them. But this is the idea. Bill has a farm which because he was in the service, Marine Flyer, he has rented out almost entirely. So that leaves him free for the summer. This is a priceless place, Jim. Horton's Bay on Pine Lake about twelve miles from Charlevoix, about three hundred miles north of here. It is great northern air. Absolutely the best trout fishing in the country. No exaggeration. Fine country. Good color, good northern atmosphere. Absolute freedom, no summer resort stuff, and lots of paintable stuff. And if you want to do portraits. You shall do them. Bill has a Buick Six that we can run into Charlevoix with when we long for the flesh pots. And it is equally good to run over to the Pine Barrens where it is absolutely wild and there are the Big and Little Sturgeon and the Minnehaha and the Black Trout Rivers. It's a great place to laze around and swim and fish when you want to. And the best place in the world to do nothing. It is beautiful country, Jim. And let me tell you about the Rainbow fishing. I don't know whether you are a fisherman or not. But you might be a rank hater of the sport and you would like this kind of fishing. Across the little Bay from where we would live is a point. And a little trout river comes into the Bay and makes a channel past this point. There is an old quay alongside and it is from there that we fish. And this is the manner of the fishing. We paddle over across the Bay and stop at this old lumber dock, just level with the water. And from the dock we run out about four or five lines into the channel. These are baited with whole skinned perch which is dropped into the channel and sinks to the bottom. The lines are run out and then we put a weight on the butt of the rod they are run out from and set the click on the reel and wait. Do you get the scene. All the rods, sticking out over the side, the clicks set, and the lines running way out into the channel. Then if it is night, we have a campfire on the point and sit around and yarn and smoke or if it is daytime we loaf around and read and await results. And these are the results. A reel goes screeeeeeech, the tip of the rod jerks under water, you run down and grab it up and thumb the reel and then out in the lake a big rainbow shoots up into the air. And then the fight. And Jim, those trout can fight. And I've never taken one under three pounds out of the Bay and they run as high as fifteen. The biggest I ever took was nine and seven ounces. And you always get a strike. A night's fishing would average three of the big trout. Though I have taken as high as seven. It is the best rainbow trout fishing in America. Just this one Bay and the only thing you can take them on is a skinned perch. And nobody knows it but us. People come down and troll all day for them from Charlevoix and never get a strike. While we will be taking them all day. An Indian taught it to me.

And they break water a dozen times and when you have one you have a regular fish. And it is the most comfortable kind of fishing I have ever found. When we feel like doing regular trout fishing, we can fish any one of the half hundred good streams for brook trout. But it's a great life up there just lazing around the old point and always have a line out or so for rainbow. There are trips in the car and runs around Little Traverse Bay to the old Indian missions and some beautiful trips. And Jim we are going to have a wonderful gang up there. Bill who I told you of is a wonder. Then there is Carl Edgar, a Princeton man of the same easy going humorous type as Bill Horne. Who reads fairy tales and swims and fishes when anyone else wants to. He's been an artillery officer during the late unpleasantness. Carl's coming up in July. Charles Hopkins, a newspaperman and general good scout and mighty fisherman and loafer is coming up whenever I write him that everything is ready. Hop is the only one that takes his fishing seriously.

Bill and I have bummed together for years and the four of us got together on a trip last year before I went overseas. Bill is known as the Master Biologist because some university decorated him with a degree, Carl as the Oil Maggot, because he owns some kind of oil business somewhere, Hop as the Wily Journalist or the Bottle Imp and I as the Massive Woodsman. This title entitles me to cut wood and build fires while the Master Biologist and the Maggot lie on their backs and praise my skill. It's a great gang, Jim, and I know you will like them. At Bill's place is his sister Kate, a rare good scout and a good talker and game for any of the parties. And Mrs. Charles, Bill's aunt, who is one of our own people.

Bill's place can't put us all up at once so when Hop comes up I'll move down to Dilworths' who have the leading house in the four house town, Horton's Bay, and have plenty of beds, good rooms in a cottage and cooking that I've been wanting to get to ever since I came back from Italy. Very reasonable rates and food and accommodations are splendid. We could have a great time, Jim. Why can't you come up? We could work and we could have a wonderful time. I don't see why you can't. It's great up there all during June, July, August, and September. And I'll probably be up there all that time so I don't see any reason why you can't come up and stay as long as you can.

I'm all up in the air about what to do next fall. Wish a war would come along and solve my problems. Now that I don't have to go to work I can't decide what the devil to do. The family are trying to get me to go to college but I want to go back to Italy, and I want to go to Japan, and I want to live a year in Paris and I want to do so damn many things now that I don't know what the deuce I will do. Maybe we can go over and fight the Yugos. It was very simple while the war was on. Then there was only one thing for a man to do. Am having pretty good luck with my yarns. If you want I'll send you a couple.

I sure wish I was starting to meet you to go to Eagle Mere, but I've promised Bill to go north now. If you don't withdraw the invitation, I'd like awfully well to be up there with you sometime. Why can't you come up North first? The good fishing and the weather begins about the middle of June.

I'll give you details about getting up there later. Chicago is the only change you would have to make. I'd meet you at the station at the other end. But when I think about that it makes me inarticulate and so I'd better quit. Let me hear from you, Chief.

As Ever,
Hemmy

Pardon the horrible typing, will you, Jim?

Jim Gamble did not accept Ernest's invitation to Upper Michigan; neither did Johnny Miller, who said he wanted to rest on familiar ground before entering the University of Wisconsin in the fall; nor did Ernest's best friend, Bill Horne. Secondary friends like Howell Jenkins from nearby Evanston and Chicagoan Larry Barnett committed themselves only to a "spell of country" in July. And Clarence, though he longed to make Ernest his "chum" (even a trip to New Orleans for spring racing was proposed), finally decided he should not leave Grace alone in Oak Park.

The friend Ernest wrote so warmly of, Bill Smith, did go north the summer of 1919 and, with his sister Kate, stopped in Oak Park the first week in May. Bill's brother Kenley and his wife Doodles had recently moved there from St. Louis and were living on North Oak Park Avenue, not far from the house where Ernest was born. One night, just before they left for Horton Bay, Ernest invited everyone out to dinner. Kenley and Bill talked politics, Kate was vivacious, and Doodles kept wanting to dance. On the ride home in the trolley, Ernest told of an Ardito he knew who had used an Austrian prisoner to demonstrate the technique of the short sword. Kate took one thrust under the right shoulder blade. That's where he put it, Ernest said. Right there.

❧ 8 ❧
Through the Dark

By the time Ernest traveled north in late May 1919, spring had advanced up the Michigan peninsula, and the breeze that still put whitecaps on the lake was softened by the smell of land. On his homecoming to Oak Park, Ernest had been flushed with the enthusiasm of a fiancé. Now there was only a tacit commitment to pick apples on Bill Smith's aunt's farm. Ernest watched the gray, lacy swells through the rain-drenched window of the lake steamer. Kate Smith, a woman as beautiful and mature as Agnes Kurowsky, was on his mind.

Ernest found the five-house, white clapboard town of Horton Bay just as he had left it two years before. There was still the empty Methodist church, still the clank and fire of Jim Dilworth's blacksmith shop across from the grammar school. Jim, a trace more gray in his handlebar mustache, had read of Ernest's heroism in Italy and was as pleased as his wife Liz that Ernest spoke only of the way Mrs. Dilworth cooked the birds he'd once brought her from Indian River and of the trout she must have missed since he'd been away. On his old cot in the empty dormitory annex, Ernest smelled the lingering winter cold in the empty room, smoked a cigarette, thought about supper. He was happy that he'd declined Bill Smith's invitation to board awhile at Mrs. Charles's farm. Late in a sleepless night, the deep silence of the woods, the cool draft of earth and pine, the moonlight through the four-paned window, so bright the shadow of a cross lay on the floor, drew Ernest out for a walk. In these woods, he had often fished and hunted alone. Still, Orion shone bright and clear overhead and made Ernest lonesome for his friends.

Because Bill Horne, Jim Gamble, and Johnny Miller had declined his invitations, Ernest neglected his fishing (though he kept his promise to the city boys, Howell Jenkins and Larry Barnett, their trips up to the Sturgeon and the Black weren't much fun) and became what his sister Marcelline called "one of the summer people."

After a day of letter writing on the musty couch in Pinehurst's screened-in porch, Ernest would amble down the sandy road from Pinehurst to the lake. Bill Smith and Carl Edgar would be there, swimming out in the cove or diving off the old bean warehouse dock or flirting with a well-built red-headed waitress, Marjorie Bump. Kate Smith was usually there, too, and "Odgar," as Ernest called him, looked at Kate with "that fried-fish look" in his eyes. "Didn't Odgar know anything," Ernest thought. "Kate would never marry him. She wouldn't ever marry anybody that didn't make her. And if they tried to make her, she would curl up inside of herself and be hard and slip away." In part to torment Carl, in part to "make" the lovely Kate himself, Ernest "scuffed off his canvas shoes, pulled his shirt over his head, and stepped out of his trousers. His bare feet felt the sandy planks of the dock. He ran very quickly out the yielding plank of the springboard, his toes shoved against the end of the board, he tightened and he was in the water, smoothly and deeply, with no consciousness of the dive." "Gosh, if I could have Kate down here," he thought. He came up in a rush to the surface, feeling water in his eyes and ears. " 'It was perfect. Absolutely perfect,' Kate shouted from the dock." Later, up on the dock in the moonlight, with the hum of cicadas and the freshwater odor of decay, Ernest lay thinking while Kate's insteps pressed against his back and she talked to Odgar.

On June 15, 1919, Ernest picked up a letter at the General Store that made him blush and stammer. It was Red Cross stationery, and from Rome. Agnes, with great economy, wrote that her duke's mother had refused to permit his marriage to an "American adventuress" and that Nicky had decided to do what his mother said. Throughout the letter, Agnes hinted that she had learned the difference between love and opportunity, and wouldn't it be fine if Ernest were her beau again. There were more sleepless nights for Ernest, but he didn't reply.

In March, just after his sojourn at Windemere, Ernest had received an extraordinary letter from his mother, Grace. On her own, she had begun to retrace her father Ernest Hall's travels before the Civil War. From the St. Charles Hotel in New Orleans, she wrote to "Dear Ernie Boy" as if she were a younger sister. Then, during the summer months, Grace insisted on building herself a private retreat on Longfield Farm. She had to have peace and quiet, she said, "a rest from you all if I am to go on living." "On summer nights," Marcelline recalled years later, "we could hear mother's music drifting across the mile of water between Grace cottage and Windemere." Clarence, disoriented by his wife's behavior, pursued Ernest as a "chum."

The first week in October, a storm moved south through Horton Bay. There had been storms in September that turned the lake gray and left piles of sodden leaves. But this was a "three day blow," and it changed the season and put the scent of woodsmoke in the air. Liz Dilworth, tired of summer people and chicken pies, told Ernest she was closing up Pinehurst, she'd been happy to see him again and hoped he'd be back next year. Fortunately, the Petoskey newspaper advertised a boardinghouse, Eva Potter's at 602 State Street. The room was eight dollars a week, and it could be leased by the month.

The day Ernest carried his footlocker up the narrow black stairs at Potter's boardinghouse, banging the banisters past the oddly placed, curtained French doors, he knew he had moved much farther than the six miles from Pinehurst. Horton Bay was the North in summer; Petoskey, the North year-round.

Eva Potter, a short, dark-haired woman with a slight cast in her left eye, showed Ernest to the front room on the second floor. There was a wroughtiron bed against one wall, a knotty pine chest of drawers, and a small fold-down desk with a lock and key. Out the broad, floor-length window, Ernest could see well down the hill toward Bear River. But the room seemed dark for such a sunny day. That afternoon, in the white-walled double parlor, he met the daughter, Hazel, a waitress in Mancelona, and the furtive, dim-witted son, Clyde.

Because Mrs. Potter did not cook for boarders, Ernest took his lunch and supper at Braun's diner on Main Street. There were a couple of tables, a long counter, and, before noon, piles of doughnuts under a glass cover. The wicker flap opened into the kitchen, where a black cook worked in the pots and steam. The menu (beans were the house specialty) was chalked up on the wall. To kill time in Petoskey, Ernest walked down to McCarthy's barber shop and chatted with white-jacketed barbers snipping away and read the stories in hunting magazines. Nights he went down to the Perry Hotel and drank coffee laced with bootleg in the red plush bar. Across the street in the Petoskey railroad station was a pile of stiff, gutted deer, half drifted over with snow.

The stories Ernest had written in Oak Park, all in his public lecturer's voice, were still, he thought, his best chance for publication. And he retyped and sent them out again. One weekend he brought a story to Edwin Balmer, the editor of *Redbook,* then living at Bay View. Balmer read the work with interest, he said, made some insipid emendations, and changed the title to "The Passing of Pickles McCarthy" from Ernest's "The Woppian Way." What was Ernest writing now? Balmer asked. Nothing much, Ernest said. He would have said nothing at all except that he'd begun a few sketches, the first things he had done since Agnes broke his heart. His sentences now were short and simple, the irony bitter and harsh, each word like his first steps without crutches or his cane.

𝄞 𝄞 𝄞 𝄞 𝄞

Crossroads—
An Anthology

PAULINE SNOW

Pauline Snow was the only beautiful girl we ever had out at the Bay. She was like an Easter Lily coming up straight and lithe and beautiful out of a dung heap. When her father and mother died she came to live with the Blodgetts. Then Art Simons started coming around to the Blodgetts' in the evenings.

Art couldn't come to most places at the Bay, but old Blodgett liked to have him around. Blodgett said he brightened up the place. Art would go out to the stable with Blodgett when he was doing the chores and tell him stories, looking around first to see that no one would overhear. Old Blodgett would come in, his face as red as a turkey's wattles, and laugh, and slap Art on the back. And then laugh and laugh, his face getting redder all the time.

Art began to take Pauline for walks after supper. She was frightened at first of Art, with his thick blunt fingers, and his manner of always touching her when he talked, and didn't want to go. But old Blodgett made fun of her.

"Art's the only regular fellow around the Bay!" he'd say, and clap Art across the shoulders. "Be a sport, Pauline!"

Pauline's big eyes would look frightened—but she went off with him in the dusk along the road. There was a red line of afterglow along the hills toward Charlevoix, and Pauline said to Art, "Don't you think that's awfully pretty, Art?"

"We didn't come down here to talk about sunsets, kiddo!" said Art, and put his arm around her.

After a while some of the neighbors made a complaint, and they sent Pauline away to the correction school down at Coldwater. Art was away for awhile, and then came back and married one of the Jenkins girls.

ED PAIGE

Stanley Ketchell came to Boyne City once, barn storming with a burlesque show. He had a forfeit posted that he'd knock anybody out inside of six rounds. Everybody was lumbering then, and Ed Paige came in with a bunch of the boys from White's camp number two to see the show. When the big scene came where Ketchell's manager made the offer, Ed went up on the stage.

It was a wonderful slashing, tearing-in battle, and there were lots of people claimed Ed shaded Ketchell. Anyway Ed received the hundred dollars for staying the limit, and he hasn't done anything much since. He just thinks about the time he fought Stanley Ketchell. For awhile people used to point Ed out. But now most everyone has forgotten all about it, and quite a few say they'll never believe Ed really did it.

BOB WHITE

Bob White was drafted and went over with a base hospital unit. About three days before the armistice he got to France. Bob told the Odd Fellows a lot of things about the war the first lodge night he was home.

Bob had an iron cross he said he got off'n a dead German officer. And the noise forty miles back of the front was wors'n right up in the trenches. Bob didn't like the French people. Some of them used cattle to plow with and all the French girls have black teeth. And they ain't like our girls. Bob was with the best French families, too, and he ought to know. According to Bob, the French soldiers never did any fighting in the war either. They were all old men and were always working on the roads. The Marines didn't really do any fighting either, Bob says. He saw a lot of Marines, and they were all M.P.s around the docks and in Paris.

The people out at the Bay don't think much of France or the Marines either, for that matter, now that Bob's back with news right direct.

OLD MAN HURD—AND MRS. HURD

Old Man Hurd has a face that looks indecent. He hasn't any whiskers, and his chin kind of slinks in and his eyes are red rimmed and watery, and the edges of his nostrils are always red and raw. Hurd's shanty is in a hollow on the forty down back of our place and you can hear him cursing his horses when he's dragging. He's just a little man and he comes up to get our swill that we always leave for his pigs in a big carbide can out back. When he finds something in the swill that he thinks the pigs won't like, you can hear him cursing us and the swill under his breath.

He's an Evan and goes to church and prayer meeting regular. Nobody

has ever seen him smile, but sometimes we can hear him singing a song
that goes:

> Reeligiun makes me happy,
> Reeligiun makes me happy,
> Reeligiun makes me happy,
> I'm-on-my-way!

Mrs. Hurd is a large woman with a big, comely, simple face, and she's
about twenty years younger than the Old Man. She's about forty now, and
when she was eighteen her father died and left her the old Amacker place.
She tried to run the place, but she couldn't do it. She didn't have enough
money to get to Grand Rapids, and in those days there weren't summer
people to work for as there is now. And she told my mother once—"I was
a right likely-looking girl then, too."

Hurd used to come up to the old Amacker place every night and not
say anything, but just look at what a mess she was making of trying to
run the place. He wouldn't offer to help her split wood or anything. He'd
just stand and look at her and the hopeless way she was muddling. After
standing there a while, he'd say, "Sarah, you'd better marry me."

So after a while she married him, and she told my mother, "the awful
part about it was that he looked then just like he looks now."

BILLY GILBERT

Billy Gilbert was an Ojibway that lived up near Susan Lake. Mrs. Billy
was the nicest looking Indian woman in upper Michigan, and they had
two fat, brown little kids named Beulah and Prudence. Billy and
Mrs. Billy both had gone to Mount Pleasant to school, and Billy was a
good farmer. Along in 1915, nobody at the Bay knew why, Billy went up
to the Soo and enlisted in the Black Watch.

This summer Billy came home. He had two scraps of ribbon sewed on
his tunic over his heart and three gold pencil stripes on his left sleeve.
Nobody around the Bay knew that the ribbons stood for the M.M. and
the D.C.M., all the boys that came back had ribbons on, some had three
and four, you could buy them at the camps where you were discharged;
but everybody made a lot of fun of his kilts.

"Look at the Injun with skirts on!" loafers would holler. And when he
rested his pack and lit a cigarette, someone was sure to say, "Oh look at
her! She smokes!" That was always good for a laugh. It wasn't the kind
of homecoming Billy had pictured.

He hiked up the road to Susan Lake and found his shack empty. The door was padlocked and his garden was sod and there was quack grass in his young orchard, choking the young trees that the rabbits hadn't girdled. Billy turned down the road to a neighbor's.

"Mrs. Gilbert?" said the man in the doorway, looking amusedly at Billy's kilts. "She went off with Simon Green's boy. Sold the place to G—— at Charlevoix. It ain't been farmed this year. You're Billy, eh? Well, they're living down the State somewheres." The neighbor stood in the doorway holding a lamp.

Billy turned away, struggled into his pack and swung into his Highlander's stride down the road in the dusk, his bonnet cocked on one side, his bare knees swinging under his kilts as they had swung down the Bapaume-Cambrai Road. His face was as stolid as ever, but his eyes looked a long way through the dark. Then he commenced whistling. And the tune he whistled was:

"It's a long way to Tipperary,
It's a long way to go."

𝖂 𝖂 𝖂 𝖂 𝖂

Ernest's best friend in Petoskey during the fall and winter of 1919 was Grace Quinlan, a fourteen-year-old with thick black hair cut short on her shoulders and a way of walking that reminded him of Agnes Kurowsky. On Saturday nights, when Hazel Potter came home from Mancelona, Ernest crossed the street to the Quinlans' tiny gingerbread cottage and picked up his "Sister Luke." Arm in arm, trying to keep the step together, they'd walk down the hill, past the feed store, over the Bear River bridge, their boots ringing hollow on the frozen planks, and down to the bright little library with its polished brass railings and staid librarian. Whispering at the broad oak table, leaning toward her to emphasize, Ernest bored Grace with involved explanations of poems by Shelley and Keats, stories by Davis and Kipling. But later, when they popped corn and drank soda together, Grace knew he'd tell her wonderful stories about the war. On their way home they occasionally heard the night train, pulling up the Boyne Falls grade, crack off its whistle in the frigid air. Ernest said that it sounded more lovely to him than all the "junk" Stravinsky wrote.

In mid-December, the Ladies' Aid Society of Petoskey asked Ernest to speak to them at the public library. None of the local young men had had combat duty, and the women wanted to hear about the real war first-hand. The gratuity, thirty dollars, was twice as much as Ernest had ever earned

with his talks before, and, dressed in his cock-feathered Bersaglieri hat
and black velvet cape, he gave an inspired performance. Most of the
women were impressed by Ernest's style and appearance, and the ques-
tion-and-answer period lasted until the librarian politely ushered the last
cluster of "historians" out the door. One lady, the best-looking middle-
aged woman Ernest had ever seen, did not join the others but asked him
into a chauffeur-driven Pierce-Arrow waiting at the curb. She said her
name was Harriet Connable, that she was a friend of his mother, Grace,
and that she had a slightly crippled, reclusive son. She proposed that
Ernest come to Toronto, live in the Connable mansion at 153 Lyndhurst
Avenue, and give her son Ralph the "right slant on life, especially as to
sports and pleasures." Ernest would get room and board and be paid
twenty dollars a week. There was a sister, Dorothy, too. She was twenty-
six, a graduate of Wellesley College, and had worked for the YMCA after
the Armistice in France and in Germany. Ernest did not need the day
Mrs. Connable offered him to decide. He could leave anytime, he said,
but they agreed on the first week in January.

As Ernest packed up and said his goodbyes in Petoskey, he got a letter
from his father:

Dec. 16, 1919

My Dear Ernest,
    I have not heard from you for some time and surely want you to con-
tinue as my "chum" and keep me in your confidence. I am very busy with
the extra duties about the place and the extra cold weather, keeping the
furnace going and the water hot to try and please a lot of very particular
sisters and a mother who is always glad when everything is 'Right!'
    We are anxious to know if you are to be home for Christmas? I surely
wish you were to be, as then I would have someone to hook up with.—
    I am to be good and like all the dear children's friends and will do my
best.

               Much love dear boy,
               Always your loyal and loving
               Daddy
               C. E. Hemingway, M.D.

Instead of going home for Christmas, Ernest sent his sister Ursula
twenty dollars for family gifts and, on December 28, got a thank-you note
for the "lovely gloves" that *"I needed so much"* from Grace. But his sense
of obligation remained, and Ernest made the long trip to Toronto by way
of Oak Park.

When he'd returned from Kansas City, Ernest had excused himself
from home with a schedule that precluded long conversations; this time

he did so again. The night he arrived, there was a dance at the "Club," and he worked his calves into spasms and didn't get to sleep until three; the next day there was a luncheon with Anson Hemingway and a touring celebrity, Scottish song-and-dance man Harry Lauder (who said the war should have been fought to conclusion no matter how many men were killed); then, that night, a drunken reunion with a dozen members of Schio at the Venice Cafe. When he left on January 3, Ernest forgot a velour hat on the rack in the hall and, according to Clarence, left his room a mess.

The Connable mansion in Toronto stood out from a wooded ravine and rutted roads like the houses Ernest had seen as a boy on the outskirts of Oak Park. Harriet Connable, whose husband, Ralph Sr., was the head of Woolworth Stores in Canada, greeted Ernest at the door herself. Behind her, standing brushed and combed, was her son Ralph. After polite conversation, Mrs. Connable showed Ernest around: there was a music room with a pipe organ, a billiard room with low-hung lighting that reminded Ernest of Stresa, and a tennis court between his private cottage and the house. Harriet Connable told Ernest that she and her husband would be leaving for Palm Beach in a few days. Besides his board and drinks (Canada was not "dry") and twenty dollars a week, Ernest would have the use of the family car with the chauffeur.

Although to his superficial friends Ernest wrote that the job in Toronto was "Peruvian Doughnuts" (the Schio equivalent of "duck soup"), he'd seen enough in Milan to know what taking care of a cripple demanded, and had learned in Kansas City that the kind of sexual problems Ralph Connable had were not so easily solved. It soon became apparent to Ernest that "Ralph was no fun. [He] was a good kid but fairly twisted up and he was that type that is stupid in his studies to the point almost of idiocy, yet extremely crafty in bringing out very intelligent remarks. You could not train him to box [Ralph Connable Sr. had said that this was just what Ralph Jr. needed], but I saw he got exercise and kept him out of trouble. But I knew any job of mine with him was hopeless."

For the female company he needed after spells with Ralph, Ernest went to hockey games and boxing matches with Dorothy Connable, attended the opera, and played bridge with Elsie Green. On weekends he went horseback riding. Because he could not bend his knees to the English stirrups, his legs dangled straight out, Indian-fashion. Ernest felt embarrassed, but his companion, svelte socialite Bonnie Bonnelle, found it charming. For his own physical therapy, Ernest got up soon after dawn, laced on the biggest pair of high-boot skates he could find in the Connables' warming house, and lurched painfully around the ice-filled tennis court. At Dorothy Connable's afternoon skating parties and impromptu hockey games, however, he had little success. One young man, another Ernest who had been a collegiate hockey player at the University of Toronto, insisted on showing off by playing with a broom and in his shoes.

When Ernest returned from Italy, he'd sought a newspaper job as security against the risk of writing fiction. With Agnes gone for almost a year, it still seemed like a good idea. Mr. Connable's advertising budget for the Woolworth Stores opened any door for him with the Canadian papers, and Ernest was hired at the *Toronto Star.*

Because he'd worked on one of the best papers in the States and had many good stories to tell, Ernest got a warm welcome from most of his new colleagues. But Greg Clark, so short he looked directly into the center of Ernest's chest, remarked how Ernest turned his l's into w's and, unaware of Ernest's damaged legs, assumed that the perspiration that kept appearing on his upper lip was caused by boyish excitement. Nevertheless, for some reason Ernest considered Greg Clark his friend. The editor-in-chief, Mr. Cranston, who wore a bow tie and kept a religious picture on his office wall, did like Ernest. He said the boy could write "good, plain Anglo-Saxon," and he had a "gift for humor" too. Before long, Mr. Cranston gave Ernest a byline and paid him a penny a word. Nevertheless, as Ernest walked through the grimy corridors filled with stale oft-heated air, past the dark, cramped cubicles, he felt he'd regressed. The shoddy four-story building at 20 King Street West had nothing like the ambient energy of the *Kansas City Star.* When his contract with the Connables expired in May, Ernest said he'd had enough of the miserable Canadian weather, of the *Toronto Star,* and of Ralph Connable. Liz Dilworth opened Pinehurst on the first of June, and Ernest wired that he'd be her first guest.

Although Ernest returned to Upper Michigan with a sense of relief, he was anxious, too. Grace, upset over a misplaced library card, had written on February 9:

Someday, dear boy, you will really come to know *your Mother;* in the meantime—may the Lord watch between me and thee while we are absent one from the other. You are always in my heart and my prayers and I know that you will be a great hearted noble man because I have faith in God and confidence in you. Not for nothing are you the great-great grandson of that noble Christian gentleman, Rev. William Edward Miller, and the grandson of the finest, purest, noblest, man I have ever known, "Ernest Hall." God demands that we be true to our heritage. He is counting on you, my son. Your own loving

Mother
Grace Hall-H.

1. Ernest Hall, his son Leicester, and his daughter Grace, shortly before Ernest Hall's death in 1905.

2. Caroline Hancock Hall, wife of Ernest Hall. Her protracted illness from cancer in 1895 resulted in the meeting and courtship of Grace Hall and Clarence Hemingway.

3. Ernest. Grace once noted that as a child Ernest looked like a little man.

4. Top, from left: Ernest, Clarence, Grace. Bottom, from left: Ursula, Madelaine, Marcelline. About 1908.

5. The house at 600 North Kenilworth Avenue and Iowa Street in Oak Park, Illinois. Grace designed much of it herself and paid for it with the inheritance from her father's estate. There were at the time six live-in servants. Dr. Hemingway's garden is partly visible in the rear. The oak tree still stands.

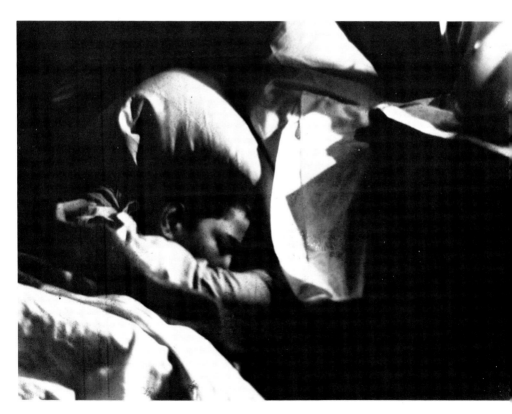

6. Ernest sleeping (or pretending to sleep) in a picture taken by his father around 1910. In an unpublished novel written in 1927, Ernest speaks of pretending to fight sleep to please Clarence.

7. Ernest at Walloon Lake, about 1913, with borrowed lever-action shotgun and willow grouse. Notice Ernest's notoriously large feet and his reluctance to hold the dead bird.

. Windemere exterior, photographed (probably ⟩y Clarence) from the end of the rickety dock the hildren dove from, nude in the moonlight. It is pring and the lake is high.

9. Windemere interior, living room. The door to Clarence's bedroom is in the center. Grace's bedroom door is out of sight on the right. The window looks over to the annex, a three-room shed where the children slept.

10. Ernest hiking through a second growth of timber. Although probably taken during his high-school years, the photo has something of the feeling of the postwar story "The Big Two-Hearted River."

11. Ernest with fly-rod case in about 1917, his last full summer in upper Michigan before leaving for Kansas City. Railroad tracks in that region were a dangerous road, but many times the only one, as in the story "The Battler."

12. Ernest good-humoredly playing the role of a naive hobo (a role he would recreate for Nick Adams in "The Battler"). In the summer of 1917, Ernest knew how to "ride the rods."

13. One of the photos taken for Ernest's high-school yearbook—far more revealing and attractive than the one he or Grace chose.

14. James Gamble. One of the Gambles of Philadelphia and Williamsburg, a Yale graduate, he was the captain who saved Ernest's life after Ernest's wounding and returned him from Fornarci to Milan.

15. Bill Horne. Ernest's closest friend during the war and his roommate in Chicago in 1920, he was to be best man in Ernest's planned wedding to Agnes Kurowsky.

16. Ernest in his dress uniform, specially tailored by Spagnoli, 1918.

17. San Dona di Piave, a town four miles downriver from Fossalta, where Ernest established temporary quarters. The small towns along the lower Piave took shelling from both sides as the front line crossed and recrossed the river.

18. The trenches along the Lower Piave looked like rat nests. Ernest brought candy, Toscani cigars, postcards, and clean water to these men, and they called him "the cheerful American."

19. An advance listening post beyond the front line. It was at such a place on the night of July 8, 1918, that Ernest was wounded by an Austrian mortar.

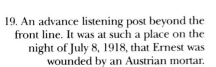

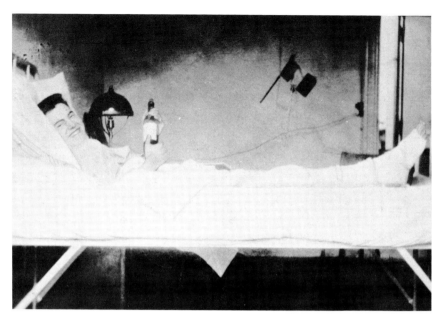

20. Ernest at the American Red Cross Hospital in Milan. Thanks to money sent by Grandfather Hemingway, Ernest was well supplied with an ineffective but pleasing anesthetic. The armoire where the superintendent of nurses, Gumshoe Casey, found his empties is at right.

21. Ernest just outside the French doors on the balcony of his room at the hospital. His pain was still intense after his first operation. The Italian carbine and cap, the big grin, suggest this was a photo for the folks back home.

22. Agnes Kurowsky, graduate of the Bellevue Hospital School of Nursing, New York, class of 1912.

23. (*Above*) Ernest was up on crutches too soon, and he suffered for it. Bill Horne stands in uniform next to Ernest. The older man sitting at the right is probably the Yak of Ernest's broken-hearted letter to Bill Horne (March 13, 1919).

24. Captain Enrico Serena, with whom Agnes had a brief flirtation the night Ernest had his second operation.

25. Ernest and Agnes, in the center, with two other nurses at the San Siro racetrack outside Milan. Ernest's right leg is so heavily bandaged that he needs to wear a special slipper. He shows two wound stripes on his sleeve. Nevertheless he has worn his leather puttees. Ernest would never again be this thin until a few months before his death.

26. Ernest posing in the black velvet cape with red satin lining just outside his parents' house on Kenilworth. It was in this cape that Ernest met Bill Horne at the dock and charmed Bill's girl, Anne Sage during tea at the Plaza. The cane, of course, was necessary. It is ironic that the cuckolded Italian duke in Ernest's youthful short story "The Mercenaries" appears in such a cape.

27. Ernest after receiving a plaque commemorating his service to Italy from Italian Commander in Chief Diaz at ceremonies in Chicago, 1921.

28. (*Above*): From left to right: Carl Edgar ("Odgar"), Kate Smith, Marcelline Hemingway, Bill Horne, Ernest, and Charles Hopkins (Ernest's friend from the *Star*). Note both Bill and Ernest are holding revolvers. Bill has pointed his upward; Ernest points his at the cameraman. Kate notices Ernest's revolver. Summer of 1920.

29. Kate Smith and novelist John Dos Passos, Ernest's long-time friend. Kate and John met, in fact, at Ernest's home in Key West, Florida, in 1929 and were married the same year. Passport photo.

30. Ernest drinking water out of a hat (amid the lumber slashings, probably up near Indian River) after World War I. Note the beret, an Italian special-forces issue, and the Italian combat boots.

31. Ernest and Hadley (with the little niece called Fronchen whom Hadley disliked) in the backyard of Hadley's Cates Avenue home on one of the five or six visits Ernest made there during their courtship.

32. Ernest, Bill Smith, and Charles Hopkins camping on the Sturgeon River, just before Ernest left to marry Hadley at Horton Bay on September 3, 1921.

33. Hadley just before leaving for the old Methodist church for the wedding ceremony. She had a terrible cold but doesn't show it.

34. Ernest's passport photo for his and Hadley's move to Paris in December 1921.

Clarence, anticipating a shared practice with Ernest in Oak Park, pressed for his enrollment in the medical program at the University of Wisconsin and wrote as "your old Scout chum, Daddy—kiss—." Then, in April, Ernest wired an Easter lily to his mother and got this unusual reply:

> My eyes are just brimming over with joyous tears to think that you thought of me—dear—it is quite the most wonderful lily that I have ever seen. They are priceless this year. I've been thinking of you so much lately—Leicester—Walloon—it seemed only yesterday that I was there with you (just five years old) you know the picture of you that hangs in your room, "Cozy Curls" you called yourself. The little lad looks so like you, and loves his Mother in just the same Bear Hug way you used to love me.
> Oh! I cannot tell you how happy you've made me, tonight, with your thoughtfulness. God Bless and keep you pure and noble my Big son.

But in June Grace's mood suddenly changed. She wrote from Windemere to Clarence, in Oak Park, that Ernest was becoming rude, irritable, and arrogant. Worst of all, he was neglecting his duties (chopping wood, bringing ice across the lake from the farm, digging the deep holes for garbage) at Windemere and spending all his time with the "summer people" over at Horton Bay. Couldn't Clarence do something to make a boy fulfill his obligations to his mother? Clarence said he would try. Actually, the cause of Grace's distress had nothing to do with Ernest's reluctance to help around the place. All over Walloon Village and Horton Bay, the gossip had it that Ernest and Kate Smith were lovers, that they met at night in fields to make love. Years later, in Paris, Ernest remembered a rendezvous that summer with Kate and wrote a story he kept to himself. Ernest was "Nick" and "Wemedge" (a nickname from Bill Smith); Kate was "Kate" or "Butstein" and "Stut," nicknames Ernest had given her.

He told how he left Pinehurst, hooked shut the screen door in the dark, and carried the lunch he'd made wrapped in newspaper across the wet grass up the road through the little town out to the Charlevoix highway. Then he crossed the creek and the field, kept to the edge of the orchard. At a copse of hemlocks Ernest put down the lunch; then he saw Kate coming through the trees in the dark, holding blankets in her arms:

> "Hello, Butstein," he said. She dropped the blankets.
> "Oh, Wemedge. You shouldn't have frightened me like that. I was afraid you hadn't come."
> "Dear Butstein," Nick said. He held her close against him, feeling her body against his, all the sweet body against his body. She pressed close to him.
> "I love you so, Wemedge."

"Dear, dear old Butstein," Nick said.
They spread the blankets, Kate moving them flat.
"It was awfully dangerous to bring the blankets," Kate said.
"I know," Nick said. "Let's undress."
"Oh, Wemedge."
"It's more fun." They undressed sitting on the blankets. Nick was a little embarrassed to sit there like that.
"You like me with my clothes off, Wemedge?"
"Gee, let's get under," Nick said. They lay between the rough blankets. He was hot against the cool body, hunting for it, then it was all right.
"Is it all right?"
Kate pressed all the way up for answer.
"Is it fun?"
"Oh, Wemedge. I've wanted it so. I've needed it so."
They lay together in the blankets. Wemedge slid his head down, his nose touching along the line of the neck, down between her breasts. It was like piano keys.
"You smell so cool," he said.
He touched one of her small breasts with his lips gently. It came alive between his lips, his tongue pressing against it. He felt the whole feeling coming back again and, sliding his hands down, moved Kate over. He slid down and she fitted close in against him. She pressed tight in against the curve of his abdomen. She felt wonderful there. He searched, a little awkwardly, then found it. He put both hands over her breasts and held her to him. Nick kissed hard against her back. Kate's head dropped forward.
"Is it good this way?" he said.
"I love it. I love it. I love it. Oh, come Wemedge. Please come. Come, come. Please, Wemedge. Please, please, Wemedge."
"There it is," Nick said.
He was suddenly conscious of the blanket rough against his bare body.
"Was I bad, Wemedge?" Kate said.
"No, you were good." Nick said. His mind was working very hard and clear. He saw everything very sharp and clear. "I'm hungry," he said.
"I wish we could sleep here all night." Kate huddled against him.
"It would be swell," Nick said, "but we can't. You've got to get back to the house."
"I don't want to go," Kate said.
Nick stood up, a little wind blowing on his body. He pulled on his shirt and was glad to have it on. He put on his trousers and his shoes.
"You've got to get dressed, Stut," he said. She lay there, the blankets pulled over her head.
"Just a minute," she said. Nick got the lunch from over by the hemlock. He opened it up.
"Come on, get dressed, Stut," he said.
"I don't want to," Kate said. "I'm going to sleep here all night." She sat up in the blankets. "Hand me those things, Wemedge."
Nick gave her the clothes.

"I've just thought of it," Kate said. "If I sleep out here they'll just think that I'm an idiot and came out here with the blankets and it will be all right."

"You won't be comfortable," Nick said.

"If I'm uncomfortable I'll go in."

"Let's eat before I have to go," Nick said.

"I'll put something on," Kate said.

They sat together and ate fried chicken and each ate a piece of cherry pie.

Nick stood up, then kneeled down and kissed Kate.

"Good night Stut," he said.

"Good night Wemedge," she said and kissed him. "Didn't we have fun?" Her eyes shone in the dark.

"Gee," said Wemedge. Then, "I wish I didn't have to go."

"Go on," said Kate. "Before anything more happens."

"Oh, Stut," Wemedge said. "You're the only one."

Kate crept down into the blankets. "I'm all right," she said.

Nick went off through the woods, avoiding the clearing and the orchard, down to the road. He was glowing, but coming through the mist by the creek bottom it died down. He was very sleepy coming up the hill. It was an effort getting up the last part. . . .

On Ernest's birthday, Grace organized a party. She invited his friends, Ted Brumback up from Kansas City and Bill Smith. Ernest, expecting the usual family ritual (lots of sentiment, a bit tear-rendering, recalling the past, was grudgingly willing to attend. After the party, as the hired girls from Petoskey cleared dishes away, Grace presented Ernest with a thick white envelope. Ernest stood in the kitchen by himself and read:

Unless you, my son Ernest, come to yourself; cease your lazy loafing and pleasure seeking; borrowing with no thought of returning; stop trying to graft a living off anybody and everybody; spending all your earnings lavishly and wastefully on luxuries for yourself; stop trading on your handsome face to fool little gullible girls, and neglecting your duties to God and Your Savior, Jesus Christ; unless, in other words, come into your manhood, there is nothing before you but bankruptcy—you've over drawn. The account needs some deposits, by this time, good-sized ones in the way of gratitude and appreciation. Interest in Mother's ideas and affairs. Little comforts provided for the home. A desire to favor any of Mother's peculiar prejudices, on no account to outrage her ideal. Flowers, fruit, candy or something to wear, brought home to Mother with a kiss and a squeeze. The unfailing desire to make much of her feeble efforts, to praise her cooking, back up her little schemes. A real interest in hearing her sing or play the piano, or tell the stories that she loves to tell—a surreptitious paying of bills, just to get them off Mother's mind.

A thoughtful remembrance and celebration of her birthday and Mother's Day—the sweet letter accompanying the gift of flowers, she

treasures it most of all. These are merely a few of the deposits which keep
the account in good standing. Purity of speech and life have been taught
you, from earliest childhood. You were born of a race of gentlemen, men
who scorn to accept anything from anybody without rendering a just
equivalent. Men who were clean mouthed, chivalrist [sic] to all women,
grateful and generous. You were named for the two finest and noblest
gentlemen I have ever known. See to it that you do not disgrace their
memory. Do not come back until your tongue has learned not to insult
and shame your mother. When you have changed your ideas and aims in
life you will find your mother waiting to welcome you, whether it be in
this world or the next—loving you, and longing for your love. (The Lord
watch between me and thee while we are absent one from the other.)
Your still hoping, and always praying
Mother
Grace Hall Hemingway

Angered by Ernest's subtle reluctance to be his "chum," Clarence told
Grace, "We have done too much. He must get busy and make his own
way, and suffering alone will be the means of softening his Iron Heart of
selfishness."

Ernest, as he always did when deeply hurt, tried to laugh off the pain,
at least in front of his casual friends. To fifteen-year-old Grace Quinlin,
he blamed all the trouble on his taking part in sister Madelaine's all-night
party at the Narrows, the "romantic" west arm of Walloon Lake. But
years later, in a novel he would never complete, Ernest wrote as though
he had known all along what caused the trouble among father, mother,
and son.

As the fourth chapter of the work begins, Jimmy Crane, twelve years
old, is in an elevator. He takes off his hat for a lady who gets in. He
notices that his father smiles and winks when the elevator stops at the
twentieth floor. Each time the elevator stops it is like a sigh inside, and
then walking feels funny. Both Jimmy and his father go into a lawyer's
office. The names, in gold leaf, are stenciled on the door. "Watson and
Watson," the letters read. There are rugs on the floor and pictures on the
wall. There are big leather chairs and magazines. There are shades over
the pictures, the rugs are thick, the chairs comfortable and deep. A volup-
tuous blonde at a desk begins to ask Jimmy Crane questions:

"Are you Mr. Crane's little boy?" she asked me.
"Yes."
"Do you live in Chicago?"
"No, I live in Michigan."
"Way up North?"
"Yes," I said. "Almost to Canada."
"Would you like a piece of candy?"

"Yes," I said. "If you've got some."

"Why do you ask that Mr. Crane?"

"Because I didn't want you to go out for any."

"You're simply darling," she said.

I didn't know what to say.

"Come over by me," she said. I went over.

"Why, you're a big boy," she said. "Aren't you?"

"I'm pretty big," I said.

"Have you a girl up in Michigan?"

"No."

"I'll bet you have, though."

"Well, maybe," I said.

"And you must see all sorts of interesting things up there?"

She stroked my head. I thought she was a fine girl.

"I saw a man stabbed on the train."

"You made that up," she said. "You naughty boy."

"I did not," I said. "I saw a man hit on the head with the butt of a revolver, too."

"I don't believe it," she said. "You adorable boy." She stroked my head again.

"That isn't all," I said. "One of the men was stabbed and I saw the blood come out from under the door."

"You say such terrible things. You darling, darling boy."

She was holding one of my hands and stroking my hair with her other hand.

"Sit closer," she said. "What else have you seen?"

"I came up in the elevator twenty floors without stopping, and I was born in France."

"You lovely, lovely boy," she said. "Would you like to kiss me?"

"Yes," I said.

"Not like that," she said. "Like this."

I kissed her and it was something like coming up in the elevator.

"Can I do it again?" I said.

"You lovely, lovely, lovely, lovely boy."

She held me very close to her [crossed out by Ernest] put her arms around me and I kissed her again.

She tasted very good and her tongue tickled across mine and she smelt clean and lovely. I was very excited and put my hand on her hair.

"Don't touch my hair," she said. "Hold me here." I put my hand there.

"Oh, you lovely, lovely, sweet, sweet, sweet darling lovely boy," she said. "I simply adore you."

"I love you too," I said.

"And to think I called you a little boy."

"I'm not a little boy," I said.

"No," she said. "You're a big, big lovely boy."

"I want to kiss again," I said.

"No," she said. "We can't kiss again now you darling."

"Why not?"

"Your father might come out. He may come out anytime now."

"I don't care," I said. "I love you."

"You're so ridiculous," she said. She took a little gold tube out from the drawer of her desk and standing up before the glass on one of the pictures made herself dark, red lips. "You're a sweet boy, though."

"Didn't you ever kiss anyone before?"

"No."

"You're so lovely," she said and sat down at the table again and looked at me and I saw the look coming over her that she had before when I kissed her. "Would you like to come once more and set here?"

Then the door opened and my father came out. I stood up and put out my hand to the girl. "Goodbye," I said.

"Goodbye, Mr. Crane," she said.

"I'll see you again," I said.

"He's so original, Mr. Crane," the girl said to my father.

"Yes," said my father, looking at the girl. We went out the door and down the passageway to the elevator. The elevator dropping down was not as exciting as the kissing but it felt much the same.

We went outside the building and started to walk down the street.

"So you made the young lady's acquaintance?" my father said.

"Yes."

"You have lip rouge all over your face," he said. "Have you got a hand-kerchief?" I felt in my pockets but I did not have one. I was blushing and my father handed me a clean handkerchief.

"Wipe it off Jimmy," he said. "Did you like the young lady?"

"Yes."

"I imagined so," he said. He was angry. (and the other night is that the way to behave) [crossed out by Ernest]. We walked along the street. There were crowds of people walking both coming and going and I kept close to my father. He was angry and would not speak to me and finally we got off on a bus that went up the avenue. We went up to the top of the bus and sat down in the front seat. My father laughed. "There are the lions," he said.

"They're fine," I said. They were very big iron lions.

"It's all right, Jimmy," he said. "I'm not angry."

"I shouldn't have kissed her," I said.

"You shouldn't have kissed her."

"She asked me to."

"You never want to say that, Jimmy."

I did not say anything.

"I'll give you a very good rule," my father said. "Never kiss anyone that asks you to."

"All right."

"You can pretend to, but don't do it."

"All right."

"Nobody has any right to ask you to kiss them."

I did not say anything.

"And never ask anyone to kiss you unless you want them to."

"All right."

"No, that's wrong. Never ask anyone to kiss you at all."

"Why not?"

"It's not dignified. Kiss people if you have to—but only when you have to."

"How will I know when I have to?"

"You'll know," my father said. He put his arm around my shoulder. "Listen, Jimmy," he said. "Don't think about it at all." And if you want to please me, don't kiss anybody at all for a long while yet."

"I liked it," I said.

"I know," he said. "You ought to. That's right. It's just that once you start it you'll find that it limits your interests."

I did not say anything.

"You'll have to take my word for that," my father said. "Take my word for it, Jimmy."

"All right," I said.

"We got some money," my father said. "Not that it interests you," he laughed.

"~~It does. Did we get a lot~~ [crossed out by Ernest]

"I was thinking," I said.

"Don't do it, Jimmy. Thinking ruins a boy. Thinking and masturbation."

"What's masturbation?"

"It's something like thinking."

~~a form of thinking~~ [crossed out by Ernest]

"Don't think, Jimmy, notice."

"All right. Did we get a lot of money?"

"Not much, but enough to go on."

"That's good," I said. "When will we leave?"

"~~That's the old Jimmy," he said.~~ [crossed out by Ernest]

"That's right," he said. "That's the way to be."

When Agnes Kurowsky refused Ernest, he had turned to Bill Horne. When Ernest had to refuse Grace, he turned to Bill Horne again. Bill wrote by return mail:

Eaton Axle Co.
Oct. 13, 1920

Honorable Bean—

Your letter has filled me with love and big words and the piss of frogs. . . .

It being now decided that we have to live together until an act of God or some woman shall us part (she being to our tutored and jaundiced eye most decidedly no act of God), now it behooves us to foregather in solemn conclave and reason when, where and how much.

Here's my dope. I expect to slither out of this beautiful city of model streetcars, white canvas shoes, quivering mammaries and world's champion baseball teams, and wait this week to take up official residence in Chicago. The boss advocates—and I agree with him—living outside in some suburb, Evanston for instance. How do you like that? It ought to be cheaper and more pleasant than being in the city. My dope is this— Catchum two furnished rooms, one to contain two beds and dressers or some such things and the other to contain deep chairs, places to write, bookshelves, and open fireplace and spitoon [sic] or other ash receiver— also a bathroom somewhere near or attached. About food I haven't an idea; but if we can find a place where we can get breakfast if we wish it, so much the better.

Or undoubtedly we can catch a three room apartment or flat somewhere and cook our own chow and entertain whoever we please whenever and however and as long as we please. . . .

It ought to be a fairly cheap proposition. I can grubstake it until you find some kind of a job. For some inscrutable reason this company pays me a fairly princely salary—compared to the local company anyhow. So we don't have to worry about money.

Now about your job. Allow me to state that the one kind of work that is least irksome, that pays most for the ounce of brain put into action, that holds the most variety of any inside work, that is the greatest and at the same time the most seething bluff at work in all of the world is work in an advertising agency. Why not give it a whirl? It's bushels of fun, keeps you writing and thinking, teaches you quite a lot about a million things, pays you a little more than enough to live on and gives you plenty of spare time to really write, and Chicago is the center of the industry. That's one sure lot, anyhow—.

But the big thing, Hemmy, is just you and me. If you need me as much as I need you, why we had better hurry—that's all, I haven't changed basically yet, but there's no time to lose in getting out the old antidote . . . come live with me and be my "life preserver"—write me P.D.Q. what ideas if any you have on where and how this sounds to you. You see I'll have to go to Chicago within a day or two now and begin looking for rooms. Do you want to delegate me as searcher for you too, or do you want to come down and help or what?

Also if you really are stony and want to borrow gasoline or car fare, why I've got some $ that is drawing no interest at the bank. You might just as well have it at the same terms, you know, old dear—write me at the Congress and Markhold—PS this is a hell of a letter but I'm too excited to be interesting.

                                                                                    Bill

✁ 9 ✂
Love and a Question

In the fall of 1920, along North State, Division, LaSalle, and Dearborn Streets, the sandstone facades, the broad windows, the heavy, gold-knockered black front doors of apartments fashionable twenty years before had begun to show the chips and cracks and peelings of incipient decay. The tenants were young, many urged to the city by a postwar resurrection of the Horatio Alger myth. Those with ambition in the arts followed the lure of the Chicago renaissance and created midwestern bohemias not unlike Greenwich Village in New York. To the new realism of Theodore Dreiser, Sinclair Lewis, Vachel Lindsay, and Carl Sandburg (championed in defiance of a cornfed culture), they brought, paradoxically, the smooth machinations of the commercial ad. The artist–advertising man could be at once successful, creative, and superior. He could make a lot of money and write his novel on the side.

Although Bill Horne found something offensive in young cynics who had life and art "all figured out," he rented an apartment for himself and Ernest on 1230 North State Street in the heart of an artists' enclave and a short walk from Lincoln Park. The landlady, Mrs. Seymour, demanded a security deposit, quibbled about Bill's stores in the cellar (his golf clubs and a collection of books irritated her particularly), and supplied a cot for Bill in lieu of a second bed. Ernest was especially pleased with the location. Kenley Smith, now well connected in business and the arts, lived with his wife Doodles two blocks away. And Kate Smith lived practically next door.

For two weeks, Bill and Ernest tried to recreate the atmosphere they had loved at Schio. They rose early, did calisthenics on the hardwood

139

floor, and usually beat their neighbors to the bathroom down the hall. A block away, at the Kitsos, they joked familiarly at breakfast and dinner with the counterman, and evenings they walked the leaf-strewn paths of Lincoln Park. (Two other regulars were an old woman who picked up cigarette butts flicked into the grass and put them in a paper bag, and an old man with a spiked cane who speared paper.) Once, Ernest and Bill saw a pair of whores, open coats flapping, dresses garish, struggling to light cigarettes in the fall wind. Usually they ended up in the back room of the Venice Cafe—the "password" was their service in Italy. Back home they drank red wine with chips of ice in it to make it last longer, read poetry to each other, and made plans as though they would be together for a long time.

The last Sunday in October, Kate Smith invited Ernest and Bill to a party at the Belleville, as her brother Kenley's apartment on East Division Street was called. Dress was informal; there would be plenty of liquor and many guests they both knew. Besides, Kate said, she had invited a school friend from St. Louis, Elizabeth Hadley Richardson. She had spoken of her before, Kate said—the girl with the beautiful hair.

Ernest and Bill, "well-oiled" after an afternoon at the Venice Cafe, got to the Belleville while the party was still new. With the elegant manners of drunks, they acknowledged acquaintances, agreed with everyone in abstruse discussions of the new poetry of Ezra Pound and T. S. Eliot, looked over the strange apartment (a half-dozen small rooms off a long corridor), and conceived an aversion to one of the four young men boarding with Kenley and Doodles. His name was Don Wright, but everyone called him "Dirty Don," ostensibly because of the way he left the bathroom. Ernest told Bill he disliked Wright's attempt at suave gentility and the petty, calculating expression in his eyes.

Sometime in the midst of the party, when everyone else had caught up with Ernest and Bill, Kate Smith gave her friend from St. Louis a general introduction. Hadley, or Hash as she was called, was taller than Kate, with softer green eyes and thick auburn hair pulled back to a knot. Slouching a bit to conceal a full breast, she gave a practiced smile and looked bitten by each word Kate said. That night, Ernest saw little of Hadley Richardson. She was taken up by Don Wright and several of his friends. But the next day, after another long afternoon at the Venice, Ernest made his way back to the Belleville.

During his hours with Hadley, Ernest was loquacious and opinionated. He spoke as a veteran of the wars, as a cognoscente of the arts, as an intimate of the low-life in the toughest town in America—Kansas City. Hadley, although she was eight years older, was struck by Ernest's knowledge of the world and by his delicate vitality. They went to dinner, then to a movie. Later, they talked for hours (Agnes Kurowsky's name came up all too frequently for Hadley) at the Red Star Cafe. On the station platform, Sunday night, Hadley felt she hadn't known anything before she met Ernest. But, for some reason, he said accusingly she knew too much.

In early November, while Bill Horne was selling for the Eaton Axle Company in Grand Rapids, he got a call from the home office in Cleveland. At first Bill thought the inarticulate secretary meant he had been fired. Eventually he learned that the company was in danger of a takeover and that management needed all road men home to gather proxies. Bill sent Ernest a check to keep "the wolf and Mrs. Seymour from the door" and wrote, hopefully, he would be home in a week. Unfortunately, as the proxy fight dragged on, Bill stayed in Cleveland at the Statler (a "depressing scene"), got drunk every night, wrote Ernest dirty jokes ("Say Bill, have you heard about the new game they're playing down on Long Island? No, I haven't, Mike. What do they call it? They call it, Bill, Button, button here comes my husband"), and formed a novel concept of education: "They ought to teach astronomy in every high school and college in the country. Then we would live more like human beings and Europeans. Hard to justify saving a few minutes on the subway when you know the city of Chicago is only a wart on the world, no bigger than a nit on the nut of a gnat, and everybody knows that is the smallest thing there is."

During this time, Ernest wrote to Bill that he'd had an interview with an Erwin Wasey (set up by Kenley Smith) to work in advertising at the Commonwealth Cooperative. Bill replied that he was going "to head into the direction of advertising, too. . . . Then we could go down to work together in the small a.m. and buy a Ford and etc. and everything." Ernest did not mention in his return letters to Bill that he was writing every day to the girl he intended to marry.

Elizabeth Hadley Richardson was born on November 9, 1891, to James and Florence Richardson of St. Louis, Missouri. She was the youngest of six children. Perhaps because two of the children had died in infancy, Mrs. Richardson was devoted to theosophy, mental science, and the study of psychic phenomena. She wrote moral essays; one, a harangue against contraception, insisted that fear of pregnancy was the basis of morality. She used religion to make those about her miserable and forced her sensitive, lighthearted husband, "Jamie" as she called him, to sing in their family music room to her accompaniment on one of two Steinway grands. For years, James Richardson drank a great deal. When he failed in the family drug business, he shot himself. Hadley was twelve years old.

The year her husband died, Florence Richardson, who had once dreamed of a career in music, hired two young women to teach her daughters the piano. (Hadley's younger sister, named after her mother, was called Fonnie.) The women had studied in Germany and had failed as concert pianists themselves. Fonnie was their favorite because she tried hard and was inept. Hadley had talent, made progress, and was abused. After a year of lessons, one of the teachers suggested sending Hadley to Germany. But Mrs. Richardson explained that Hadley suffered from hysteria and congenital weakness, she walked in her sleep, and now with menses she had fainting spells.

Nevertheless, when Hadley was seventeen, Florence Richardson herself took her daughters on a summer European tour. Just after their return in August (headaches, fainting spells, and the Italian heat made the trip an ordeal for Hadley), the family suffered a terrible loss. Hadley's eldest sister Dorothea, trying to put out a brush fire near her home, ignited her kimono. Third-degree burns covered half of her body. After giving birth to a stillborn child, she took two days to die. She was the only one, save her dead father, that Hadley had loved.

Because Hadley knew something of painting, literature, and aesthetic theory, had a musical education, and could write clearly (she had graduated from the Mary Institute, a rigorously efficient women's preparatory school in St. Louis), she did well in her first year at college at prestigious Bryn Mawr. Also, she discovered that she was not as weak as she had been led to believe. After a summer in St. Louis, Hadley expected to join the sophomore class in the fall. Florence Richardson, however, had other plans.

On short breaks from Bryn Mawr during their freshman year, Hadley and her roommate, Edna Rapallo, had traveled north to Windsor, Vermont, to be among the artists and iconoclasts in a cultural retreat. Maxfield Parrish, the painter, and Howard Pyle, the author of an American version of *The Merry Adventures of Robin Hood,* lived on the town landmark, the Winston Churchill estate. Hadley and Edna played tennis and "bummed around the hilly country roads in an old surrey." On dates, they teased young men from Harvard about their earnestness and their "careers." Edna's mother, whose husband had left her some time before, was at first sight enamored of Hadley and determined to make her an intimate friend. Also, Mrs. Rapallo retained something of the native Italian's taste for casual physical intimacy. She greeted Hadley with strong kisses, loved to see her eat heartily, sat up with her during the long hours of Hadley's sleepless nights. Ironically, Hadley came to feel that Mrs. Rapallo couldn't get along without her. Mrs. Richardson, to whom Hadley wrote almost every day, suggested that Mrs. Rapallo, and perhaps Edna herself, were lesbians. Frightened and confused, Hadley broke with the Rapallos and withdrew from Bryn Mawr.

The fall of 1911 was a desperate time in Hadley Richardson's young life. Her beloved sister Dorothea had died horribly, and, though she never admitted it even to herself, she had been made to feel she was sexually abnormal. In heart-to-heart talks, Florence Richardson convinced Hadley that her withdrawal from Bryn Mawr and the break with the Rapallos had been all for the best. The piano, Mrs. Richardson said, would be Hadley's university and, in the long run, her best friend.

As if to underscore her convictions, Mrs. Richardson dismissed the two young women who had studied in Germany and arranged for Hadley to be instructed by a young St. Louis aesthete, Harrison Williams. Like the women he replaced, Harrison had studied in Europe—in Italy under Busoni. Mrs. Richardson thought him "poetic" (i.e., sickly, cynical, playing the role of artist manqué), and she knew he collected female friends. Twice a week, on fall and winter afternoons, Harrison Williams tortured Hadley with technical exercises designed to dazzle an audience, preached the virtues of Liszt and Wagner, and, in fits of emotion, stalked out of the Richardsons' yellow music room. Hadley worked very hard to satisfy a perfectionist. For the first time in her life a man needed her; she suffered for him and fell in love.

For Harrison Williams, Hadley was that exception among the women he knew, the odd one who didn't play at being in love. She wanted to work for him; she believed in him; she was sure he could do great things. Unfortunately, Harrison's role as the arriviste who never arrived suited him just fine. And Hadley's enthusiastic acquiescence to his judgment and taste, her expectations, her proddings to take risks turned him petty and mean. One afternoon, on a picnic at MacKensie Lake, Harrison told her he loved her very much as a friend. Knowing how much and how little that meant, Hadley was crushed. Over her mother's objections, she broke off the piano lessons and began dating a forty-eight-year-old cancer specialist, Leo Loeb.

In the late summer of 1920, Florence Richardson learned she had Bright's disease. It was hopeless; she had only a few months to live. Instead of turning to her favorite daughter Fonnie, who was well ensconced on the first floor of the Richardsons' house on Cates Avenue with her husband Roland Usher and two unruly children, Florence moved in with Hadley on the second floor. Each day, Hadley watched her mother—lying in the spare room, made more spare by a new single bed, a night table filled with bottles with typed labels—fight death with only her vicious will. Finally, with coma, even the will was gone, and Hadley, in the foul air of the sickroom, wiped her mother's face with alcohol, then folded the cloth over yellow, sightless eyes.

When Florence Richardson died in October, Hadley was stricken and exhausted. But she was relieved, too. When she got Kate Smith's letter from Chicago, inviting her for a long visit to meet "interesting and exciting friends," Hadley couldn't wait to go.

Ernest Hemingway knew the first time he saw Hadley Richardson that he would marry her. Hadley was not sure they would marry, but she found him irresistible. During the nine-month courtship, they met five times, only once—a week they spent together in Chicago—for more than three days. But they did write wonderful letters to each other, usually presenting themselves as they wished to be.

Beginning in early November 1920, Hadley, often wearing her brown fur-collared coat over her nightgown, her slippers leaving strange pointed tracks in the snow, hurried down to the corner mailbox with "special deliveries" covered with six two-cent stamps, looking as if they were going overseas. To amuse Ernest, she addressed the letters sometimes to 1230 North State Street, sometimes to the Belleville, sometimes to the Commonwealth Cooperative on Wells Avenue. Then, every morning she waited for the jingle of the mailboy's bicycle bell, the door downstairs closing, and Fonnie calling, "Hash!" In nine months, Ernest wrote a thousand pages to Hadley, and she wrote as many to him.

At first, Ernest and Hadley pretended they were self-sufficient, that love was sport, and the objects were winning and fun. Hadley, hurt by Ernest's remark at the station—"You know too much"—wrote the day she got back to St. Louis that it had caused her "ruinous sorrow" and mentioned several men: Bill Horne (who had liked her stockings), George Breaker, and her boyfriend Dick (who saw she hated to leave Chicago). But the one she missed "most awfully" was Kenley Smith. She couldn't wait for the portrait he'd promised her. Also, she wanted to keep the blue kimono Doodles had given her to repair. Ernest, stung by the attention Hadley paid to Kenley Smith, told her of his one-night romance with a woman named Maude. He had dazzled Maude with his dancing, Ernest said. (Hadley had never learned to dance and hadn't yet learned from Kate the reputation Ernest's size eleven feet had gained for him.) But he admitted admiring Hadley as a "drinker" and compared her to "Falstaff," himself to "Prince Hal."

By late November, the first rounds of sparring had ended, and Ernest

began to write his letters to Hadley with all his energy and skill. She said
they were "running, rippling, and polished too," and she read sections
("only sections," she assured him) to friends. She wanted "to run down
and holler my undying affection into your far too distant ear." Once, in a
telegram, Ernest told her that he might have the mumps. Of course, she
knew what the mumps could do to a man, he said, and he released her
from her explicit and implicit obligations. "You know," Hadley wrote,
"the 'great mumps gram' swoll me and the entire household with pleasure
arriving sonorous and epigrammatic as it did at about 11 p.m. on a particularly stupid evening." Hadley was sick, too, she confessed. She had a
heavy cold in her bronchial tubes and, wrapped in a scarlet eiderdown
blanket, Doodles's blue kimono, and lingerie Ernest had bought for her
in Chicago, she sipped quantities of Dr. Hemingway's remedy: lemon
squash. Ernest had accused her of taking "this attitude of olderness" with
him. Hadley reassured him, "How much more of the world you know
than I." To prove it, she asked for "some kind-hearted man to tell me all
about dancing and salads." Ernest said that his best friend, Bill Horne,
had told him not to write too much, not to seem too eager. "If a girl were
unresponsive," Hadley said, "that might be good advice. But how much
more responsive could I be?"

Soon Ernest confessed "something deeper" to her. He and Don Wright
had attended an Armistice Day celebration in Chicago. Coerced by "Dirty
Don," he'd laughed at the clumsy, maudlin "patriots" and their bad taste
in wiping tears from their eyes. But Ernest, though he did not show it to
"Dirty Don," was so moved "by those other fellows' sacrifice" that he himself had shed hidden tears. Hadley felt "obliged, obliged, obliged, obliged,
obliged to love you" but wouldn't, as Agnes had done, call him "Kid."

At the end of November, too, Hadley wrote a "very warm, affectionate
letter" to Ernest from a place called "The Clubhouse" in Allentown, Missouri. She was there on a party of sorts with Helen and George Breaker
and Ruth Bradfield. They did a lot of walking, smoked, popped corn, and
drank "plenty of booze." Hadley wanted to know what the difference was
between his and her writing. She knew that hers was filled with abstrac-
tions (she said she could probably write a good morality play). But there
was something more. In all of Ernest's sentences, the accents fell naturally
on "the correct quantitative place. . . . *I* have to scratch lines under important words." She remembered how she'd loved to hear him roll into
Kenley's room and "just have to read to me what you'd written, hot from
the mill." She also admired Ernest's "loyalty," she said. Doodles was leaving for an extended stay at home in New York, ostensibly to study the
piano seriously, again. For her going-away party, Ernest furnished "the

146

ALONG WITH YOUTH

spirits, and the physical comforts for everybody": "You carried the entire dinner party on your back." Ernest was very good at getting someone into a corner and making "him (or her) feel your inward happiness," Hadley said. Ernest wrote that her letters made him feel as if he were sitting in front of an open fire on a cold, dreary November day.

On Saturday, December 3, against her sister Fonnie's advice, Hadley took the early morning train to Chicago. Ernest met her at the Wabash Station at eight o'clock that night. Striding on ahead, forcing her train-deadened legs to keep up, Ernest paced Hadley the sixteen blocks to his 1230 North State Street apartment. It was a lovely night of cold bright stars, clear air, and a dusting of snow. Ernest, head hunched in his worn Mackinaw, hands stuffed in the pockets, said nothing. Hadley was afraid, though glad she had come.

Ernest dismissed Mrs. Seymour (who thought young Bill had got back from New York) and brought Hadley up to his third-floor apartment. Hadley was delighted by how clean Ernest kept the place. He took her coat, kissed the top of her head, and gave her a welcome tumbler of good Italian wine. Later on, at the Kitsos, Ernest told Hadley all about his new job at the Commonwealth Cooperative. He had been hired, Ernest said, by an unctuous do-gooder who seemed a sycophant of Kenley Smith's. The boss at the Commonwealth Cooperative was Richard Loper, a deep-voiced, forceful man, who spoke with the tone of Moses and considered the society members the children he would lead into the Promised Land. Frank Parker, whose wife was the treasurer, supplied the money.

Ernest showed Hadley a copy of the Commonwealth Cooperative's magazine. On the cover, beneath an eagle and the subtitle "The Weekly Magazine of Mutual Help," there was a pitiful, bald-headed man, designated "the consumer." He rode on the shoulders of a strong young man, "The Cooperative Movement." In the background, ugly faces peered from the brush, and the caption read "Profiteers." As Hadley looked over the copy, she smiled at Ernest. There was the Cooperative exchange. The Cooperative business directory listed bakers, chemists, carpenters, brokers, caterers, dressmakers, florists. The gift for new subscribers was a set of Rogers' silverware. The magazine was sixteen pages long. The whole thing, Hadley said, had something of the "con" about it. She could feel it in the paper and smell it in the print. It was hardly the place to begin a career. But Ernest told her that the advertising business had suddenly gone sour, men were walking the streets (and women, too), and that even "Dirty Don" Wright was about to be fired out of his job. Bill Horne, traveling somewhere between Grand Rapids and Cleveland, was about to be fired, too. But he was still sending more than his share of the rent.

Doodles's room at the Men's Club was now open. Ernest wondered if this was the time to move. It was terrible for Bill, Hadley said. But then he could always go home to New York. Before he brought her to the "crummy old train shed" on Sunday night, Ernest made love to Hadley on the davenport. But at the station platform: "You didn't hold me very close, Nesto, no you didn't. And I felt funny about it. I thought maybe you really didn't want to kiss me good-bye. I was shot to pieces 'cause I certainly didn't want to leave. Maybe I felt so bad there wasn't any way of holding me close enough."

Hadley assumed that Ernest's pensive mood those days in Chicago was explained by his distasteful job. As she told him, it seemed a poor place to begin a career. But Ernest, in fact, had far deeper concerns. At his father's chicken-pie Sunday dinners, Ernest had, for the past month, noticed Clarence would sweat profusely and stare off absentmindedly. Also, Clarence's face had become gray, and all his collars suddenly seemed too large. He still moved with his usual vigor and solidity, but he often spoke of the past when he and Ernest had "palled together," of the Indians in Michigan, and of his trip to the Smoky Mountains, where, for his companions from Oberlin, he cooked blackberry pie sweetened with honey he found in a hollow tree.

After her trip to Chicago in early December, Hadley was determined to write Ernest carefully composed letters every day. She sent encouragement: "If you write for the public the way you write for me, it's going to be a really good thing." She acknowledged his poetry: "Yes, Lake Shore Drive in winter does look like 'white piping on gray ruffles, indistinguishable from the sky.' " And she reminisced: "Do you remember the room at Kenley's: the piano, the couch, the victrolla [sic], the big window, the rugs pushed aside and two people dancing?" Ernest wrote that, though he loved her, he couldn't make enough money yet to satisfy his "wicked worldly nature" and to support a wife, except by giving up his writing. Hadley countered that by the time he could earn enough, she would be "old (though only in the matter of years, never in thought, I think)," and he "would be finding another person just right for you at the time." But she "would never want to block a good man's chances," and "maybe it would be easier to break up now." It was his decision, Hadley said. In answer, Ernest bought her a lovely platinum ring.

With both parents dead and her brother Jamie somewhere "in the East," Hadley dreaded the prospect of Christmas with the Ushers downstairs. Thank God, she felt, for her music, the friends she'd earned, and the forthcoming visit of that "charming Princetonian" she'd met in Chicago, Bill Horne. Hadley helped to organize citywide caroling. ("How horrid it is," she wrote to Ernest, "to have to indulge 'indefinite people,' who can't be counted on to do a thing.") She rode in a new " 'lectric" with Dick to the ballet to see Pavlova and to see her screen love, Douglas Fairbanks, in "something." Hadley told Ernest she'd met a "new guy" at a dinner party. He looked a lot like Bill Horne, "the awfully nice slouching sort . . . smokes a pipe . . . knows enough to guess about books and music." He had brought Hadley home from the party, she said, and they now had two engagements. Nevertheless, couldn't Ernest "possibly make it down to St. Louis for Christmas Eve or at least for a New Year's Eve party Helen and George Breaker are giving?"

On December 23, 1920, Ernest answered:

I'd be much happier too, Hash darling, but I can't come. You see I hate and loathe and despise to talk about seeds [money]. But I haven't been home since 1915, I think, and I more or less threw a family debt Christmas for the kids. And am consequently broke. Embarrassing of course. Could much easier have lied to you, and mentioned acceptance of a half-dozen New Year's dates. All of which I'd have thrown over in a minute for a sight of you. I've always had this fearful truthtelling habit with you. You can make me jealous and you can hurt me most awfully. 'Cause my loving you is a chink in the armour of telling the world to go to hell. You can thrust a sword into it at any time. Hate to think of you going to the party with Dick instead of me. But I'm broke because of the Lord's Birthday. Not a question of regard for seeds or anything you know. But why go into it. Feel terrible bad. . . . Saw tragedy tonight. I was in a something shop opposite the Marigold Gardens and a girl was telephoning in a booth. She was kidding someone over the wire. Lips smiling and talking cheerily away and all the time dabbing her eyes with a handkerchief. Poor kid. It was terrible bad whatever it was. Dear Hash, you can surely hurt me a lot when you want to. About the platform and the train. I thought I was loving you. If I wasn't I never could and never would love anyone. Guess I was thinking about how much I didn't want you to go. Don't you believe I love you??? Don't know how I can make you believe I didn't want to kiss you goodbye. That was the trouble. I wanted to kiss you goodnight and there's a lot of difference. I couldn't bear the thought of you going away when you're so very dear and necessary and all pervading. When you tell me how nice Dick is, I ought to counter with Mae or Lyn, and how nice she looks topside of a horse. But when I think of anyone in comparison with you, you are so much clearer and I love you so much. What odds kidding along about them. Course I love you. I love you all the time. When I wake up in the morning and have to climb up out of the bed, and the sun splashes around me glare, I look at your picture and think about you. And that's a pretty deadly part of the day as you know, and a good test of loving anyone. And in the evening it's too much to stand. Sure, go on—go to the party with Dick. But maybe once pretend

I'm there. Discovered Siegfried Sassoon this afternoon and so feel kind
of better. . . . Night my dear Hash. I'd like to hold you so and kiss you
so that you wouldn't doubt whether I wanted to or not. I love you.

Ernesto

Christmas in Oak Park had for a long time been the major event in the
Hemingway family's year. Besides its spiritual significance, observed in
the customary way, it was the winter equivalent of Upper Michigan in
the spring. Starting early in October, Clarence prepared for the holidays
by curing a slab of beef in the fruit cellar. He would go down and rub
salt and saltpeter on it every day. In December, he'd make "hockies,"
boiled, highly spiced pork hocks which he'd set out in the back yard in
stacked porcelain bowls to cure and freeze. Then, just before Christmas
Eve, Clarence would bake, then freeze in the back yard, a stack of mince
pies. On Christmas Eve, there would be a feast at the yellow oak table in
the dining room. Clarence would open his stores of preserved fruits and
vegetables from their Michigan farm, serve his hockies, homemade pickles,
mince pies, and cut the oven-roasted beef so thin the slices curled.

Christmas in 1920, however, was different. In late November, Grace
had left with little son Leicester for an extended vacation in Bishop, California, at the home of her brother, Leicester Hall. Grace thought it fine,
she said, to reinstitute the trips her father, Ernest Hall, had made each winter for so many years. Besides, Leicester Hall was now a well-to-do lawyer, and, Grace said, she needed now and then the atmosphere of success.

With his wife in California, Clarence settled for opening a few jars of
his fruit, bringing up a few dozen pickles from his barrels in the cellar,
and baking a few extra Sunday chicken pies. Ernest tried to brighten the
affair by leading carols off-key—how could anyone be too embarrassed to
sing listening to him?—by telling stories about his Italian Christmas, when
everyone made Christmas last as long as they could, eating and drinking
with vigor and sleeping and then eating and drinking again each day,
and about how lonely it had been two years ago eating the tough roast
beef and all-flour gravy and the soft, tasteless canned vegetables at Woolf's
Restaurant in Kansas City.

On December 27 at "just dusk," Hadley, forgiving Ernest for leaving
her alone in a crowd on Christmas Eve, gave him just the kind of present
he needed. Coming home from a party at the Atkinson's, "I had such a
glow about your old dear self, somehow all cold like that, having to be
hugged into a cozy warmth of being by me. To be perfectly frank, I mean
to say, not you so much having to be hugged, as me having to hug you—
wonderful feeling to express something so good, isn't it? Would you like

it baby? . . . I was once so very unhappy not to have you down here
Christmas Eve it was, and now I'm sort of used again to the idea of not
seeing you for a long time. You are a dear and I love you so much and I
have no opinion about your reasons for staying on in Chicago."

About the present Ernest had sent her, Hadley wrote:

> How much longer can I keep from falling on your shoulder about the
> bag. It's an exquisite, lovely thing and I am very much in love with it.
> The things on it look mysterious and submarine and are very soft to the
> touch. It's different, as we advertising men say, and charming. You're
> generous and sweet to think of such lovely things for me. Did you notice
> the little frill on the side edging the lining. I'm very fond of it, and have
> already used it and had it heartily admired by lots of people that couldn't
> help it. Darling Nesto, thank you for it. Do you think I could kiss you
> some way or other? I feel as though you need to be kissed, and I'm not
> there. . . . My sister Dorothea was the same kind of loving, understand-
> ing person as your delightful sounding Ura [Ursula]. She understood me
> by tolerant affection and died just before I went to Bryn Mawr. I think
> you are the nicest lover a person ever had, really. I feel matched up and ap-
> preciated and taken care of the way I did the night I rolled so fast and
> scaredly down the sand dune in the dark and you whirled me up and
> kissed me—Kate and Bill being conveniently, to be nice, seen out of, not
> seeing, in the firelight. I want to be picked up now Ernest. I want you
> here tonight around me. I feel small and lovely and lonely (but happy)
> 'cause I know that if you were here you would be around me and domestic
> and needing to be necessary. Do you ever feel that way about me? Big
> and lonely, only, and needing?

On Wednesday, December 29, however, Ernest wrote that an old Army
friend, Captain Jim Gamble, had proposed they spend a year together in
Italy at Jim's expense. "Jim Gamble is great," Ernest wrote, "and I love
him a lot. But not like I love you." Clarence favored his going, Ernest
said, but what did Hadley think? Because she was hurt and angry, Hadley
wrote that she'd be going to the Breakers' New Year's Eve party at the
University Club with Dick and that Harrison Williams, "the person I
loved so much a few years ago," would be there. "Those years," she continued, "were so full of torture for me. Thought I couldn't force myself to
live through it. Guess 'tweren't any worse than something you had to endure. Don't think such things do anything in the long run, but make us
wiser and more understanding and lovinger and stronger to endure the
things that come up to be endured." There would be "lots of booze" at
this party, and Dick, if he didn't get sick drinking, would want to kiss her
all night long.

On New Year's Day, Hadley wrote Ernest a report: "Dick did indeed

get sick from drinking, he danced with everyone, and flirted with Pere
Rowland's girl." Hadley took the "good crowd" back to her place. Harrison tried to "get me going about the guy in Chicago," but only "screwed
out pitifully unimportant things . . . Dick did everything he could to
make me kiss him, and I did in the quietest way." She added, "I suppose
it would be just as much fun to write and hear from you in Rome as in
Chicago."

This was not the response Ernest had hoped for. His threat to go to
Italy with Jim Gamble had been a test. He had already cabled Jim on
Christmas Eve:

> Rather go to Rome with you than Heaven. Stop. ~~Not married~~. But am
> broke. Stop. Too sad for words. Stop. Writing and selling it. Stop.
> [written on the side of this page] ~~Unmarried~~. Don't get rich. Stop. All
> authors poor first then rich. Stop. Me no exception. Stop. Wouldn't we
> have a great time. Stop. Lord how I envy you.
>
> Hemmy

Since their first night in the parlor at the Belleville, Ernest had hinted
he'd been an emotional cripple after Agnes Kurowsky. At first, Hadley
had said nothing, then she sympathized a bit, then she was annoyed:
"You're a jolly, healthy Nesto." His Italian love affair was another instance of his "passionate love for the good." "Hit or miss," Hadley wrote,
"it gives you an understanding and a genuine working basis. . . . I think
it is true you have a lot of blind believing. It is a most lovely thing—intuition—inside dead sure of stuff. And it'll get to be more and more."

Ernest wrote that Bill Horne had ended the year with the same dreams
he began it. His convictions were still as firm as ever, too. In a couple of
end-of-the-year letters, Bill had written his impressions of the girls in St.
Louis: "Ruth [Bradfield] is a complete loss. Hadley is either polite or a
damn poor judge. Ruth is slender, tall, very dark, built large, low and
tantalizing, with big legs, but practically no allure. She is pretty in the
same way the Madonnas of the Early Italian Masters were. Dark and Jew-
ish looking. Fonnie, however, is not a Gorgon. She's a vivacious, married
woman with four children—a bit too eager and earnest. She asked me
what lasting and fundamental effects the war had on my cosmos, religion,
and philosophy." Then, Bill reported that the widow "H" he had been
pursuing broke their tacit engagement for a "sad egg." Bill asked, "Is
there a God? . . . What have I done for such a kick in the teeth?" He
was going to be fired, too, Bill said, and Ernest better find someone to fill
the cot or move into Doodles's vacated room at "The Club." Their "married life" was, at least for the time, over. The five hundred dollars he'd

lent Ernest, the "National Debt" as Ernest called it, should be forgotten for the time being. "I'm backing you in a marathon," Bill said, "not a fifty yard dash."

Ernest moved over to Kenley Smith's "Club" at 63 East Division Street on the seventh of January, 1921. The other boarders—Bobby Rouse, Don Wright, a boy named Saltzenbach, and Nicco Philes—welcomed him after a fashion with their best bathtub gin and a pliant girl named Irene. The room Ernest took smelled like Doodles. She always wore a particular New York perfume with the fragrance of gardenias.

Ernest knew there were advantages to moving in with the Smiths, especially for someone with his eye on a writing career. People like Kenley Smith—with not much talent but a sense for where it could be found and how best used—managed to know magazine editors like Harriet Monroe of *Poetry: A Magazine of Verse* and Margaret Anderson, who published *Little Review.* Because of his "connections," Kenley Smith could lure to his weekend literary soirees nightlights of the Chicago renaissance: Carl Sandburg, a midwestern imitation of Walt Whitman; and the current "ingenue" of American letters, forty-four-year-old Sherwood Anderson.

At the first party Ernest attended, he read aloud from *The Rubaiyat of Omar Khayyam,* and Sandburg, fond of bardic presentation himself, praised Ernest's sensitive interpretation and style. Anderson, however, now married to a "new woman" (Tennessee Mitchell, who used her maiden name and slept in her own apartment), had accomplished *Winesburg, Ohio* in 1919. All the cognoscente at Kenley's place called Anderson "Sherry." But Ernest, deeply impressed with Anderson's mastery of the simple style which conveyed profound emotions and complex states of mind (just the sort of thing Ernest had attempted in his best work so far, "Crossroads") enthusiastically accepted Sherwood's invitation to visit him at his rural Palos Park home. On the long walks they took together amid the manicured hills and copses, Anderson talked about the life he had rejected (the kind of life Ernest believed Clarence Hemingway had cowardly embraced), about his father (a cavalryman in the Civil War), and about his belief in the salvific power of a "good woman."

During January 1921, Ernest told Hadley in increasing detail of the other women in his life. First there was "that corking little Irene" at the Men's Club, who liked Ernest best of all. "Wasn't it good of her to tell you when it got to be too much for her," Hadley wrote, "and in such a selfish way." Ernest said, too, there was another contender for his heart, even more aggressive than Irene. "The other girl sounds horrible," Hadley said, "and I don't get it unless she tried to force herself on you or

accused you of fooling with her or something." Hadley had never had
"an infatuation with a man. . . . There's got to be other interests."
Ernest had been "press-agenting," Hadley maintained. She herself "never
had a friendship with someone I didn't admire."

With all his talk about the women who found him attractive and who,
in the spirit of the times, felt "anything goes," Ernest was indeed "press-
agenting"—but not so much with inflation of ego in mind. His purpose,
rather, was "testimony of authority," to prove to Hadley he was worthy
of her love. When Kate Smith wrote to Hadley that Ernest was "in body,
mind, and spirit" the most wonderful man she ever knew, he expected
Hadley to be pleased. What Hadley did write was, "I want the person for
you you need most—me or if it changes, somebody else." On the back of
the envelope, Ernest wrote with a flourish, "Hash loves you."

The dominant theme in Ernest's letters to Hadley during the winter
and early spring of 1921, however, was not his charm for women, his concern for his father Clarence, or the fatigue and frustration he felt in his
"stinking" advertising job. He was living, he wrote, on ten dollars a week
and changing the other forty-five into lire. As he had told Jim Gamble
in 1919, Ernest was willing to "die for this great and glorious Nation, but
I still hate like the deuce to live in it." When he wrote of his and Hadley's future together, he wrote of Italy.

On January 12, Ernest proposed that Hadley go with him to Italy, make
"the bold penniless dash" to Milan. They could leave as soon as Bill
Horne and maybe Howell Jenkins were able to go with them. There
would be an apartment with piano, trips to the Milan Cathedral, and
da Vinci's *Last Supper,* which they could see, if they wished, every day.
"To hell with the beaten path," Ernest wrote.

Hadley's reply was oblique though not ambiguous. Impulsive foolishness was not inspired spontaneity, and in the man she loved she expected
a lot more: "I'm glad you think we could love each other a long time
because I'd be frightened to even start otherwise. I'm so terribly in need
of just such an adorable warm-hearted sweet and tender darling to love
me. But even more than that I need someone to give my lots and lots of
lovingness to. They have to honestly make me look up to them or I
couldn't keep it up. I know myself (of old) how often I've tried, dear, to
make a person be the ideal I dreamt for them. It's probably very prehistoric in me but I do think I can't get along without awfully much wor-
shiping the goodness in a man I'm to love for always. I have such an
initiative, healthy, put the other fellow first, kind of goodness and you
have a heart that I undoubtedly adore! Don't you ever let me down,

now—not that I think you could—and don't forget that I've awfully much the same idea of 'goodness' as you have. You could never be afraid of me— to talk to me when you wanted."

Hadley thought that Ernest should consider an editorial job he'd been offered at a new magazine, *Brackett's Weekly*. But Ernest persisted: "Let's take the good things now. . . . We don't know about the future, and we can't plan." No one knew that better than she, Hadley said. But this should be "thought out, not felt out." His ambition was of great value, and poverty in Milan would make her "not your helper but your hindrance and force you to put your work in a background position." But life in Chicago was making him "fat and bald," Ernest said. That was all right, Hadley reassured him. She could get fat, too, and a loss of hair wouldn't hurt his "classical" face.

As the weeks passed, Ernest made the return to Italy and the risk involved the touchstone of their love. Hadley, despite the dreadful memories of her mother's European tour, finally wrote that she now thought of Italy so much that the "country is riddled with my thoughts." Each time Ernest's letters stopped, if he missed even a day, she feared all was off. "There isn't any arms in the world I want around me as much as yours. There's no heart like yours for me."

Hadley had been reading, as Ernest suggested she should, G. K. Chesterton's book on Browning in Italy, the chapter headed "Marriage," she said. She loved him "so highly and lowly and like a boy and girl warmly," and it was "so hard to mail these letters. It's like putting yourself in the mailbox." "Oh Ernest," Hadley said, "I'd like to be walking with you in a forest. A very soft dark green. There would be things to do there that would be more beautiful than anywhere else. The atmosphere would be light enough for the commonest things to pass through so that love and understanding would scarcely have to express in one before the other knew it. Only probably the only thing that made the medium there was the love we had ourselves. Do you think we could make it like that?" In part for rescuing his lady fair from the dragons of her past, Hadley, quoting from Chaucer's *Prologue to the Canterbury Tales*, dubbed Ernest "a verry, perfect, gentile knight."

₦ 10 ₦
The Pragmatist

By mid-January, 1921, Ernest and Hadley were ready to marry. But a lesson Ernest felt he had learned with Agnes Kurowsky stood in their way. Couples starting out need money, he said. Referring to their plans for Italy, Ernest wrote: "The sloop doesn't need many [dollars] but there's beachcombing at the end of the cruise." Maybe with the help of his "old friend" Greg Clark, he could become a foreign correspondent for the *Toronto Star*.

Since October 1920, Ernest had been sending slick, quick-paced articles in his public-speaking voice to the *Toronto Star Weekly*. A handful had been published, and he'd made a hundred dollars or so. Unfortunately, despite a barrage of letters from Ernest, each bursting with reasons why a man who knew Italy in wartime and had learned his politics in Kansas City could give readers the understory of European reconstruction, Greg Clark put him off with noncommittal, "professional" notes each hinting at success but promising nothing. Hadley called the reports "encouraging." She said Ernest was skeptical because he needed a rest. In just two months, two weeks together, Hadley said, they had leapt toward marriage. Maybe it was time to get better acquainted, to tell each other many things. Ernest agreed.

To begin with, Ernest said he had been hurt by Hadley's lukewarm response to some of his work. He'd read her "stuff" after a movie, they'd made love, she was very tired. "All men lose their balance on the subject of their own work," Hadley said. "But listen here, I simply said, in effect,—I forget the words—that I don't get it. . . . I like to take time to all good things."

Another thing Hadley didn't get right off was the cause of Ernest's inordinate interest in the upcoming heavyweight championship fight. The European champion, Georges Carpentier, would fight the new world champion, Jack Dempsey. Carpentier had written a book on the science of boxing. He was a natural light-heavyweight, very fast, a splendid athlete who could hit like a mule with both hands. Carpentier thought, he said, while in the ring the way Ty Cobb thought stealing a base. He had a famous French chef at his training camp, wore formal clothes in the evening, and believed a training camp without women was like a monastery: good for the spirit, bad for the flesh.

The Dempsey image was far different. He was the saloon brawler from Kansas, with shoulders a yard wide and a face toughened by soaks in brine. In his title bout, he'd broken all Jess Willard's ribs, his jaw, his cheekbone, his nose. Ernest hated Dempsey and claimed all his opponents were "has-beens" or "canvas-backs." He assured Hadley that when the fight came off that summer the European gentleman would embarrass the American pug. For reasons of his own, Ernest said he was having friendly bouts with Nick Neroni, his wartime buddy, now a staffer at the Italian consulate in Chicago. Hadley wrote she'd "like to see but not feel *your* wallop . . . like to sit reading to you and rubbing you and loving you."

Although Ernest wanted Hadley to know he could take it and to learn from him how to be truly tough, he didn't hesitate to complain—"bellyache"—about physical ailments: his throat (which had been chronically inflamed), his spastic back, his hemorrhoids aggravated by hours at the desk. He needed sympathy, Ernest said. He sent a "gram" about the "Grim Reaper"; he was "terrible depressed." Just after Christmas he had written his mother, Grace, of all this. Grace's reply—"I don't believe God ever does the things that people can do for themselves—it would be poor ethics. He stands for self-control, self-government, self-determination and self-destruction if you choose to go that road"—was just what Ernest expected. But Hadley wrote that she knew "it is awful to be sick, even if you're not very sick, 'cause the mind rots idly about, conceives of its owner often as a very poor specimen with a cheap past, a sick present, and no future worth mentioning." But how could he be so "discouraged about yourself and hold any opinion of my judgement at all?"

As Ernest sat aging like a wheel of Wisconsin cheddar in Chicago, Hadley wrote she was out skating—"my stroke is shaping up more every day"—the "high and pure air out there" made her feel like the "kid" she'd never been. At night she darned, mended, smoked, read Chesterton on Browning, and did the laundry. Was Ernest as good at picking out hats as he was at selecting handbags? Hadley wondered. She wrote she "wanted to look my best while you can look anyway you wish." But then he had those "beloved brown eyes . . . and that sweet, clear look."

In late February Hadley said she was back at the piano. At the University Club she played Malagueña, Jeux d'Eaux, and a Brahms ballad. Also, she'd met a nice Englishman who taught advanced writing at the University. She was getting "those stomachaches" again, and she needed Ernest's "way of comforting a person that is better than anybody elses." When Ernest criticized the "casual tone" of her letters, Hadley wrote she was "thinking about you every minute . . . always thinking how the everlasting ache goes out of living if you could once be with me and do little things for me and let me do oh so awfully much for you." The poison in Ernest, from "whence all your badness comes," Hadley said, "is all parental stuff," and of course she understood. If she were in Chicago, she'd come up behind him, typing in the office, and kiss him. No, she's not "irreligious, anymore than you are. I've never seen anyone have it better than you," Hadley said.

Speaking freely to Ernest about her difficult year at Bryn Mawr, Hadley said that she'd been invited to join a sorority, until the girls found out her mother was a theosophist. Because she was blackballed, Hadley named the sorority "at home to the infinite," and the name caught on. "After that day they weren't so serious, and the Lord was probably grateful." Ernest sent Hadley his poems. "Dreamy things," she called them. Nevertheless, what she really wanted to be was "picked up and loved to death—won't hurt you a bit or me either . . . any woman with a gram of sense would adore you." Hadley said she was certain their love was secure:

> First and foremost, we love each other—then we respect each other's minds and capacity for judgment (and with me that is a quality in you I love and I hope to be able to go by that in you rather than the open results of your judgements). I don't think a mistake is anything but a patch on the motive back of it, do you? Well, anyway, as I was saying, we have all this, and I'm crazy about the way you write and you like my playing and I know from the way I play backcourt in tennis doubles that I'm good at backing up my partner's serves—and Oh, a sense of humor and yards and yards of tolerance both of us and somewhat the same impatience I imagine and love of people and—Oh, you know all the other things, darling Ernest—concerning ourselves very clearly.
>
> And then in addition to all that I adore you and I am never bored by you and see your enormous power of living and how inside intuition stuff comes through to you very, very often and gives you new food for tho't. Wish I could make you see what I mean—I have it too—not in the same degree—it's really the best gift I know of so don't tell anyone I said I had it. A very obvious example of it is your power coming to you probably unsolicited. But the great beauty of it is ideas just appearing in your mind

that make you understand the way things are—or sometimes, the way things are going to be when adjustments are made that seem impossible now. Do you see what I mean? Simpler way to say it is that your *intuitive.* But that's so overused a word it hardly has a muscle left.

Well anyway you can see that I think a lot of this side of you. And all the other sides—the loving side, and virile side and the responsible side, and the flexibility side, and, Ernest I love you—madly—come here.

Nevertheless, Hadley wondered, "Who is the lady on the mantel occupying the center of the stage in your neat room with your coat on the chair and your typewriter on the stool?"

Each time Ernest wrote to Hadley about his lack of money, however, she was less than sympathetic. "Love the obsessing sense of what it's up to him [the artist] to do for the world," Hadley said. "Then if he's really an artist, he'll have to create *anyway,* and he'll find time and money for it. . . . I'm no longer for dandying artists in the lap of wracking poverty, We won't have to lose their best creative years."

Hadley was hard on Ernest in another way, too. Although she rarely mentioned Kate Smith to him (perhaps because she knew they had been, and perhaps still were, lovers), when she did she was frank and sincere: "The story of how you gyped Butstein makes me weak in the knees for my own future. . . . I say, it would be unscrupulous to work me that way, Ernest. . . . Now you just quit before you start . . . hear?" Hadley said she would like to be where Ernest was, "but not clapped up to you every minute." She knew he'd "be wanting every sort of contact with the wonderful good guys," and he didn't have to worry " 'cause I'll just sort of be there."

Strangely enough, Ernest wrote very little about his family to Hadley. He and Hadley were engaged before she knew Dr. Hemingway was a physician and not a minister. But on one occasion he composed a panegyric on his grandfather, the military hero, "The Great Man." Her own grandfather, Hadley quietly replied, wasn't any hero. But he was a fine man, an educator of boys, and had founded the Weston Military Academy in Massachusetts. As far as she knew, Hadley said, she came from as "fine and well-bred people" as Ernest. She wished she could see Ernest doing "those wonderful things" with his aristocratic body. Ernest replied he would write about "one part of your body every day."

In mid-February, Hadley and her sister Fonnie began attending a Mr. Halstead's Mental Science Class at the University Club. Prancing home afterward, Fonnie wanted to talk about "first principles" and such things, but Hadley told her that Ernest was the "first principle" as far as she was concerned. Ernest went more deeply into male–female psychology than Mr. Halstead would ever go: "How men must work and women must weep—with sympathetic assistance for the women weeping." Only a few women understand where they belong in the scheme of things, Hadley wrote. "So many of us force ourselves into business that's none of ours and leave off in business where we're the only ones who can do it." Ernest was reading Havelock Ellis, all about the "sads and mads" who love mortal pain. Hadley thought all women get something out of pain: "If it's a male does it to 'um, . . . it's a low woman's thought, but they do."

Ernest believed that the techniques of all art forms had a common ground, and he wanted to know all Hadley knew about music. Once she wrote lyrically of what one needs to play well:

Tuesday afternoon Feb. 15th 1921

Just the kind of afternoon for the afternoon of a faun. Wouldn't we have fun together with days stringing along to bring us different moods. A day like this, balmy and fresh, a really blue sky, and such emotion in the air that it brings you anticipation instead of memories. It's so clear it comes to you with both vigor and tenderness. . . . All day long I practice. Hands getting some semblance of control—can order the muscles to do pretty near what I want—it's a ticklish point where I've often failed cause the power does carry you away if you don't look out, and the quiet inside feeling of the piece loses its tender contour. —You know, maybe.

On Valentine's Day, Ernest and Hadley exchanged telegrams. Ernest warned her not to believe anything Mrs. Charles (Bill and Kate Smith's guardian) said about him; he hated "Auntie" and "the doctor." Hadley wired that she'd rather be an old maid than to be "peppy and tied up to a sad old party without a joy or sparkle."

Because Hadley couldn't come up to Chicago, Ernest said he was being driven toward one Ruth Lobdells—"Ruth Lobdellswards," as he called it. Hadley wrote back "she sounds the sort of girl who would chew you up." In answer to his recent letters about the war, Hadley said she couldn't "have stood it unless I could have done something for you. But you had someone then. Sorry the end of that threw you into a chaos of mind and body and spirit. But then you ended up a mellow and clear-sighted man." She herself had found much to delight her in other men, though nothing to satisfy her. But Ernest was "a joy to heart, a delight to eye, a darling friend, a peach of a worker, an imaginative mind, and a creative 'creatch' all together." Ernest, Hadley believed, was "untouched by anything, no matter what you do that may meet with the disapproval of Mrs. Charles." "We're simpatico—fit in every way."

One "bathnight" in February, Ernest wrote he was coming to St. Louis

in two weeks. "It's about time," Hadley replied. "I'll eat you alive." Enclosed in this letter was a mass of Hadley's auburn hair, "For you, Ernesto
Mio," she wrote. "Had a wonderful big lot of it cut out a year ago to
make the knot a manageable size . . . but this piece is for you. Kept it
the length and size for you to shape it as you will. My hair is this color
when I dry it in the sun. Put it in the sunshine and see."

Ernest said he'd had many reasons for not coming down to St. Louis
before. He was too poor, too tired, too plagued by worries over his job.
Also, Hadley had written that the obstreperous Usher "kids" from downstairs were constantly bursting in and out, sometimes before breakfast,
when Hadley's "brain was slow and I couldn't quite control them as I
would my own." One night in December, "Fronchen," her sister's daughter, "a rather unpleasant little party—a she-devil at times," had succeeded
in annoying even the "sweet as peaches" Bill Horne. Ernest was also
afraid, he said, that he'd seem ignorant to Hadley's high-brow friends,
and, like bullies with a kid wearing glasses, they'd be inclined to attack.
But because the best way to handle bullies of any kind was with your
fists, Ernest was sure he could take care of himself. Besides, he thought he
would bring along Kate Smith.

On March 11, 1921, Friday night, Hadley met Ernest at the Union Station in St. Louis. He wore a three-piece suit (the jacket and vest he believed made his "corrugated ash can in human form" figure look trim)
and carried his scuffed-leather, copper- cornered, bulging valise he'd bought
in Milan. He was pale; he limped a bit; there were dark circles under his
eyes. On the ride to Cates Avenue in Helen Breaker's electric, Hadley
strained to make conversation. Still, she was happy Ernest had come alone.

The next four days, Ernest slept in Hadley's "frilly feminine" room
that smelled of lilac and where anything he used made him feel as if he
were violating a decorated cake. Hadley slept on the living-room sofa
under a print of Michelangelo's *Creation*. Each night she kept coming in
to get "things." They both slept through breakfast time, ate lunch at a
little table in the den, sat by the fire in the evenings, and commiserated
with each other about how ill they'd been. Hadley had had acute intesti-
nal distress and a stubbornly painful tooth, and she was desperately fighting against the recurrence of her nighttime attacks of nerves. "I'm too
good, I respect myself too much," she said, "to be afraid to go to sleep,
and have such a sickness of which so great a part is fear and low depression." Besides his sore throats and back spasms, Ernest told Hadley he'd
been afraid to sleep, too. When they were married, Hadley said, she
would hold his head to her breast until "you just sailed swiftly off to
sleep." Then she would "kiss you very tenderly and go away . . . but not

very far and listen for when you weren't maybe happy in the dark night of the dreams, if the dreams came again."

For the three nights Ernest stayed in St. Louis, he and Hadley did not worry about sleeplessness or dreams. After a late supper and cups of Ernest's Italian wine (he'd smuggled the bottles down from Chicago, he said), she listened to him roll out his stories in a voice she found "the nicest in the world." Later on, Ernest told Hadley the details of his wounding in the war, of how proud he had been of himself and how near he'd come to losing a leg. He loved Italy, Ernest said, not because he fought for it but because it was a civilized (that meant tolerant) country.

When the crackling logs in the fireplace had burnt to ash and glow, Hadley, sporting a new navy French blouse, played softly on the piano for Ernest. Forget the serious music, she said. It was the hour for *"Avalon, Sandman,* and *Mammy's Arms."* One night they went out to the Orpheum, and Hadley "watched your face and loved it and the spirit behind it and got so deep in it I couldn't pull out." She behaved "normally" afterwards, but asked him to leave his scrapbook with her.

Although Hadley had warned Ernest of the intrusions they could expect from her sister's undisciplined children Fronchen and Roddy (who, in his rough plaid coat, woolly cap, and hands-in-pocket way of trudging, looked like a small Ernest), Fonnie saw to it that Ernest and Hadley were left alone. She herself, however—a lovable, pretty badly dressed, high-minded Puritan, according to her sister—made sure she looked Ernest over enough to pronounce him selfish, unsympathetic, and very young.

When he returned to Chicago on Tuesday the fifteenth, suffering all the way with a bad throat on a drafty, miserable train, Ernest wrote a "letter" he never sent. In it he made an ideal of what Grace, then Agnes, had taught him to fear. But he treated the "idealist" with gentle irony.

🖉 🖉 🖉 🖉 🖉

Portrait of the Idealist in Love—
A Story

The elevated tracks were just below the open windows of the office. Across the tracks was another office building. Trains passed along the tracks and stopping at the station shut off the view of the other building. Sometimes pigeons lit on the ledge of the office windows and flew down to light on the tracks. Moving trains did not cut off the view of the buildings opposite but showed them through open windows and the quick segments of the platform. It was lunch hour and there was no one in the office except Ralph Williams who was finishing a letter to the sister of the girl he was engaged to. He took the last sheet out of the typewriter and read over the letter.

My Dear Isabelle,

I am taking this means of talking to you because your ideas and mine are so greatly different on various subjects that it would be extremely difficult to come to any conclusion through talking.

I have seen that something growing between us, something that I do not wish to see. If I am wrong I want to remedy my errors. Those feelings have been hurting me more than you can imagine. More than the slights which you told me you noticed when I first came down to see Irma. Those days to me were wonderful for I was awakening from a sleep which I thought was everlasting and was perhaps my reason for seemingly neglecting small attentions toward you—because I was finding the love that I had looked for and, after finding it, did not wish to lose it. I tried to make amends after you told me about them sitting in the North Shore Hotel quite a few long months ago. I regretted them and was sincerely sorry for my negligence. My efforts in that direction, however, seem to have been in vain and are apparently a failure. It is hurting me to think that a member of the family that I have learned to love reflecting through Irma has found a place in her mind for ill feelings and ill will toward the man who hopes sometime to be her Brother in Law. It is not that my feelings toward you have lessened. You are simply permitting yourself to think so.

The nature of my living, my experiences, my feelings, and my ideals have caused me to think a little more than the average man of my age. And I know why you are allowing these feelings to enter your mind.

Through 23 years of my life I have, through some unknown reason, reverenced an ideal peculiar to mankind, an ideal which has grown in magnitude to such a high estate of thought that even the slightest reference to it causes a feeling of resentment to show in me from within, and I cannot help it showing. So I am going to continue feeling as I do but with the determination to try and keep it within my heart whether it may wound or not.

The difference between a person with an ideal and one who lacks an ideal is the difference between the person who guides his life by what he thinks and sees materially and the person who has enough of the visionary in him to adopt as his guide a dream which has not yet come true or perhaps never come true. I am adhering to mine. It is all in giving a little more than what I would ask or take. I have always thought, and thought, and thought perhaps too much so, but always placing myself in the other person's position and thinking what I would do under the circumstances in their position, then continuing in the path of what I think is just. When one continues to do what is right he can never go very far wrong. You have read of men, men of wealth, who have won place and power and happiness by means and methods which have stirred up the ill will of their fellow beings causing an indifference to their standing with their fellow men because of an ideal.

Like mercy, thoughtfulness, consideration, and good will bless both those who give and those who receive it. They are virtues worth cultivating and practicing, not merely at Christmas, but from January to December. That is and has been my policy. You perhaps will not agree with me on this subject. You may say, I do not practice these things. If you still think that way, I am sorry, I can do nothing more than I have been for when one shows a kindness for others, when one thinks less of making themselves happy than making others happy, they feel unselfish, they are thoughtful and they come nearer obeying the commandment, "Thou shalt love thy neighbor as thyself."

Unselfishness, consideration and good will are built primarily on honest, unstinted, and unselfish good will on our own parts. It is the deliberate cultivation of good will by playing up to people's prejudices, their natural likes and dislikes. That is what I have tried to do many times. It is why Irma and I love each other; it is why I love all of you folks. To you these feelings of mine may be prejudiced, but they're only that in your mind—to us they are reasonable likes and dislikes. You do not understand why I should have it. That Ideal to me is You, a woman. Then what do you suppose the nature of that Ideal is in the woman I love? You do not like it because I do not enter into the things you like with as much zeal as you wish, and I know that you are not the only one that feels that way. You did not like it because I did not smile or laugh at the object of your humor the other night. With the amount of modesty which my ideal of a woman possesses, you among them and also Clara, I could not see the humour or amusement in the nature of form of a woman's limbs that you could, making comparisons with others.

My idea is a woman, the works of a Greater Being than Ourselves, of nature, no matter what forms they may take, and, when that ideal is marred by casting un-called-for reflections upon them, my reasons for resentment are apparent.

I know that I do not enter into a lot of jests and humorous pastimes, bringing forth amusement, and I have seen that it has been noticed at different times before this. I have regretted it always. Years ago when I was much younger, when attending picnics or parties when I did not enter into the amusements and mirthful pranks with the enthusiasm that perhaps I should have, it was noticed and I was often told about it. I have often tried to overcome these feelings so that they might not show on the surface, but I see I have not been successful and that they are still noticed.

I do not like to see things which do not add charm or grace to a woman because of the nature of my living and the formation of my ideal, because I think deeper and have a higher standard for such things than the average man has. Ideals are the most powerful forces known to man, but they entered my mind, I think, before they should have, and I made them entirely centered on that one object. We all must have them, why I chose that one, I have never understood, but I am glad I did. I do know that the man with ideals, the man who refuses to tarnish, lower, or barter his ideals or ideal, no matter how high the price or what the cost, can never feel abjectly poor, can never feel alone in the mind and spirit and soul.

These likes and dislikes so you make yourself think they are something uncalled for and to you, you think I am prejudiced against some act, some word or statement. However, they may be very reasonable after all, since people have them and since you want the thoughtfulness, good will and love, it is necessary that you overlook some of them or that thoughtfulness and good will cannot be obtained. Sometimes other people like very bad things, and our way may be a better way of doing the same thing. It is then the natural course for us to fight for our way to the death that sometimes people will see the reasonableness of our method and think of it in the same way.

Now I am willing to go more than halfway to accomplish and overcome my feelings, to do my part to try to please everyone and if you are willing to come a little way we will forget what has passed.

I have always had a policy of when I wanted to make a friend the only way I found it can be done is to watch for opportunities to do them a service. To do this or that person a favor, and with persistent actions it seldom fails. For good friends appreciate those things; whether they show it or not, you know they are your friends. If I find that I may lose them, I look for some repulsive habit and then try to remedy it or rid myself of it entirely. Isabelle have I in a way succeeded in doing it entirely? Isabelle have I in a way succeeded in doing that with you even in part, by writing this letter to you?

I haven't the slightest idea what you will think or how you will accept this letter, but I am hoping that I have to some extent been able to tell you why I have felt as I have.

If I have caused you to feel indifferently towards me, if it is my fault that a growing dislike for me has entered your mind, all that I can say is that I am sorry. I have simply been myself, my natural self, and regret that I have made you feel in such a way.

Sincerely your humble brother to be,
Ralph Spencer Williams

He had been eating his lunch while he read the letter. He corrected an awkward sentence in the fifth from the last paragraph, addressed an envelope on the typewriter, folded the letter, sealed it, and placed it in the basket for out-going mail. Then he put the paper his lunch had been wrapped in into the wastebasket, blew the crumbs off his desk, and walked over to the window. He looked across at the drugstore under the elevated on the other side of the street. What he wanted was a good, cool, double lemon coca-cola. It was a good, cool, stimulating drink. A man was better off without stimulants but sometimes they were a good thing. They had their place like everything else and the thing to do was not to abuse them. He put on his hat.

⚑ ⚑ ⚑ ⚑ ⚑

Against her sister Fonnie's advice, Hadley surprised Ernest by following him to Chicago on March 17. There was "something about your eyes" that made her want "things to be good in them," she said. It was terrible that a person who had "all the goods" had to be "giving out and giving out forever without new stuff from somewhere or somebody putting in." Ernest's friends (Howell Jenkins, Kenley Smith) had told him that being tied to a woman was bad for a gifted young man. Bill Horne had said it was the best thing that could happen, if you had any talent to start with, and Hadley "blessed dear old Bill." She was relieved that Kate Smith had gone south to Arkansas to visit a "soul mate" for the winter. Hadley loved to watch Ernest "tramping down the street and know that the new lines in your face are firmly implanted in my mind and heart." When Ernest told her he didn't like her new coat and her hair comb, Hadley said "that made my loving deeper."

During the long train ride back to St. Louis on the twenty-ninth, Hadley wrote, "In Italy there won't be anything but love and peace to form a background for writing. All the seething, writhing mass of creation going on inside you now and busting loose now and again despite the lack of any opportunity, will be given ample play. Why, you will write like a great wonderful breeze bringing strong whiffs from all sorts of interior places." He was her "Little Prince." Hadley ate a "marvelous breakfast at Union Station and took the luxury of a taxi home."

April Fool's Day, 1921, was bright and clear in St. Louis. Hadley said the sky was "full of nice little clouds to keep it from looking too clear and lonesome." Ernest had written that they were each other's children and yet could be married, too. Hadley replied that she "likes nothing better than what I'm going to be and for that I'll miss you in the other role." Very few people could have kept from frightening her, and he was one. She was happy her banking grandfather had left her "a little packet of money for us." How bored she'd been sitting around listening through open windows to that horrible electric music down the street and discussing the *Harvard Lampoon* with some boring members of the University Club.

It was wonderful, though, she wrote, that "those two 'old' fellows [Sherwood Anderson and Carl Sandburg] think so much of your work." And Ernest should not be embarrassed by his "publicly placing of kisses on the top of my head." To tell the truth, Hadley said, she'd been disgusted by the attitudes at Kenley Smith's "Club" the last time she was there: "All those drunken people running in and out, Carper [Howell Jenkins] showing up with whores. Only Horney Bill seemed to know how squalid the whole situation was." Ernest, now keeping "friendly company" with a woman named Frances, thought he was lonely even with Frances around. That was good, Hadley said, because having "an affair when you really don't want to out of a sense of boredom or obligation with someone you're indifferent to, is a sin." The poem he sent her, though, was grand: "Isn't that way of having things done for you wonderful? The image springs up of itself; it is a surprise, though always expected. You feel it there, don't you, like a pregnant woman senses a child. It is the basis of your work."

When Ernest sent her that delightful "alley cat necklace and earrings," she promised to bake, next time he was down to St. Louis, a chocolate custard the color of "canton crepe." "You pour cream on it and eat it cold. It melts in your mouth." Hadley hoped Ernest didn't mind her not putting quotation marks around his words when she repeated them to friends. "We're more or less the same firm. . . . I love you and am living for you." He left "folks falling into fits of admiration" about him: "boxing, fishing, writing, selling, teaching Horney Bill you can't expect ever to be attractive and good simultaneously, getting war medals, playing bridge, swirling about in the black cape with the ermine cassock, wopping it at the Plaza, swimming, paddling, tennis, charm, good looks, knowledge of clothes, love of women, domesticity." She would fall on him anywhere, Hadley said, "like a chamois leaping from crag to crag."

Early April 1921 was a bad time for Ernest. He had sprained his shoulder; his stomach was pale and tumbling; he was homesick for up North. Teasing Hadley about the "lovely Jewess Irene," he asked if he shouldn't write to a girl so terribly lonely. He hated his job at the Commonwealth Cooperative but endured it because it was just a snakeskin to be cast off, just good in its day. He told Hadley to read Rudyard Kipling's *Kim* and *The Red Lily,* a "passionate book about insane jealousy" by Anatole France. It would leave her breathless, he said. He was disturbed a bit that she was going out into the country with Marguerite, a sculptress. But Hadley explained that Marguerite had been "in life class all winter. . . . She's seen nothing but males. . . . Finally, in despair, she called me to help her out. . . . I feel very fat. . . . I will pose in some reeds, holding up a big bowl."

Their wedding would be "simple and small," Hadley wrote, just what Ernest wanted. But she hadn't told anyone because "I don't want to betray you as the domineering type." Then Hadley wrote proudly that she'd handled her life "well today: tennis, darting about light as air, clouds above like in Constable's landscapes." Still, she loved her afternoon naps. "Thank goodness you and I are going to a country where a siesta is one of the, as you say, 'decencies.' . . . God, how I love you." Speaking of

Ernest's favorite sister, Ursula, Hadley wrote, "It's truly adorable the way she loves you. . . . Got a tremendous soft spot for her and you could give her my love and be absolutely on the safe side."

These days, Hadley said, she felt a virtuous woman, brimming with domesticity, anticipating their own "domicile in Milan." She "thoroughly cleaned both dining room and den and the shades are now at half-mast mourning for the tons of fine, fair dust that have gone out the windows. Everything is clean, even the inside of the radiators and electric light globes and the mop boards. These things could have been neglected by a light-minded woman." Somehow she had the feeling, though, Hadley said, that Ernest would "despise" her if she were dirty, even though she was working for him.

In *The Red Lily*—"a white hot love story it is"—Hadley noticed that "the heroine Theseus [cast in the mold of Emma Bovary] achieves a fourth dimension, more than length, breadth, and thickness. It's because each step toward tragedy is familiar yet nonetheless terrifying and delicious for that." And yet Hadley was sure that marriage, "though a trap biologically and socially . . . is still the way to get furthest in every way." Yes, Ernest agreed with her. He would not be afraid of Anatole France, Flaubert, or D'Annunzio. "We'll show them they can't run the world, won't we," Ernest said.

In mid-April, after eating and smoking and drinking too much at a party—where she walked miles "in ice cold air; everything was sunshine and green"—Hadley rode home in the back seat of a roadster:

> I thought of you and me together in some mountains somewhere, walking along, kind of tired, towards the sunset, with the slanting rays casting shadows on the hills of that cropt looking grass cows make so smooth and soft in country where pasture is scarce, and there'd be dark trees along side lots of time and freezing torrents of a river coming near every once in a while as we followed the winding road at the time of day when you begin to trudge instead of walk with a spring. We'd be hungry and finally fall into the door of an Alburgs then splash about in cold water from the stream while someone got us an awfully good, plain supper. . . . There'd be probably some funny old boys sitting around there in the evening as long as we could keep awake. . . . You and they would trade stories in some goat's cheese dialect or other, and the sleeping we'd do, not a bit lonesome. And right on top's the world afterwards.

Ernest told Hadley she was a dramatic woman who would frighten a lesser man. "You're dramatic yourself, you know," Hadley said, "and never frighten me. Only your so light touch, besides. . . . I suppose that scares me."

In mid-April, too, Ernest wrote that "from over-work and under-cared-for" he'd become "stale, flat, tired, uncreative." He was doing many sit-ups each day, but he needed a woman to make things go again. Hadley was surprisingly sympathetic: "I feel so helpless and want so awfully to help you. Why if I could help you in any way I'd be a worthwhile person. You see I love you so very very far in I can't even tell you about it and part of the result is that I must do something for you. Rita Rommilar sounds (and looked when I saw her) as though she could furnish the 'anything' you crave so to have happen, 'cause you're stale. When she first came out, I thought she was the loveliest thing ever—marvelous hair and reed-like legs can be a wonderful thing."

The sculptress, Marguerite, told Hadley she was a "classic beauty." But Hadley didn't like the "too hippiness of the 'Psyche' " Marguerite had done. "She worked on the nude figure of a girl with me as the girl. The girl's figgah really looked like me. There's to be a man in the picture—sort of a composition, you know. Three women in the centerpiece . . . the Three Graces." Knowing how Ernest felt about her posing, Hadley added: "Oh Mr. Hemingway, how I love you. How exciting you are. How a lot of things happen around you. And besides all that, I love you anyway. How I love the way you love me. And your flannel shirt seems a strangely beautiful thing, and it smells so good besides. Some day, if I don't watch out, there'll be a poem on the smell of a clean white shirt that'll raise up the hair on the dead."

Greg Clark suddenly wrote Ernest that there was a good chance of a job for him at the *Toronto Star*. As he knew, Clark said, Ernest had been a favorite of Mr. Cranston all along. It was a resident position, though; there was nothing for a foreign correspondent. Ernest said he was very much tempted. He would double his Commonwealth salary at the *Star*. He wrote Hadley that a "planned separation" was probably good for couples. But Hadley knew otherwise: "I've about reached the conclusion that if you love someone very much, know definitely that it is someone you're going to care about permanently, that you love personally and impersonally and respect, then the way to show it is to give that feeling tender, loving attention and care, watch to see what it needs, like a child or a garden—and—be doing for it all the time. I don't mean constantly hovering—that would be insufferable—must let the sun and the rain and the will of the gods have their play. . . . But a love where planned separations are required is a scrawny, little love. . . . You go anywhere you want, do anything you want, and I'll be back of you with my wits as well as my heart, old dear."

In order to carry her own part of the load for their "Woppian Way

Money," Hadley agreed to rent the home at 5739 Cates Avenue and take an apartment downtown. Between the money from the house on Cates and the rent on the apartment, there would be a profit of eighty dollars a month. "After all," Hadley said, "Italy did offer a more sophisticated life . . . a tolerance of differences because it's so old and has seen so many things, a privacy in the midst of people"—the kind of privacy that Ernest would never find in Chicago or Oak Park.

At the end of April 1921, Ernest began his first novel. "Kenley should give you Don's corner room," Hadley said, "because you need the sense of a sacristy." The novel "busting loose now" in his brain was all about the adventures of a young man, Nick Adams. Ernest said he knew he could get three chapters done right away, but they would probably be juvenilia. "Pooh," Hadley replied. "Thank the lord some young ones gonna write something young and beautiful; someone with the clean, muscular freshness of young things right in him at the moment of writing. You go ahead. I'm wild over the idea."

Ernest said he was going to start with "real people, talking and saying what they think"; he would send her "page by page." Hadley said her feeling for him was like his feeling for his writing: "No one can take it away, though they can make it painful and hard." Alluding to his affair with Agnes Kurowsky, Hadley wrote, "maybe your work calls for another, harder wreckage . . . but you're not going to get it from me."

Because Ernest was about to hurl his sticky old newsroom typewriter against Kenley's refrigerator, Hadley promised him a "Corona" for his birthday. Two-story bags, Gladstones, and the traveling kit would come with it, too. "Do you think I'll be like all women and when your head is full of a novel, I'll waltz in and insist on being caressed—we shall see what we shall see. . . . Isn't it a good thing you and I know so well we love each other . . . (rather ghostly the way this pen repeats itself below the line) . . . Don't let's ever die, Old Sweet . . . let's go on together. . . . I'm sure we're a pair preconceived by the Maker. Maybe we'll be going somewhere else together someday." Then Hadley added, "Never mind, I think we've got happiness all right now."

Nevertheless, Hadley was very much distressed, too. Fonnie's husband, Dr. Roland Usher, had left her and their two children, and Fonnie was worried about money. Fonnie and Roland never had much of a marriage, Hadley said, because they weren't good enough for it. What was needed? She had some clear ideas:

> The idea is you've got gifts, loads of gifts, wonderful strange beautiful gifts, that I love and adore, and even others that I haven't the inkling of, maybe. And then there's me. I have my own peculiar endowment. You

know the few things all mighty well. Think you know everything about me to date. But am always changing, just as you are. I really am a most surprising person. Well, here we are. Two nice gifted beings (with most of the weight on your side). My thought is how tremendously when we're made into a unit or firm or whatever 'tis, gifted we'll then be. "Why, I know I don't write novels and stories and so forth, but Ernest does, so you'd better keep friends with me, 'cause it's practically the same thing." All your gifts of lovingness and thoughtfulness and kindness and good guidance belong to the firm and we pool everything precious we've got. Everything I've got is yours. But I don't give it to you. There's no volition on my part. It just belongs to you, Ernest, 'count of love.

Would she pray with him at the Milan Cathedral (as Agnes would not)? Of course she would, Hadley said. In fact, she felt, "I am doing the best thing a woman can do for a man. Bringing you back to religion. Not any set beliefs, though. Most of my belief is: 'We don't know the half of it.' . . . But I'm grateful to something ungraspable, a kind of loving purposeful force that made things like that [Ernest and Hadley's love] not only possible but necessary." When Ernest wrote her he was still living on ten dollars a week (saving forty-five dollars for Italy), Hadley warned him to do "the right thing about lunches. Remember how you'd feel if I didn't eat enough and good enough food." Yes, she knew how he'd felt on the steamer pulling out of Gibraltar [Ernest and Agnes Kurowsky had parted uneasily because she would not come home right away]. "No sea breeze, no matter how fresh, can blow away the staleness of yourself. Nothing in the world can, except getting out of yourself, or something, don't know exactly. But you did it for me. Never did expect to find anyone into whose life I could fling my spirit."

To earn money, Ernest was hiring out as a sparring partner for some middleweights at a Chicago club. The next-day pains were worse than a hangover, he said, but nothing to "the devil of loneliness tearing at you." "Dear old beloved boy," Hadley called him. "I'm crazy about ye," but worried about "your tendency toward the complete thing." "The last time we were together, I did worry about that a little, but I threw it right out of my mind because of much confidence in you. So I know nothing could shake me from my desire to be everything to you. . . . Being everything to you is the only thing that can satisfy me physically. I hate rather, to have loved you that way. Seems as though you were too good for it. Funny, if it had been anyone else but you loving me, I'd have felt it was very wrong. I know there's a fine, clean quality in you, it runs clear through, that evaporates nauseating memories."

Ernest was the first who'd ever satisfied her, Hadley said, "as having the capacity to go the whole wonderful circle intellectually and spiritually;

'cause you have miles to go and wonderful miles they'll be and you're panting to be off definitely laboring toward an end, aren't you?" Hadley was happy too over his insights "that rush to the open channel that you are." When Ernest worried that she wouldn't think so much of him if she'd ever seen him drunk, Hadley replied that he'd been "drunk that night at the Venice . . . and I knew it, blind as *I* was at the time." She intended to use everything he had to give her, "use it very hard."

The first Sunday in May 1921, Ernest found no letter from Hadley on the icebox at the foot of the stairs, and he took the train out to Oak Park for his Sunday chicken pie, feeling "low." After dinner, Dr. Hemingway, dressed in his best three-piece suit and looking pensive and gray, took Ernest into his examination room. He told Ernest that he was "in the clutches of angina pectoris." It came from his diabetes, Clarence said. Try as he could to be cheerful, he felt full of doom each time he climbed the stairs. Grace knew nothing of his condition. It didn't matter. He would leave the bulk of his estate to his son. Ernest should come next week to make formal plans.

That night, Ernest wrote Hadley about his father. He was comforted by her reply:

> I'm so mad I didn't have that letter for you Sunday, poor dear. That's a hard visit ahead of you, but your father gets the kind of comfort from you that you're able so wonderfully to give. If only he is open to it. . . . Well here's wishing the best to that poor, mangled set of feelings out there. He's been terribly square about the money business, hasn't he. Funny, I had never thought of his dying or of you getting any money from anyone except a shadowy grandfather, living somewhere in the world. I do love you so dearly, and I feel all sort of wretched in my heart for you to have been jerked about. Had a lot of wonderful, young affections just simply worn away by unnecessary pain.

Sherwood Anderson had invited Ernest out to Palos Park. He should go, Hadley thought. It would be a "good antidote to your trouble." "I expect," she wrote, "you'll be infinitely better than all of these writing men. More power and more balance and I'm crazy for you to have your chance." Out of her own "soul struggle," Hadley had found the capacity "to make a better place and companion than you've had before."

Besides the ordeal Clarence Hemingway's illness had created, Ernest was plagued in May with the sort of things that usually go wrong at the worst of times. First, Doodles, after her mysterious sojourn in New York, was coming home to what Ernest now thought of as "his room." Rooms were scarce in Chicago, but he'd have to find one because he couldn't endure living at home. Then, Greg Clark at the *Toronto Star* had sent a letter that sounded as if Ernest's six-month-old proposal (to be a foreign correspondent in Italy) had only just been made. And Bill Horne, for some reason, had broken down and seemed to be proposing to every girl who would give him a date. To "ease the pain," Hadley sent Ernest a packet of pralines, sympathy for the throat that was tormenting him again, and a lovely rendering of St. Louis spring:

> It's something to see every spring, how the shadows change as the foliage spreads; how the laundress next door clenches her pins as she puts up the clothes; how the auto-delivery wagons chugg out in the streets and the lawn mowers chugg down in the back yard; while I, sitting in the bedroom window, absorb the morning sun.

Although the spring air, even in Chicago, was fresh and clean at night, Ernest was not sleeping again. Hadley said *she* was sure she could get him to sleep in ten minutes. "It seems funny that you'd be marrying an inexperienced baby," Hadley said. "Well, I'd challenge the world to say many girls lived more intensely, just the same. I really know awfully little, but I know that little awfully well. I'm not a baby, but very, very old, and yet still always going to be young. . . . I think you look great in the sunlight, and people that are nice in the sunlight must have something so superior about them."

Ernest wrote Hadley a long letter about trout fishing. He said that once she learned she'd probably do it better than he. "That's ridiculous," Hadley said. "You know that your writing proves more than my playing does and both of us know that and like it." "I've got a lot of stuff that you would like in me, maybe even need in me, just simply because I did hang on so many years and thought and thought of that one art that's of course very representative. One year, had to lie on the floor on my back fifteen minutes after every half hour of piano, Ernest."

Dr. Charles, Kate Smith's uncle (though an optometrist, he insisted on the title *Dr.*, and Ernest resented this), had been treating Hadley for acute pink eye: "One eye wept all the time, and the other felt like something scratching under the lid." The prescribed treatment was cold compresses, and while Hadley lay with crushed ice in a facecloth across her eyes, thinking of Ernest, she thought of his hands: "I love your hands. I think it's wonderful when anything is both great and strong, don't you? I'm thinking of your hands but you really are that way all ways, through and through. Your hands can make me do all sorts of nice things to you by the littlest touch, make me want to, I mean, but then so can your eyes. I'd do anything your eyes said. Gee, it's your eyes have such fine control—

no, wouldn't lay it all to the eyes 'cause there's lots of things—endless—guess I'll stop analyzing. How healthy and fine it will be when we're not rushing to make every minute count because we'll be pretty soon separated again."

Ernest said he wanted her with her hand on the comfortable part of his shoulders. "Sometimes I feel so close to you," Hadley said. "I feel the same air were being breathed by both of us." Hadley loved physical beauty but could seldom disconnect it, she said, from breadth of mind. For example, "a crummy body, well-defined mind in Krebs." After Ernest confessed he'd taken Kate to a party, Hadley wrote she'd always thought he and Kate "would eat each other up." Her brother Jamie, still in the sanatorium, had somehow managed a wedding gift of two hundred dollars. There was now more money to buy lire, Hadley said.

In preparation for Ernest's visit on Decoration Day, Hadley, to trim off the "winter pounds," played tennis every day up on the hilltop court in the park. Her new racquet was a "humdinger." At home, she would bathe and let her hair, laid out on the picnic table in the back yard, sizzle in the sun.

Hadley was "wild" over the stories Ernest sent her (usually with a letter of explanation mashed down in the envelope). His style "eliminated everything except what is necessary and strengthening." Hadley was "wild over the way you pounce on a strong word and use it in the right place, without any of this damned clever affect most present day writers have." The "War Story" he sent was terrifying: "All about black and ugly and you bright yellow." Ernest wrote that he wanted very much for people to like his stories and needed Hadley to reassure him they did. "That's not conceited of you, Ernest," Hadley said. "That's just right."

When Ernest was plagued by "constant headaches" (he could do nothing but take aspirin and lie down until they passed) and "felt like hell" about what Hadley called the "filthy lucre check" she'd sent him for lire, she comforted him with her "dreams." Lovers such as they "get so bad you want to be immersed in a sea of their presence. You can see how just a couple of days can make up to you for all you've been through without them. Then, the wonderful feeling of peace and foreverness comes in about three minutes. . . . It's hard because a person wants another person, and not for some sneaking, swilling little length of time, wants them for a dead sure thing, wants to go to sleep for a long time and be sure that there he'd be, still just as big and just as wonderful."

Because his love for Hadley was still the "chink in his armour of telling the world to go to hell," Ernest sent a story he'd written in Toronto while shepherding Ralph Connable around. Perhaps Hadley would appreciate the tragedy of a Kansas City thug whose "flaw" was his love of music.

🙚 🙚 🙚 🙚 🙚

The Ash Heel's Tendon—
A Story

In a former unenlightened time there was a saying, "In vino veritas," which meant roughly that under the influence of the cup that queers a man sloughed off his dross of reserve and conventionality and showed the true metal of his self. The true self might be happy, might be poetic, might be morbid, or might be extremely pugnacious. In the rude nomenclature of our forefathers these revealed conditions were denominated in order—laughing, sloppy crying and fighting jags.

A man with his shell removed by the corrosive action of alcohol might present as unattractive an appearance as the shrunken, mishapen nudity of an unprotected hermit crab. Another with a rock-like exterior might prove to be genial, generous and companionable under the influence. But there were men in those days on whose inner personality alcohol had no more effect than a sluicing of the pyramids with vinegar would have on the caskets within.

Such men were spoken of as having wonderful heads; the head being popularly misconceived as the spot of greatest resistance in the body's fight against alcohol. As a matter of physiological fact, they were the possessors of non-absorbent stomachs. But you couldn't build a barroom saga around a non-absorbent stomach. That would be almost as difficult as persuading a badly shot up doughboy that he had made war on the German government and in no sense had opposed the German people.

This yarn deals with non-absorbent stomachs, shooting, and the Hand of God and the true seat of the emotions. It does not handle them in that order, however, as it begins with the Hand of God.

Back in the days before cocktails were drunk out of teacups Hand Evans was a gun. Now a gun is a widely divergent character from a gunman. A gunman, and present styles seem to tend toward the two-gun man, is an individual with chaps, a broad-brimmed hat, a southern drawl, a habit of working his jaws so his cheek muscles will bulge in the close-ups (the same effect can be acquired by chewing gum consistently) and two immense pistols in open holsters tied low on his hairy pants. He may look hard but he is really very kind-hearted and will come out all right in the last reel. Usually he is someone else in disguise anyway.

A gun has not a single one of the gunman's predominant characteristics. Instead he is a quiet, unattractive, rather colorless, professional death producer. His form as a killer may vary, but as a class, he likes to work in pairs and to work close. The gun's preference for close work may be accounted for by the fact that he is often an execrable shot. There is small opportunity for practice with the automatic pistol in a city, but at ten feet no great skill is required. Also every gun has his weak point, what Jack Farrell (who, while he was on the force, had seen the rise and assisted at the fall of most of the killing brethren from Killer King to Kansas City Blackie) called his ash heel's tendon. The first two members of the trilogy of W.W. and the Song claimed many. All had their vulnerable spots.

Hand Evans was the exception. Hand was short for Hand of God. That irreverent specimen of the nomenclature of the underworld had followed him east from Seattle. After he had done his first job in the middle west Rocky Heifitz, who ran the saloon at Ninth and Grand, held forth to a brace of initiates who leaned on the bar while he punctuated his harangue with stabs of a pudgy forefinger.

"If that bird is the Hand of God, I'll say the Lord has some straight left. That's what that bird is—Gawd's Straight Left. And I hope to tell ya it's a left like Peter Jackson's, too. One of these that shoots faster than you can lamp it and won't take no for an answer. You gaudy dancers that are sacking around here and making a play to be bump-off artists better not run in with The Hand."

Thus spoke Rocky as he sliced off the surplus collar with a wooden spatula.

There were elements of style about Hand's execution of his first commission. Certain requests required the erasure of one Scotty Duncan, who was possessed of more than a desirable degree of knowledge and was suspected of being in communication with those representatives of the law known as "The Flatties." Hand's terms were "two hundred down, getaway money, and two hundred mailed General Delivery, Chicago." This of course was an exorbitant price for a single bump-off job, but as he explained, "You take or you leave it. I ain't no working stiff. Get some cheap hyjack if you want a sloppy job." They took it. For the demise of Scotty Duncan, because of his police protection, must have none of the earmarks of a local accomplishment.

So, shortly after noon, as Scotty Duncan emerged from Wolf's, where he habitually lunched, Hand Evans, a cool, short, swarthy-faced little figure, stood in Heifitz's corridor, the outer swinging door ajar. With the unhurried accuracy of a champion billiard player making a shot requiring some little skill, he took a squat, ugly automatic pistol from his pocket and as Duncan appeared across the street in front of Wolf's he shot once, watched Duncan slump face down to the pavement, and then, replacing the gun in his pocket, walked to the bar.

Rocky set a bottle of whisky in front of him and Hand poured a half-tumbler full.

"The head," he remarked conversationally to Rocky, the barroom being clear by arrangement, "is cleaner, neater; and using soft-nosed stuff, you know a job is finished."

He drained the whisky, refused a chaser, and taking a soft hat and ulster from a peg on the wall, picked up a travelling bag and started for the rear entrance. "Say Hand!" boomed Rocky, coming out from behind the bar, "I'd like to shake hands with you." He wiped his big hands on his apron and smiled admiringly at the dark little man.

"Don't call me Hand," said Evans, very calmly, and opened the door that led into the alley. "And I don't shake hands with nobody."

And that was all the city saw of Hand Evans for some time.

Occasionally reports filtered back to the city about him. He was in New York. He'd done a croak there. He'd left New York. No one knew where he was. He was believed to be in the West again. Then he killed a man in New Orleans and was not heard of for a month or two until he appeared in Chicago again and there was another killing. The sequence was always the same. Hand Evans appeared in town. There was a killing with no witnesses or only favorable witnesses. Hand Evans disappeared. He worked for the highest bidder and he worked alone. He gave allegiance to no one and he split with no one.

The members of the oldest profession could get no hold on him and his only possible weakness was drink. He drank a great deal too much. But it had no visible effect on him. While his companions at the bar grew maudlin or quarrelsome, he was always Hand Evans, with all the rattlesnake's deadliness and without the serpent's warning signal.

So when he was seen at Rocky Heifitz's place after an absence of two years, his coming bred conjecture, consternation and in two cases, cold, deadly fear in those citizens of the city who would be aware of his coming. There was conjecture on the part of the entire district who were in the know; the coming of Hand Evans was a far surer presage of death than the most reliable banshee wail in Ireland. The district wondered who was going to die. There was paralyzing, gnawing, sinking fear at the pits of the stomachs of Pinky Miller and Ike Lantz. And there was joy in the heart of Jack Farrell.

Scotty Duncan's well-conducted exit had not stopped the leak that threatened to enlarge in the dike of security that protected the interests, and with a sudden pouring rush to carry them all on the flood into that dreader bayou of the discovered, the penitentiary. Pinky Miller and Ike Lantz knew of adequate reason why they should be called upon to shuffle off in the interest of protection. Fear that Hand Evans was in the city as an agent of that protection, that their loose-lippedness threatened, nauseated them, and they pictured Scotty Duncan lying on the pavement in front of Wolf's with a neat round puncture in his forehead and a hole big enough to put an egg in at the back. So they went to Jack Farrell.

"Hand Evans is in town," said Pinky, looking across the desk at the square-jawed, ruddy complacency of Jack Farrell, the czar of the Fifteenth Street police station.

"I know it," Jack spat accurately at the cuspidor in the corner and reinserted his cigar.

"What are you going to do about it?" demanded Ike.

"Nothing," returned Farrell, looking at them amusedly from under his bushy white eyebrows.

"Nothing," almost shouted Pinky in his phobia. "Nothing. He's going to croak us. That's what he's going to do. And 'nothing' you say."

He pounded on the desk, and his face was pink with emotion. "Don't you know he's out for me and Ike?"

"Sure," said Jack Farrell, and again scored on the cuspidor.

"Don't kid us, Jack," said Ike, who had himself better in hand, "we know we're stools. But I seen Scotty Duncan. Don't kid us, Jack."

Farrell removed his cigar, tipped back his chair and looked the two stool pigeons in the eye.

"I'm not kidding you birds. We ain't got nothing on Hand Evans. We know he bumped Scotty, but there ain't any proof."

"How about Heifitz," cut in Pinky whiningly.

"Heifitz. Heifitz, he'd swear he'd never seen Hand. There's nothing of him anywhere's. All we can do is vag him or hold him for investigation and neither of them will hold him for more than twenty-four hours. He ain't no vag and there's nothing to investigate that we ain't went into already. Somebody's due for a one way trip to the land out of which's bourne no travellers return. You ain't afraid to die, are you, Pinky?"

"Don't kid, Jack," said Ike, his racial fortitude giving him dignity beside the whining Pinky. "Ain't there nothing that we can do?"

"Bump him yourselves and make a getaway or get something on him and I'll jug him." Farrell puffed complacently on the cigar.

"You know we can't bump him. We ain't guns," pleaded Ike.

"He drinks, don't he? And he'll drink with anybody. Maybe he ain't after you boys after all. Get him full and maybe he'll spill something. Get him full tonight at Heifitz's. I'll look out for you all I can, boys."

"The hell of it is," whined Pinky, "it ain't as though he was just an ordinary gun. We might have some chance to get him, or we might get someone to croak him. But this guy's death. There ain't anybody could get him and he ain't got any weak points. And he'll kill anyone that tries to even pinch him."

"Everybody's got weak points," said Farrell. "Now you birds get along out of here."

The two stool pigeons opened the door and slipped out.

Farrell reached for a desk phone and called a number.

"Hello, Rocky? This is Jack. Anybody in the place? All right. Yes. I know he's after me. The two stools were just up. Scared to death. But we haven't anything on him. Yes. I understand why you can't testify on the other. The stools are going to try and get him oiled tonight. He's to get me tomorrow? I'd do the same thing in their place. Why bother with the stools when they can get the man higher up. All right. Yes. Get this Rocky. I'm sending a record over for the phonygraft. Tonight at about eleven thirty I'll call you from Wolf's across the street. Start the record. The one I sent over. He'll be drinking with some sacks the two stools will have there. Be ready to duck after you start the record. Yes. All right. So long Rocky."

He hung up the receiver and clapping on his derby found a fresh cigar in the top drawer of his desk and started out of the door whistling.

That night Hand Evans stood, short, olive-faced and stony-eyed, his right foot elevated upon the brass rail of Rocky Heifitz's bar, his left hand encircling a bottle of whisky from which he regularly filled the little glass that was before him. After filling the glass he drank it with his left hand. His right hand always hung by his side where there was a bulge in his coat pocket or rested on the bar where it could reach the other gun that he carried in the holster under his armpit. His eyes were on the mirror that paralleled the bar back of Rocky's head and that showed the panorama of the room and the swinging doors.

During the evening several men had approached Hand and offered to buy him drinks. To all he made the same reply. "I'm buying my own liquor." After that conversation was rather difficult. There was small likelihood of Hand spilling anything. If there is any truth in "In vino veritas," Hand's shell, peeled off, revealed only another and much harder shell beneath.

At a half hour before midnight the phone back of the bar jingled. Rocky answered. "Hello? Wrong number," and slammed down the receiver.

"Say, maybe there's one you ain't heard," he said, and reached for the top disk of a pile of phonograph records.

"None of that damn jazz," said the swarthy little man in front of the bar.

"This ain't jazz," replied Rocky, adjusting a new needle. "This is the genuwine high-brow stuff. This is soup and fish music. It's called Vesty the Gubby."

He started the machine and the great tenor's voice poured out of the sounding box in Leoncavallo's soul-searing music. "Laugh, Pagliacco, though your heart be breaking," sang Caruso. Hand's face brightened, then clouded, and his eyes dropped to the floor. All through the singing of the heart-broken protest of the fool against the fate that forces him on to jest while all his life has tumbled about his ears, Hand looked at the floor. The shell was broken.

Hand didn't see the swinging door open, and Jack Farrell standing in the doorway. He only heard Caruso's mighty voice ringing out in Canio's soul-tortured lament. At the last note he raised both hands impulsively to applaud.

"Keep 'em up!" Jack Farrell's voice cracked like a shot and Hand turned to look into the muzzle of a forty-five in the Irishman's big freckled hand. "Keep 'em up, Wop!"

He ran practiced fingers over Hand's coat, extracted the two pistols from the pocket and the shoulder holster, and then laughed into the swarthy face.

"Didn't have a weakness, eh? Couldn't be pinched? Kill anyone that tried to pinch you, eh?" He slipped a pair of steel bracelets on Hand's wrists. "You can put 'em down now. We got enough on them now so that Rocky here can tell what he knows of Scotty Duncan without any risk."

Hand Evans stood immobile, looking at Farrell with all the poisonous hate of a back-broken rattlesnake in his eyes.

"You didn't have a weakness," Farrell went on, gloatingly. "Liquor didn't bother you. You didn't care any more about a woman than a slot machine. You were going to kill me tomorrow. But you had a weakness all right. Your real name is Guardalabene, ain't it?" Hand had not said a word since his arrest, but all his concentrated hate was in his eyes. His face was as immobile as ever.

"Guardalabene is his name, Rocky," said Farrell, turning to the bartender. "And what brought his hand away from his pocket was the wop voice. Your ash heel's tendon, Mr. Guardalabene, was Music. Call the station, will ya, Rocky?"

♮ ♮ ♮ ♮ ♮

When Doodles Smith came back from New York in mid-May, Ernest moved into another of Kenley's apartment houses at 100 East Chicago Avenue. It was a small stone-faced building, with a spiral fire escape and a little plot of grass out front. Ernest's room on the fourth floor had been Hadley's during her October visit. Again, the furnishings were "yellow and lady-like," Ernest wrote, but he had his typewriter, a wonderful desk, a nice bed, and a fine view of the Rush Street skyline. Nevertheless, he got hardly any work done his first week there. He couldn't wait to see Hadley on Decoration Day, and a spring heat wave had turned his room into a fried egg. He couldn't think either Ernest said, but Hadley's nighttime thought that "doctors deal with keeping physical life going; artists with keeping spiritual life going; and psychiatrists are sort of the middle ground" seemed as if it were true. But Ernest wrote that he didn't want her reading Fonnie's book on sexual relations. Mature people, after all, have to gauge things for themselves, he said.

⋈ 11 ⋈
A Sense of Proportion

On Friday night, May 27, 1921, Ernest and Bill Horne left the LaSalle Street Station bound for St. Louis. For the first time there was a tension between them. Ernest's life was coalescing; Bill's was falling apart. Because he knew Bill hadn't found work, the "National Debt" (Bill's five-hundred-dollar loan to Ernest in Chicago) drove a wedge, in Ernest's mind at least, into their friendship and threatened to split it apart. "Go to hell with your talk about seeds," Bill said. "If I can't grubstake my best and bosom buddy for a while without making him feel he owed money, then I'm a weed and it's time for the Supreme Lawnmower." Then, too, Bill's courtesy would be tried by his weekend partner, Hadley's best friend Ruth Bradfield, and Ernest knew it.

At first the train ride was difficult for Ernest. An hour into the trip he had back spasms and restlessly paced the aisles alone. Eventually, though, Bill's flask of quality New York gin was emptied, essentials were remembered, and they got to Cates Avenue early Saturday morning comfortable with each other and in good cheer.

Although she'd had a "miserable night of sleepless anticipation," Hadley cheerfully cooked sunny-side eggs and Canadian bacon for four. She squeezed fresh oranges and toasted homemade bread. That afternoon at the hillside tennis courts in the park, she ran down every shot and apologized for hitting out. It was her newly strung racquet, she said. Later, Ernest and Hadley, Bill and Ruth visited a Mrs. Offenclause, "a fine healthy-minded, able-bodied old lady." She had the wrinkles of a prune, Ernest thought, or of an apple gone bad. But Hadley said her body was springy and her face was scarred by life. Sunday afternoon they went

181

canoeing. Ernest and Hadley worked well as a team, Ernest in the rear steering. But Bill, steering too, beached the canoe several times, and Ruth was weak from "women's fatigue." Finally, they landed on a grassy bank, had lunch and cigarettes, and Hadley suggested they leave Ruth and Bill alone.

On Monday, Ernest challenged Hadley to a singles match at the Triple-A Club, and, while Bill and Ruth looked on, he ran down Hadley's drives, punched every shot to her backhand, and hardly laughed at all. Hadley was pleased she was not easily winded and could give Ernest a game. Back home, Ernest said that paddling the canoe had aggravated his back, and, despite the drinks he took for anesthetic, his face looked fired down by pain. Hadley told him, "I have had people like my hand on them rubbing" and gave him a vigorous massage. Then she told him, "You're a baby, but you look more aesthetic that way."

When Ernest complained that he hadn't gotten in any swimming that year, Hadley got angry. "I've missed most of the things that men find important in their lives." Then, for some reason, she told him a strange story: "I went out one day with Eleanor Smith in a rowboat during a terrific storm. A man on shore shrieked to us to come right in; Captain Davis signaled wildly from the lighthouse. But I really kept right on. It was raining and the waves jerked and plunged the little boat about, and I can smell it all now: salt water smelling on a gray day with clouds."

When Bill Horne went off into another room with Ruth for some necking, Hadley said Bill was too eager: "A girl, a girl, my kingdom for a girl. . . . He's a verra fine fella, but Horny needs a good girl bad or a bad girl good."

Hadley confessed that recently she'd been a bit of a bad girl herself. The week before, she'd been picked up by Dr. Tony Day in his Ford, had gone off "to Lillian's for a frappe and zoomed out to Clayton Road for a cute little dinner. . . . You eat in funny little screened-in houses," she said, "and feel that you are meant to take some devilish advantage of their privacy, but never do." Later, the doctor had taken her up on Litzminger Road to "look at picnicing places."

Ernest said that for the past month he'd been getting chest pains climbing the stairs to his room and had started taking the old elevator. That night, Hadley said the worst thing for a woman like her would be to discover that the man she loved could have gone further without her. That night, too, Hadley herself went further with Ernest than ever before. But the next morning she said she'd "do it over again . . . and be worse."

By the time Ernest left for Chicago, the date for the wedding had been

set (the first week in September); a "producer," George Breaker, "a magnificent stager of great spectacles," had been enlisted; and a honeymoon
at Windemere had been planned. Kate Smith would be in the wedding
party, though Hadley had trouble understanding that "you love her like
mad; but at the same time I'm to remember that you don't love anyone
but me."

The first letter Hadley wrote to Ernest after his Decoration Day trip
to St. Louis was twenty-eight pages long. She had had a lovely time "sitting under the trees, but I was sick the last day so left the dishes and
smoked and drank and read." Helen Breaker had promised to give her an
announcement party. Hadley said she would make herself "magnificent"
and lie about Ernest's age in case anyone was curious enough to inquire.
On the wedding announcement, Hadley called Grace Hemingway an
"architect." She said her own mother was sort of an architect, too, an
architect of Hell. Hadley was "ground down to the root of myself" when
she'd met Ernest in October and "felt that that root might be dead." Her
mother, Florence Richardson, made "a terrible storm come for me and
things would get said that would lay like lumps of lead in my heart." Had
her mother lived, Hadley might have killed herself, she said. In fact, she
was sure she would have killed herself years before if not for her friends.
"You're absolutely a flame of love and understanding and sweetness and
strength," she told Ernest. "I miss you often in that terrible, black, sick
way—not physical, like you say. It's like being a great firm river that's cut
off from its channel, and you get black and poisonous and frightfully
unhappy."

Ernest apologized for his behavior in St. Louis on the canoe trip: complaining too much, being obnoxious, getting drunk. If she wished, Hadley could attribute it to his "acknowledged fear of storm." There had
been thunderheads threatening all that day. "Foolishness," Hadley said.
But she did love having the razor he'd forgotten. "Can sort of see you
around the place; this trip much better than before." She herself apologized for having a "Puritan upper" that made kissing less fun. "Sure hope
it doesn't ruin me for you. That four-poster sounds nice, and we'll love
each other in that room."

Ernest was still worried that Hadley was eight years older than he. "I
know a composer, wonderful, marvelous man, married a wife ten years
older," Hadley said. "Man is David Gregory Newson, and my what they
wouldn't do for each other. But then, wouldn't we?"

In early June, Hadley got some bad news. Fonnie had consulted a
Dr. Schwab, a psychologist Mrs. Richardson had selected to treat Hadley

years before. He said Hadley should not marry at all; but since she was determined to do so, she should not, in her delicate mental state, have children for at least six years. Hadley was beside herself. She raged at Fonnie, said all she felt, and when Fonnie reminded her that the outburst proved just what the doctor said, she forbade Fonnie "ever to speak to me again." She knew that Ernest wanted to be "atavistic, to tear beauty out of chaos and dark things and get it done in some manner." "Your biggest value," Hadley wrote, "is your resounding reaction to everything." She would never, for her own "mental health," try to "level you down to smooth even feelings and thoughts. I haven't any sense of humor about this at all. I'd rather do anything than do that. I know that some of the time I'll be sick and a weight to carry, but as little as possible 'cause I truly love you and want to help."

Bill Horne hadn't mailed back Ruth's pajamas yet, Hadley said. Maybe he would "nail them up on the wall like rattlesnake skin."

There would be thirty people at the wedding announcement party. "We're going to curl our hair and break the news," Hadley said. But "if you aren't sure you want to marry me, let me know by return mail as the invitations will be mailed Friday of this week."

Hadley hoped that she wouldn't faint at the party. When she thought about it, her heart "beat like mad." She had told a friend that Ernest was "the first American killed in Italy." When Ernest wrote that there was no need to fear Dr. Schawb's counsel, that he didn't want any children for a long time, Hadley sent him her mother's article on contraception. "This is whom you're in league with, when you take this stand," she said. Perhaps it was his severe headaches that made him think that way, Ernest wrote by return mail. "For the life of me," Hadley wrote, "I couldn't stop thinking of you leaning over me out on the porch, that very porch where I lay on a comfy sort of wicker lounge, talking to Marguerite. . . . The main thing you gave me was the strong feeling of loving protection or protecting love." She would endure the announcement party, Hadley said, "but the wedding has got to be simple and beautiful. Small wedding, reception roundabout the church door, quick reception at the Dilworth's, then run in Bill's Buick."

She hoped that Ernest would not judge her fear of "big events" to be cowardice. There was something about having lived with brutal, selfish people that made her love informality and detest duty and rules. When Ernest wrote that in her own home Hadley had lived through horrors war couldn't provide, she told him about the Rapallos and her first year at Bryn Mawr.

Oin darling:

This is the most understanding and loving letter about how irritable I was in the home. As to Mrs. Rapallo—pooh. She's quite a little fool and a perfectly charming affectionate person— [She] went wild over me and knew I was sick. I sort of appealed to her as a helpless little somebody—as I was—. In order to help me out, she managed to show me how much pleasanter life was with her and Edna—best friend at college, freshman year—, tremendous amount of jealousy. Then this rotten suggestion of evil—and being very suggestible, I began to imagine I had all this low sex feeling for her and she for me. Quite sure now it was nothing but a very spoiled, absorbing affection. Certainly did make hell between me and family. Got awfully tired of her though, because she couldn't get along without me. And of course it cut me off from the small amount of young stuff I was able to do at best. Finally was persuaded by Mama that it was very bad for me 'cause I was tired of her, you see, and frightened her to death by saying mysteriously I was afraid she was going to get this here frightening shock someday.

It's only occurred to me recently what this low thing could be. Certainly never was the remotest suggestion of such a thing. Poor old dear. She hated to break up since,—and you know I'd have busted it up ages before if I hadn't been so pecked about it. Tell you what, Oin. If any concrete sin had been committed, I couldn't have felt more guilty. 'Cause it was bad for me. If home had been different, I wouldn't have wanted them. They lived so attractively and affectionately. By George, I'm fond of her still. She was a lady to the end. She never insulted my family or anything, and she knew what they thought of her too. She was very good company. Friend of Jay Marlowe and Maxfield Parrish. And studied with Howard Pyle, and loads of wonderful people. No reason why I shouldn't have gotten fun out of her. They did. Oh, you needn't fear me on that side, my dear. There was a time when someone liking me that much made me think I liked them that much. But I know now that I don't. I like other kinds better—very few women and a great many kinds of men. . . . I ain't mad at all. Feel fine. Only thing is to have anyone alive thinking you're marrying such a queer, abnormal somebody.

Ernest wrote that, temporarily at least, Kate had refused the invitation to "support" Hadley at the wedding. But he felt she would probably change her mind. His little sister Carol was down to the room for a day, and, fussing and straightening, she looked so much like Kate. The poems he sent Hadley he'd submit to Harriet Monroe's *Poetry*, too. He was thinking of quitting his job at the Commonwealth Cooperative again, Ernest said. The stench from the bilge had reached the bridge. Still, he hated it that a bounder named Munson had just stepped into his kind of job with the same power and the same pay.

In mid-June, Hadley got more bad news from a doctor. After a thor-

ough examination, a Dr. Royston (recommended by Helen Breaker) cautioned Hadley about giving birth in a country like Italy. Anesthetic was
not widely used there, especially in the delivery room, he said. But Hadley was confident: " 'Twilight Sleep,' a marvel of modern medicine which
brings the Mama through very marvelously, I understand it's for nerves,
is practiced to some extent in every country, must be in Italy." Besides,
"if we don't take Italy now," she wrote, "when might it be shoved off
to? . . . Only maybe the free life we planned there being somewhat
threatened by our bambino, might make it not worth so much to you?
'Cause the nicer the place and the 'Dolce' the atmosphere I have to enjoy
and love one baby in, the happier I'll be." Then she went on: "When are
you going to tell Haddam about Caporetto? Love to hear about the boxing, too. Know pretty well the way you manage your body—it is panthery
and beautiful. Haven't a professional viewpoint, of course. Still, have a
viewpoint. Aren't you glad?"

Perhaps because Ernest had been writing a great deal about his rooftop
boxing, his friend Nick Neroni, how "funny" he felt asking the guys in
the wedding party to wear white pants, Hadley composed a manifesto for
one. "Of course marriage is a particularly unfitting state for you," she
said.

It takes a good bit of courage on my part to stick on in spite of it. . . .
Courage that I didn't have at first because I kept planning and thinking
what I would do to make it all that you wanted. All I could do seemed
too little if this blessed state of matrimony was going to lead you away
from the main road into a temporarily agreeable by-pass. That's when it
finally dawned on me that it was scarcely at all what I did and aimed at
that was going to work the wonder for you—though of course I am not
aimless in my purpose and love—but just something that I happen to be.
That is not of the head entirely, nor the heart entirely, nor the spirit or
body entirely, but an essence of all—that is made to blend with your
own beautiful elements and make wonderful happiness, wonderful peace
and satisfaction, and many many concrete things come about naturally
and without the unnecessary struggle and pain you go through to accomplish things when you're unhappy or even unsatisfied. I'm just as sure
as sure that we're meant to be happy, to enjoy work to be done. I hope we
never lead the hand-ruled scheduled life most people do. We couldn't
'cause the best things that come to both of us come pretty much unsolicited.
Which means that I think that if you plan for what you want you may
get it, but if you just go on loving, bringing sort of hope and an appreciation, something (it can be more precious and beautiful and of a fibre
absolutely unknown to you in a mental state) will suddenly be sort of
alive in you. That's the kind of thing happens to you so much. That's
the kind of thing I've had some of—much slower than you, but still

there's always been some of it there, all the time—and we do our realist living that way. When we're black in mood is when we think this inspirational sort of thing has left us. It's all over—never a creative thought again. You're equally frightened, I think, of that happening. And probably equally sure that no matter what depths we go to, we'll always come back and feel this power again. A few years back, I couldn't have married because I had ambition and passion for music and believed that married, I couldn't have satisfied either.

It ought to be wonderful, our living, knowing something heavenly was gradually being worked out and developed around the house. It kind of does something for a house, don't you think so? Free fine thing for young "Ziochs." But the best thing in his young life will be his Papa.

Darling. Don't think marriage exactly changes two people that are well-mated, dear. If it's the right sort of love. It just makes them grow into what they're meant to be. I feel awfully sorry for all your adoring friends, 'cause I know just how they feel about you. Not only selfishly at losing you as the perfect free-lance playmate. But on your own account, for your work, especially. Do you realize that what they're seeing, your friends, in the effect I have on you, is all necessarily very romantic and elemental. . . . But it generally bores the onlookers. . . . "Oh Hemmy's different, always wants to be alone with that girl. Not adventurous, etc." By the rules of society and convention, we set ourselves before their gaze with apparently no sense of proportion in living. But they will see, I think, dear old thing, when we've had a chance to gain a fit setting for our little play, that our life will be very beautiful and full of very kind of human friendship.

Hadley still wondered "sometimes, wouldn't I have rather had you maybe for *my* Papa." Ernest said he thought that there was something awfully appealing about being a "Papa." It meant love and guidance—a protecting love, as Hadley had once put it so well.

Ernest wrote that he had "battered his hand" in the elevator door and had been given an office without windows. "Of all the people obviously made to breathe great tons of air in a single intake," Hadley said, "you are the chief. You should speak up about it to someone." Hadley herself had a sore, "speckled" throat. Yet, "after drinking last night," she and Ruth had "walked barefoot in the rain, wet and cool, all the way home."

Hadley wanted to wear a veil in their wedding. Ernest said it would make the "best man" have to wear formal clothes. "Too bad," Hadley said. "Ought to wear a veil for a church wedding. You know what St. Paul says about women's heads." Ernest wrote that just before the wedding he needed a week with the men. "That's fine," Hadley said. "What kind of bathing suit do you like me in? . . . I immediately hate whatever you

don't like me in. . . . Like the gingham dress and the speckled hat."
Ernest said he "evolved my tales lying on a pillow, saturated with cigarettes." "Dear old beautiful Nesto, seems as though I have to hold your
head close to me tonight and look down at you. I'm so lonely dear. My
hair is turning a nice shade of red it never looked before. I love to have
you love my hair. I love yours. Love to pet it back from your forehead.
Wish I could have been there when you'd boxed and bathed and felt fine
and stretching and lazy. It's a fine time to be with ye. This time next year
we'll be in Wopland together."

On June 12, 1921, Hadley sent Grace Hemingway news of her engagement party. She was apologetic and at pains to be ingratiating. She copied
the letter over for neatness twice:

> Dear Mrs. Hemingway—
> I knew you would be interested to know about the party Helen Breaker,
> one of my very best friends, is giving for me tomorrow afternoon. It is a
> small tea, about 35 people asked, and Helen is going to stand by me and
> tell the world of my engagement to Ernest. Invitations are very discreet,
> you see, to keep it a surprise. I'm enclosing one to show you. Helen's
> house is terribly pretty and it will be a lovely party. I do wish you and
> the girls were here to share the place with me.
> Ernest has written to me from time to time of your sweetness and gen-
> erosity in planning for our happiness in September. I can't think of any
> better way to spend our honeymoon than North and in the woods. Of
> course there are not words big enough to thank you for putting the op-
> portunity in our way, but I do thank you nevertheless, from the bottom
> of my heart.
> I have never had time to acknowledge your two songs which came some
> time ago. I was terribly pleased to have them and the picture. And as-
> tonished and surprised at your being a real composer of songs. I've always
> been afraid, though I had no training in that direction at all, that com-
> position would always remain over my head, though I'd rather do that
> than play, very much.

That same June evening, Hadley wrote to Ernest recalling how her
own mother, Florence Richardson, had "protected me into neurosis. . . .
I wasn't allowed to go into cold water for years because of the 'shock.' I
still have a hangover of scare about it. Never forgot my trepidation walking down the hill wondering whether I'd be ruined for life or what."

"I usually love you lightly, lovely, and gaily," Hadley said. "But tonight
my love is heavy and breathless like the air." Ernest's presence to her was
"like the cool moist breeze that won't come tonight and stir and lighten
the heavy dark leaves of the trees. It lifts a person's heart up to a light,
even place where it's comfortable and dear and loving to live. That's what

we want, isn't it? To be where it's light and beautiful. To be happy and as tender and as deeply loving as we want."

Ernest had written that Kate would not meet his eyes except in a crowded room and that she talked about the future in glib, sarcastic way. Perhaps asking her to join the wedding party was cruel; perhaps he had a duty to her. In answer, Hadley said he must be true to his heart. "None of this artificial search for duty and wanting to do right by sacrificing something or somebody." Hadley was distressed when the next letter Ernest sent to her was addressed by Kate Smith.

For months Ernest had been sending Hadley everything he'd written, most of it in the lecturer–journalist voice and headed for the *Toronto Star Weekly*. But some pieces were in his "serious style." "You're very funny," Hadley wrote. "But I admire the straight ahead stuff a little more than the funny ones. . . . Guess I am in love with style in all things. Not just in a superficial sense, either, 'cause your style is the outcome of a deep feeling and not just intellection. . . . You've got a good ear for rhythm and tone and lines. . . . You've written me paragraphs that come right straight from the highest things there are. Wish people besides me could hear some of the priceless things you've said to me alone. Course they'll get others, but a person hates to think of a fine thing not being reflected in a big mirror for all to see."

Despite Hadley's eloquent assurance that she loved him, understood and valued him, and wanted to help his life "go" with hers, Ernest wrote that he'd been playing tennis every day with the "svelte Jewess," Irene; had been practicing his Italian with Nick Neroni (he was getting as fluent as a cabby in Milan), and had been picturing them in Italy, he "gossiping with old loves and old comrades—co-males and human warriors—scarcely seeing her at all." Nevertheless Hadley replied, "In the midst of some high adventure, you will feel a timid plucking at your sleeve . . . and who will it be but Hash, begging you to come and use your linguistic talents on the *First Cause*." Ernest wrote that he was boxing with Kenley Smith up on the roof. He wore a top hat to show his contempt for Hadley's favorite, poetic friend, and Kenley didn't look so long and cool after three serious rounds. Then Ernest said that he and Kate were entering a dance contest.

Life is beautiful and serious, Hadley said. There was no place for petty jealousies in "such a richly endowed creatch" as Ernest. "What bugs me about Kate is that it's someone I can't help caring about that's losing out. It sure is bum for her. And of course I can't ever do or say anything. Bad thing to know, as I do, exactly what it feels like, and it's very hard for you, Nesto. Please don't think I don't know that. I think you did wonderfully right and well and worthy. It's amazing you happened by some chemical accident not to fall for her, hard. Worth about three of me, anyhow, and probably be a better lover and worker for you, and everything. My but it's queer the way things happen, and if you didn't want me pretty hard, as I think you do, I'd make you throw me over and do yourself justice."

The confessions Ernest made about Agnes and Kate hurt a lot, Hadley said, "but even when they're hard to tell and hard to hear I feel terribly way inside happy that you bring things like that to me. It's after all the only way for us to do because either one of us would guess or feel things the way they really are. And to know that you feel about me the way I feel about you—maybe it's just my feminine reaction to finding a lover like you—I feel sort of bound up in you and part of you and dependent only on you for my happiness. But if that is the case, I must not have anything that I have to hold back from you. It would *poison me.*"

In late June, Ernest wrote that the job at the *Toronto Star Weekly* still hadn't come through. He was working like a pig at the Commonwealth Cooperative, writing "Boy's Personals, The Country Division, Miss Congress's fiction, bank editorials, children's stories, etc." He had written her a nine-page "hot weather letter," but he tore it up. On the back of the last page of the letter he did send, Hadley found a poem. Ernest and Kate had won a dance contest at the Red Star Cafe, and Ernest had been reminded of Oscar Wilde:

Lines to a Young Lady on Her Having Very Nearly Won a Vogle

Through the hot pounding rhythm of the waltz
You swung and whirled with eager, pagan grace
Two sleepy birds, preening in their wicker cages
And I am dancing with a woman of the town.

"Why tear me to bits," Hadley said, "asking me to come up and play with ye on the roof?" Especially since "I felt very lonesome yesterday, and the evening came up such a blowing, pouring storm, and I went out on the porch, sat down humbly in a niche, watched the foliage whirled into wild shapes by the wind, smelled the drenched, cooled grass, and let the thunderclaps terrify me, the lightning cut me blind. And when I didn't see how to go about anything, I wished the lightning might have settled the whole shebang for me."

Reading Somerset Maugham's *Of Human Bondage,* Hadley thought, "The girl is unattractive as the deuce, for some reason: But I think he makes her unattractive by unresponsiveness." With Ernest, Hadley said, she could never be that way, because Ernest "would have been an alchemist in the Middle Ages, or a Galahad." Why couldn't he "write a short story about Horney's [Bill Horne] 'affaires de coeur.' It would make a good one." When she had tried to disillusion Bill about women in May, Ernest had leaned over her chair and told her quietly, "Horney doesn't like to be talked to that way." "A girl would have to be a tremendous actress to get away with a romance with Horney," Hadley had quietly replied.

After offering her honeymoon wardrobe for Ernest's approval (pink nightgowns of pussywillow—"I'll be the best-dressed lady in nightgowns you've ever seen"—a stunning one-piece swimmer, tan with decorative stripes, green and black shirt, orange belt, bathrobe, two camisoles, and a waist with brown frill for "traveling with you the first time"), Hadley brought up the question of childbearing again. She said her doctor friend, Tony Day, believed the best place to have a child was in France. In Italy, he said, they never use anesthetic. Another friend, Otto Simon, confirmed this. Traveling in the mountains of Bardocase with Hadley and her mother in 1910, Otto had had a "frightful abscess. . . . The local physician lanced it without anesthetic and laughed at Otto's agony."

Mrs. Otto Simon, however, had "a genius's sympathy for misery," Hadley said. "She thought I could do anything and college was wrong for me. . . . But my mother considered it foolish to take me out of school before graduation. I came back from Europe to the dusty, prosaic schoolrooms of the Mary Institute, and American jokes, and stupid schoolgirl stuff. This woman was able to make me hear the component parts of musical things I was too lazy with. I became essentially musical with her. Floated in sounds—yet understood them with perfect security and marvelous speed as in dreams—without stepping on the ground."

Ernest wrote that he had a new boss at the Commonwealth Cooperative: J. Clover Momna. It was destiny's voice, he said, and time for him to get out. Also, he wanted to reassure Hadley that, despite his confessions, the intimate details of his love affair with Kate he'd kept strictly to himself. Hadley replied:

Ernest, I know that Kate's affairs in relation to you are kept to yourself. You told me some of the points so's to keep close to me—in every way. Anything was touching you so hard + so close you felt maybe a little unfair not to confide in me? That's the way I'd feel about you. Feel kind of guilty not to be all there, dear, standing straight before you. It's strange how it seems hard, as you go along, to come out with confessions that bring a little dismay + disturbance in their train. Must, if we're sensitive at all. But I honestly think we're right to have kept things as open as this. We'll probably always do it. Keeps us up with ourselves. There are lots of things I could tell you, but either they were of no importance or simply induce a vague outline to everything of that sort. Very seldom made any response to obvious attraction I'd have for people. Don't mean many, but just ordinary amount. Honestly had no feminine ambition for scalps. Please don't think I'm classing you and Kate in here. . . . You're a clean-cut romantic. Be it understood I instinctively should not, and because you say so, [would] never under the sun, mention Kate's feelings for you to her. She's a dear old, puzzled, mussed-up thing, and I love her very much, and feel a good deal more than you guess how probably I'm not the person I could have been in her eyes.

Ernest had been sending more articles to the *Toronto Star Weekly,* articles entitled "Booze Situation," "Condensing the Classics," "Carpentier–Dempsey–Exploding the Superman Myth." Hadley told Ernest to say "the hell with the funny stuff." "It hasn't got your vitality . . . *your* way of saying it is ingrained in the style of the serious stuff." When he wrote well, Hadley said, "I feel like someone in a crowd adoring someone up on a raised place." When Ernest called her "a beautiful fool" for her naivete about Kate and hinted that his love affair with Kate had produced more than guilty feelings, she wrote: "Ernest, you're about to make a big, fat, generous, Ernestique mistake. . . . Honestly, darling, I think she'll [Kate] yank ourselves up and out of all this stuff, and we've more chance of being for each other than any two I ever saw." Because Bill Horne had advised Ernest to "think twice about your duty to Kate," Hadley wrote, "What I really think is that Horney should hang for his impertinence to you and to Kate and to me."

Ernest was still saving, he told Hadley, forty-two out of fifty dollars a week for their time in Italy. He was working hard, not only at the Commonwealth Cooperative but on the "stuff" he sent her, his stories and his poems. He wouldn't blame her, Ernest said, if she was "surfeited." But Hadley replied she "had a place to keep everything you send. . . . Do you realize how many important threads you're weaving your life with these days?"

Hadley wrote that she had gotten "a great little note from Ursula. . . . Gee, that child made me feel nice. Leave me advise you a person couldn't be better than this 'Ura.' " Ernest was happy Hadley liked Ura, he said, because for a long time she was the only one of the family he could stand the smell of. But then, he had had a hell of a nose, good on a bird dog, useless for a man. Hadley disagreed. "You've got the nicest nose, my favorite nose," she said. When Ernest wrote about Capracotta, Hadley said: "No better place to work and keep in physical trim. . . . Being with you and you working on fine stories and maybe a novel . . . sounds like a natural life. . . . Sounds like what a person dreams of when things press around him too hard."

The Chicago veterans of Schio were planning a reunion at the Venice Cafe, Ernest wrote. They were all going to wear their uniforms. But for some reason, he felt he couldn't wear his. "What's in honor of you is in honor of me also," Hadley wrote. "What's beautiful in you is a gift the gods give to me in the most wonderful ways. And my inmost thoughts are yours to use. Everything in me is for you, Nesto, or I can't be any good. . . . Ruth is in the clutches of Calomel and her eyes hurt and she's lost her glasses and she can't read. But I feel *fine*."

After the reunion of the Schio boys at the Venice Cafe (to which he did not wear his old uniform), Ernest wrote that he and Nick Neroni boxed a long time on the roof. Because of his "funny story," "The Woppian Way," Hadley said jokingly that she had assumed Nick Neroni was dead. But in winning Ernest thought he'd broken his hand.

Hadley said she didn't mind Ernest "putting out Nick Neroni's candle," but "make sure you don't light Doodles's torch." Doodles's passions were a lot like Harrison Williams' aesthetics, Hadley said. "He had me going that way 'til finally, being a bit too healthy for such bloodless exclusiveness, I suddenly found myself all 'agin him. . . . Ideas were all right for him, but it took me a long time to find a world of art and life to love and admire again. . . . *I starved on him,* didn't realise I was walking into the desert. I had to work to build things up to make them grow . . . and Harrison, poor old boy, has lived to see the day for my much pooh-poohed sympathies with all sorts of things and people and art appear to be the fruitful thing."

Imagining what their life in Chicago would be like, Hadley wrote: "I want to meet you and walk down by the lake the last stretch together. . . . And then you bathe and dress and I'll dress and we'll feel fresh and you sort of weary and maybe slouch a bit reading and what fun it will be, Oin. . . . And then in the fall, before dinner, the streets smelling leafy and the fresh odor of the Lake mixed in, and you come up in the dark elevator and into the old 'H' with a warm lamplight shining against the duskiness and the windows and sofa and books and the piano." She said she wanted to "feel the soft little part of your cheek on mine and then kiss your brow and lips . . . better not write about—guess."

For walking in the country, Hadley had bought herself a scotch plaid cape. It was not lined but very pretty with a leaf hat and ribbing for the steamer. "It is the only wrap I'm going to buy. It'll be fine in Italy. I've taken the old brown, sober as a judge coat and made a fur collar." Ernest wrote that, at night, he felt her holding him close. Hadley said she felt that too, and "I thought I was imagining it for my own joy, but since you feel it too it must be something mystical. . . . Good thing I'm busy, otherwise the restlessness would be too much for me to stand."

By late June, Ernest was well into his novel, he said, but he was having problems with "conversation." "Nothing to do but practice," he wrote, like five-finger exercises on the piano. "You know, it takes a lot of humbleness," Hadley wrote, "to hold yourself down to truthfulness in an art. And up to the day of your death, you'll probably find yourself slipping with technical ease into poor psychology. You have little excuse for such because you do know and understand so many human types. But 'course it's just as hard for you as for anyone else to be honest—by George. I think that's the hardest thing there is. But also, no one has a better chance to be honest than you because you've the will to be, and the power of discerning in others. Couple the two and you're there. Add boning the way you're doing and honestly, you'll suddenly find yourself doing marvels of stirring, potent stuff. More than you thought you could do before, I suspect. Can't imagine a better thing than this practice if done for a while anyway. I'm so wildly in love with this side of you, Oin. . . . Think maybe some writage might occur at Windemere, evenings maybe, just play writage, but something nice might happen." Hadley promised to think of him when she washed her hair that night with Castile shampoo.

As the Georges Carpentier–Jack Dempsey heavyweight championship fight approached, Ernest wrote that he was betting heavily on the European champion—"seven hundred dollars and change." Part of the money to cover his bets Ernest intended to make boxing a rooftop exhibition with his Italian sparring partner, Nick Neroni. Hadley wrote she wished she could be there, "not at the ring, but for the pride and loving afterwards." She wanted him to wear something of hers into the ring. His lavender trunks looked very good, she said, but "revealed a man's form awfully." Ernest said he hoped he'd do well, but he'd have to tape up a broken knuckle, and something under his left jawbone was making him feel rocky. "When we're in Italy," Hadley said, "you'll probably prance off some and give me a lonely feeling. 'Women must weep so.' When you come back, I'll find an excuse to smother you with loving." Ernest said everyone urged the "Boxer," with his broken hand, to fight. They don't care if it's good, only passionate.

Like all boxing between good friends, the Hemingway–Neroni bout was a show of sportsmanship and a test of skill. The "crowd"—members of Kenley Smith's club, literary friends and neighbors, and the building janitors—was unanimously disappointed. On an applause decision, Ernest lost the winner-take-all. Worse yet, Dempsey beat Carpentier like a rag doll and knocked him out in the fourth round. Bill Horne was heart-broken over Carpentier's defeat, Ernest said in his "sad little letter" to Hadley. "But not me."

Hadley soon found out, however, that Ernest was more than heart-broken, and the cause was many things. On July 6, Ernest wrote that for the past few months, burdened by his job at the Commonwealth, by worry over his father's illness, by being put off at the *Toronto Star*, by headaches, sore throats, back pains, hemorrhoids, and too many sleepless nights, he'd found himself yearning for death. He couldn't forget that night at the Red Star Cafe when Hadley had told him to stop acting like "you're nailed to the Cross" and that the only word for his affair with Kate was "obscene." "Besides," Hadley had said, "it isn't such a wicked word . . . and it fits in and you know it does." Now, Ernest had to think of reasons not to, when he "really wanted to go."

Hadley wrote immediately, Special Delivery:

> The meanest thing I can say to you on that point is to say that remember it would kill me to all intents and purposes. Horrid to have to think of a reason against it. . . . Don't ever get confused when such a moment comes. Don't ever forget that responsibility to me. You got to live. First for you and then for my happiness. I know how it feels 'cause I have so very many times wanted to go and couldn't on account of the mess I'd leave some other people in. Remember one of the few nice things I've ever done—and I really shouldn't tell you about it—but remember the eventful day I managed to find out all this psychological, mental mystery about myself. Could see just afterwards that Mama was terribly frightened having told me—so I went for the family party with numerous people and Bragdens and Ushers and you know, and took um all down to the park that afternoon. Mama couldn't understand why I was so smiling and happy—still worried—finally I doped it out that she was afraid that a bad moment would come and I'd think *I was too queer to live or something.* So I went and told her I had made up my mind never to kill myself. She blossomed like a rose. Really had been scared. *That day was the first day of life in a long, long while.* . . .

Hadley continued:

> You mustn't feel so horrible unworthwhile, dear Ern. It's because you're sick (throat). What you should really do is give way physically. . . . Draw the sheet tight as skin over a matress [sic] and prop head up on finished pillow. Have book and paper handy but chiefly leave um unread. Electric fan for stirring the air. Not on you, but around cool in the room. . . . Me arriving Saturday [July 9] to love you closer than for a long time. . . .

Hope I hear from you, dear old thing, I'm so very lonely for you. . . .
Bow down before you about the word *"obscene."* . . . The word obscene
has been used slangly of late and I've allowed my sense of it to be
warped of late. I've got thousands of secrets you'll hear sooner or later, too.

The next day, Hadley read that Ernest had imagined the end of their
engagement, "every detail, and all the pain." Again, she wrote back immediately to tell him she was "glad you wrote it all out; I know it was
hard; don't mind your saying it all. I think we both might feel a little
happier if we could see each other right now." On July 8, Hadley tele-
grammed: "Bringing racquet and cape . . . want you terribly . . . love
EHR." Ernest wired Hadley: "Please come . . . stay here . . . all my
love, EMH."

Unfortunately, all Ernest's love that weekend proved much less than
Hadley had hoped for. Their first night together, he took her to the Red
Star Cafe (as a gesture to sentiment, he said) with his new friend Ricco St.
Larietto (whose smile was "so easily forthcoming") and with Kate Smith.
Showing off the prize-winning form he'd developed, Ernest danced one
set after another with Kate. Back at the table, he called attention to Hadley's dress, the styling of her hair, and encouraged her to dance all she
wished with St. Larietto. That night, too, Kate told Hadley she'd wear
what she pleased at the wedding. "That's OK," Hadley said, "if you look
as pretty as you really are." Understandably, Hadley drank "a lot of white
wine" and worried over "having Ruth Bradfield [enamored of Bill Horne]
and Kate Smith in the same wedding party: both are losing someone they
love."

As Ernest and Hadley stood on the grimy LaSalle Street Station platform, with the smell of coal and metal and the smoke of departing trains,
he confessed to her that his friends, particularly Bill Smith, were "busted
over my marrying plans. . . . There's something fatal to success in them,"
he said. Hadley was furious. Bill Smith, she said, was a hypocrite, as were
all the Charles clan. Ernest should know that

Practically the first thing I heard, almost, when I came down from Chicago when I met you was that the whole Charles family, including Bill,
had told Fonnie you weren't estimating yourself low enough from the
point of view of literature. . . . For goodness sakes, do your friends justice, don't stop telling me of my forcible insertion into an hostile camp.
There are so many places I want to go, so many things I want to do, so
many new things I want to learn and think about, so many people I want
to love and like, it seems terribly unreasonable that I should have picked
this place of all places where the people hold out so long and hard
against such good things. It makes me frightfully sad (no use being angry,

except the unavoidable instance of immediate reaction with childish ideals) . . . no use in saying I'm the perfect woman for you—might be an enormous healthy mistake. I'm sure I don't know. God hasn't told me a single secret about it. Just the same I think in the same way he hasn't told them a thing either. About this "talented" business. When Fonnie, who may so easily have misquoted the Charles [sic], told me that stuff about you, all I thought to myself was, at Oin's age I overestimated certain things in myself of the dazzling sort and usually underestimated others of far greater importance. And if Oin is doing that too, he can't help it. Anyway, I'm proving so terribly fond of him and I believe in him and I want to be with him whatever the stages are to enjoy and love. Never have seen any overestimation that way. But then you are an old dear. And I'm your quite critical, rather artistically made up loving friend.

But after a lonely train ride home, Hadley felt that she had said too much in Chicago, hadn't shown how she understood, how sympathetic and tolerant she intended to be. The night she got back to St. Louis, Monday, July 12, she sent Ernest another Special Delivery:

I see you Ernest in a white city where the sun is too dazzling, but you keep on trudging along the way you do, and getting things done just the same, and somehow the heat and the worry and the responsibility that you endure make you more and more lovable. Can see your head dropped forward a little, but your eyes looking straight ahead. It's enough to make a person rally from any depths to see you that way. Honey, you're doing some of the best things that you've ever done in your life right now and every single one of um is as devilishly hard as possible. . . . I'm awfully sure you're going to ease through.

Ernest wrote back that if anything he'd done in Chicago had hurt, "I was sorry before I did it."

After their first fight and their first reconciliation, Hadley wrote that she was "looking forward to the honeymoon tennis at Windemere . . . looking forward to both of us playing so much better, as we know how. And getting meals. That's fun with you. And the cold nights at the fire and pillows and the books with each other and the tang in the morning and evening air of September in the North." Ernest said he felt better about his job at the Commonwealth Cooperative. He'd been given a splendid new office, and now he had his own phone. He sent Hadley his number and exact instructions for when she should call. Ernest wrote that he'd started a porch garden with some seeds and cuttings his father had supplied, and he'd shown some of his serious stuff to the new editor-in-chief, Mr. Stockbridge. The boss had, "with his clear eyes," found it good.

Doodles had taken to snubbing him, Ernest wrote, but Kate was still

198 ALONG WITH YOUTH

going to dinner with him. His throat though was bad again, and his black maid, Annie, said to gargle. "Do as Annie says," Hadley wrote, "and all will be right soon." Besides, they had a "wonderful invitation to the Fuller's farm outside Walpole [Massachusetts] when we go east. . . . Elizabeth Channing, a fine old college friend of mine who married a rather interesting bolshevik youth, Willard Fuller. Nothing like us. But we've a whole side devoted to their kind of stuff. Charming. I've spent time there, fine time. Three sons, good books, and charming oldstyle New England farmhouse." Ernest wrote that he thought the farmhouse idea charming too, but three sons were hardly enough. They ought to have at least fourteen children. They'd have to call the first Nick Hemingway, though.

Hadley wished that they were lying "somewheres on a high bank or stream today reading your stuff and talking impersonally about it and smelling the dry, hot September air and looking over landscape and summer sun, and cries of birds on the still air. Not closely conscious, but deliciously, nonchalantly, sympathetically conscious of one another's personality. Smoking a cigarette, maybe, and kicking the heels in the air. And very late one September evening, sharp cool came on, trudging homeward with hunger and fatigue and contentment filling us. I love the way you trudge, lamb. It's so big, and patty, and rhythmic. Makes me keep going so comfortably by your side. Evenings of such a day we'll sleep early or I'm a bad guesser. Funny thing lately how marvelously clear and clean I've slept. Even the heat couldn't stop the spring I felt from it."

When Ernest sent her a poem he'd written for Kate—"Why did you send me that poem"—Hadley wrote of how she had modeled her wedding dress at Helen Breaker's: "It's the loveliest thing I ever imagined. Manages to be exquisite without any of the sentimentality of lace. Makes me look like a Human Hazelnut. . . . I feel small and want you to pick me up in that nice way and fling me down somewhere and love me."

When Ernest said he worried about their fitting into each other's personal ways, Hadley assured him "nothing would satisfy me but to have you deeply and to have you for my surest companion. It's a sad, wonderful thing to find yourself helpless against such a need. . . . Think we'll be good at fitting into each other's personal ways. All mixing of stuff will be charming. Think seeing each other doing the little things to get ready for the day, and seeing them put away for the night, will be so dear. Like the beauty of moonlight, sweeter and lovelier when you don't try to keep your eyes fastened on the moon, exactly. . . . I want to pull your darling head down, let you lie there head down by my side like a little child having to be cuddled in a lonesome moment. Then, after your loneliness has been loved away a little, look at me."

Hadley reported that Kate Smith's uncle, Dr. Charles the oculist, had agreed to give her away. There were "lots of hard feelings," Hadley wrote. "I wish I could have been given away by my brother [Jamie]. . . . But he can't come 'cause he's too hard up and I guess pitiful, too. He's in the sanatorium, for T.B., and he has to return to the sanatorium in the fall."

When Ernest wrote that Hadley was "the most beautiful girl I have ever seen," she replied, "I'm just a red-headed, freckled girl, but I suppose that affection lights up the face for you." The "Corona" she'd promised him could be forgotten about, Ernest wrote, "since it's a great strain on you [financially]." But Hadley insisted, "I'm the fella that's going to give you the Corona." The new poem he'd sent her, a distillation of a short story he'd read to them all in St. Louis, lost none of the story's vitality, Hadley wrote. Ruth Bradfield, to whom Hadley had shown the poem, said she found it "weak." "There's always someone who'll say that sort of thing," Hadley said. "I myself am undecided but lean very heartily toward the new version." Nevertheless, she said, " 'Sweats' [a word Ernest used in the poem] is quite dripping and stark. A chilly line. Do you think so at all? Think that's maybe a childish inflexibility on my part. Just the same. I think it's awfully good. Get an awful lot out of it."

Hadley planned on only a few announcement cards—a hundred or less—and she wanted to know the name of the church where they were going to be married. Also, there was the money. "Those who'll send it instead of gifts or of coming. . . . How practical it will be to get the money."

"We'll be together so soon, a week from this night," Hadley said. "That will be July 27. . . . Saturday's your birthday," Hadley wrote, isn't it? Will you be thirty-one? But glad it's only twenty-three [actually, Ernest was going to be twenty-two]. Like you just that way."

Ernest worried that with all the wedding preparations Hadley was forgetting all about him. "I'm thinking of you even as I work on my wedding dress," she said. Still doubtful, Ernest hinted there was something hidden in her getting his age wrong on the birthday greeting, and Bill Horne was back in Chicago and sick and needed nursing, and why hadn't the birthday Corona arrived yet? Nevertheless, he sent Hadley the "loveliest wedding gift . . . suited to our taste, just what I like: a plain gold watch, not laid down with diamonds . . . nothing to weigh down the soul with responsibility. A plain small (not too small) gold watch with gold grain ribbon and gold clasp. Inscribed, H.R.H. I promise to love you all ways that are pleasant to you, Ernest," Hadley wrote.

On July 25, Ernest sent Hadley a special story. She thought it "the most wonderfully keen and superbly done thing. I simply went wild, wild, wild, wild, wild about it . . . charmed by it, shaken by it. . . . Oin," she went on, "it's—well maybe you don't think of it as well as I do—maybe I better not say it at all. . . . Well, I'm completely under its power . . . simple— but as fine as the finest chain mail. It's the best prose you've ever written that I've seen. Maybe the best of everything. But comparisons is bad things when you get to using words 'better' and 'best,' huh? . . . Don't see how I couldn't go on loving you forever. . . . Don't see how I could ever help myself."

🦋 🦋 🦋 🦋 🦋

The Current—A Story

Stuyvesant Byng grinned at the maid who opened the door, and, as was customary when Stuyvesant Byng grinned, he received an answering smile.

"Miss Dorothy will be down, Mr. Stuyvesant. May I take your things?" She looked after him with more than approbation in her eyes. Women usually looked that way at Stuyvesant. On his way to Dorothy Hadley's that night he had stopped in at a telephone booth and two girls as they came out of the next booth nudged each other as he passed.

"That bird sure does an eye good," remarked the first, following him with her eyes as she drew a lipstick from her vanity bag.

"Yeh, he's too good to be true. I'm weary of them too darn handsome guys. No collar ads in mine. Give me Henry the foundry hand who pays for what he gets, and gets what he pays for." She laughed mirthlessly at her joke.

"Come on Evelyn, don't look at the door where he's went out all night. Handsome Harry has passed out of the picture."

"I guess," said the first, finishing her lipstick operation and considering herself in the mirror of her bag appraisingly, "I guess he was too darn good looking. But I'd like to have a date with him for tonight."

"I'd like to be Lady Astor—but we ain't. We got to blow down to Peccarraro's and maybe we rate a supper. Come on old war horse. We got to shimmy along."

Stuyvesant Byng was unconscious of this of course. He didn't know that women usually looked after him and often commented on him, and tonight he was particularly unconscious of everything, because he was going to Dorothy Hadley's for a very definite purpose. He was going to propose to Dorothy, and he wasn't at all sure what her answer would be.

Stuy had proposed to girls before. Once in a canoe up at the lake, with the moon aiding and abetting, and once in his car going well over fifty miles an hour with one hand on the wheel. But he'd always come out of them all right, and his elder brother had pulled him out of the last one. Let's see. The last one was still quite vivid. He'd proposed aboard Harry's yacht. But he'd had the moon with him then, too; and there had never been any doubt as to the answer. Tonight was different. He was going to propose to Dorothy Hadley, and he had a hunch that she was going to turn him down. He lit a cigarette and substituted smoking for thinking for a moment. Stuyvesant Byng could never be really accused of thinking, but when he smoked he used his brain less than normally.

Then Dorothy came into the room, her hand outstretched. "Hello, Stuy," she smiled at him.

"Howdy, Do," he grinned back and flicked his cigarette into the open fire.

Her hair was the first thing about Dorothy that everyone noticed. It was the raw gold color of old country burnished copper kettles, and it held all of the firelight and occasionally flashed a little of it back. Her hair was wonderful! The rest of her was altogether adorable and Stuy looked at her appreciatively.

"You always look wonderful, Do," he said as she sank into one of the deep leather chairs before the fire. He sat on the arm of her chair and looked down at her glorious hair!

"What have you been doing since you got back Stuy? You haven't been around for ages?" she asked looking up at him. Stuy considered.

"Oh a bunch of us were up on the Nipigon last August. Sam Horne and Martin and Duntley and I. And then I went way up back up of beyond in Quebec with Sam Horne and we got a moose. Sam got it, to tell the truth. And I've been down at Pinehurst just lately dubbing around. Nobody much there."

Stuy took out his cigarette case and offered it to Dorothy. She shook her head. Dorothy was the only girl Stuy knew that didn't smoke, and it always gave him a pleasant feeling to have her refuse. She thought he was merely thoughtless.

"What are you doing in town now Stuy, you old wild man?" Dorothy smiled and stroked his arm. It was peculiar with Dorothy. When she stroked your arm she did just that, she stroked your arm. Other girls—but not Dorothy. It meant nothing to her.

"Came up for the opera," grinned Stuy.

Dorothy laughed tinklingly, like the chiming of one of those Chinese wind bells. "You never went to the opera in your life that you weren't dragged. What are you up for, Stuy?"

"All right, Do. Now's as good a time as any." His voice took on a different tone, his hand rested on her shoulder. She didn't shrink away, but looked steadily up into his eyes. "I love you, Do. I want you to marry me."

His hand still resting on her shoulder, she laughed again but this time not so merrily, and her eyes still looked up at his. "Oh Stuy! You're so funny. I can't marry you. And you don't really love me you know." Stuy's hand had fallen when she said "funny."

"Funny peculiar, not funny ha! ha! I mean," she said gently and put her hand over his. "I think the world of you Stuy. We've always been pals. But you've been in love with twenty girls while we've been palling around. You could never be really in love with any one. And besides, you're too good looking. I've got a snub nose, Stuy. Oh yes I have. I could never marry a man as good looking as you are. I'd never go out and have people say 'Who is that red-haired girl with that wonderful handsome man over there?' "

"You're the most beautiful girl in the world!" said Stuy fervently.

Dorothy smiled quietly at him and pressed his hand. "I wonder how many times you've said that, Stuy? You're fickle, boy. You're inconstant." Her voice was very gentle. "Oh I know I'm hurting you. I guess I mean to. You've never stuck to anything. You play a good game of polo. But you never would stick to it. One year you were runner-up in the National Open. The next year you didn't enter. You play lots better polo than at least two internationalists that I know, and you know the game of golf you can put up. But you're not a sticker, Stuy. And you'd be the same way in anything else. You're a philanderer, Stuy. I know that's an awfully old-fashioned word—but that's what you are old dear." She stroked his arm again.

"Let me say something, Do." Stuy's face was carmine and he was so good looking that Dorothy longed to be in his—well, Stuy was handsome. "I've always loved you Do, ever since we were kids. I loved you from the time you were a little red-haired kid till now. It's been the big thing in my life. It's been the big strong current. It's like a river. The current always flows along, but the wind on the surface makes white caps, and it may look as though the river is flowing the other way. But the white caps are only on the surface. Underneath, the current flows strong, always the same way. My love for you has been the current, and any other girls have only been little waves on the surface. Don't you see, dear?"

"I see, Stuy dear. But seeing isn't believing," said Dorothy very tenderly, and if Stuy had taken her in his arms then the story wouldn't have amounted to much for the reader. "But I'll give you a chance, old boy. You've never stuck to anything. You've always philandered. Pick something out and make an absolute, unqualified success of it. Show you're a champion, not a runner-up. Don't always be an also-ran, Stuy. And then you can come and ask me again."

"Do you mean business?" said Stuy, dolefully.

"Not necessarily. It's no harder than anything else and you've plenty of money anyway. It wouldn't be right to get any more. Anything hard, Stuy. And make a success of it. Be a champion, old boy."

"By Gad, Do, I'll do it." Stuy was on his feet and had Dorothy's hand in his great paw. "I'll do it, Do. And then I'll—."

"Come back here," finished Dorothy for him, and he went out of the room with his mind alight with her smile.

At his room he called up Sam Horne, his best pal. Sam was out. "Ask him to come over as soon as he comes in. It's very important." Stuy hung up the receiver and began to pace up and down. After a while he went over to the cellaret and poured himself a drink. Just then Sam Horne burst in.

"What do you want with me at this time of night, you crazy Bingo? Solitary drinking, eh? Well, we'll soon remedy that. Where's another glass? What's up? Spill it out to Uncle Sam. Some girl going to marry you?" He circled the glass with his hand and put his feet up on the table.

"I've got to be a champion, Sam," began Stuy earnestly.

"Easy!" said Sam. "You cast the best fly on the Nipigon."

"She wouldn't accept that," returned Stuy.

"She, eh?" said Sam. "Oh yes, of course She! Well, who is She? And why have you got to be a champion all of a sudden for She?"

Stuy explained at length. Sam, his feet still on the table, his top hat pushed far back on his head, poured himself out another drink, and as Stuy reached for the bottle Sam's fingers closed around it. "Not for you boy. This isn't the stuff to make champions at anything but elbow crooking. Let's see. You couldn't ever make it at tennis. Not against Johnstone and Johnson and that crew. You might have once at golf, but not anymore. There won't be any polo to speak of for a year. You're out of luck Bingo."

"You've forgotten something, old wiseness," said Stuy.

"No, I hadn't forgotten it. I just didn't know whether to mention it or not. You know what Dawson said about you the last time you were down sparring at the club. 'If Mr. Byng would go into the game there isn't a man in the ring today that could touch him at 154 pounds.' I know that. And I know how much love you have for it."

"She said—something hard," mused Stuy.

"That's hard all right, all right. It's the hardest, dirtiest, worst game in the world Stuy old Bingo," returned Sam.

Stuy got up and assumed a fighting pose. "How does Slam Bing sound as a nom de guerre, Samivel? You see before you, old son, Slam Bing (the late Stuyvesant Byng), the future middleweight box fighter champion of the world," said Stuy impressively.

"Gentlemen, Mr. Slam Bing, the Hoboken Horror," nodded Sam and filled his glass.

The first eight months were awful. Stuy had always hated the thought of fighting, he hated punishment and was always in a cold sweat before he climbed through the ropes. He didn't have to take much punishment, though, for he possessed a left hand that was a shade faster than anything that had ever been seen in the middleweight division before, and a right that wouldn't have been any more effective if it had been ballasted with the concrete-filled glove. He utterly outclassed the first few men he fought in preliminary bouts and soon possessed a more than local reputation. But he hated the whole thing. The smelly dressing room, the crowd, the smoke-filled close halls he fought in, the smell of everything, and all the faces that shone white and red from the ringside seats he loathed.

Sam Horne and old Dawson, who had been sparring partner to Fitz-Simmons, were always with him. Dawson made his matches for him, trained him and counseled him. Sam swung a towel to drive the air into his lungs between rounds, while Dawson sponged off his face and chest and chafed his legs and kneaded his arms and thighs, and poured advice into his ears. Stuy won all his first fights quickly. After the first few set-ups he ran up against some better opposition. He learned what it was to take punishment, to be hit hard and often. He had his first black eye, and he learned the thrill of the knockout. That feeling comparable to none when the perfectly timed punch crashes home, and the man who has been battering you slips down to the resined canvas floor unconscious.

And one night when, after eight rounds of fast and bitter fighting, Stuy's right swung to a spot a little to one side of the point of the jaw of a certain Hebrew Gentleman with an Irish name, and Stuy stooped and putting his gloves under the unconscious Celtic Semite's arms carried him to his corner while the crowded auditorium shouted and yelled for Slam Bing, he realized that he was very near the top of his profession.

"You got him, Bingo! You sure knocked him for a goal, old boy! Oh you've got the old wallop, kid!" Sam exulted as they forced their way through the crowd to Stuy's dressing room. Dawson was following with the bucket, sponge, towels and other paraphernalia. Stuy lay on his back on the couch in his dressing room, breathing heavily while Sam raved.

"Oh boy, when you were lugging toe to toe there in the sixth, I thought little Sammy would go clean off. And when you got him in the eighth, I hit old Dawson so hard I nearly knocked him up into the ring. I fight as hard as you do, Stuy."

"It was a fight," said Stuy in a tired tone. "He was better than I thought. He jolted me a couple of times."

"Yeah, and you jolted him, old Grampas. Eh, Dawson?" to the trainer who was coming in the door.

"Jolted him! You couldn't have hit him any harder if you'd had a fist full of lead. You hit him with everything but the water bucket. You're a heavyweight above the waist, Mr. Byng. That's where you have it on all these other middles. Well, there's only one better than that one you rocked to sleep tonight." He uncorked a bottle of liniment. "We get him next, Mr. Byng. How do you feel?"

"I'm all right, Dawson. But I wish to hell it was over with. All of it. Twice tonight I thought I'd give anything if I wasn't fighting. What do I fight for anyway? I don't have to fight?" he said testily.

"Oh yes you do, Stuy," said Sam quietly.

"Yes I do," said Stuy resignedly. "But how I wish it was all over. When do we take on McGibbons, Dawson?"

"In about a month, Mr. Byng. At New Orleans. It's for twenty rounds."

"You know I never fought twenty rounds, Dawson." Stuy's voice was grouchy.

"You won't have to Mr. Byng neither," grinned Dawson.

In McGibbons Stuy was meeting the champion of his class and one of the greatest, although one of the freakiest fighters that ever entered the squared circle. He was actually Irish, a rare thing in a pugilist nowadays, and was squat-built, with a simian face and the long arms of a gorilla. No one had ever knocked him down, much less knocked him out, and either of his hands carried the deadly knockout potion. He was a past master of every trick of the ring craft and saw no reason why he should not hold the championship for years to come. When his manager spoke to him about a match with Stuy, his ugly ape face was distorted by an evil, fang-revealing grin.

"Society Willie, boy, ain't he a pretty looker? All right, make it for twenty rounds if you can and he'll not be so pretty. Offer him an eighty–twenty split."

After a lengthy session with Dawson, Seidman, Ape McGibbons' manager, returned to his principal. "Did you make it eighty–twenty?" asked the sour Ape.

"I got something better than that, Mac. A winner-take-all. You got it all over this Byng thing. He's a set-up for you. You'll butcher him. Old Alec Dawson that used to spar with the Cornishman is handling him, and I took him for it. That gives you twenty-percent more. Ain't it a good move now, Mac?"

"I said eighty–twenty, you Jew swine. Now what if accidents happen? Why don't you do what I tell you?"

"There won't be no accidents, Mac. Believe you me. There can't be no accidents. There gotta be no accidents! You just knock him for a goal. Won't you now, Mac?"

"I gotta now, you hooker. But eighty–twenty listened a lot better to me. This winner-take-all stuff was all right in the old days when you hadda have it. But eighty–twenty means you get the eighty no matter what happens. And there's always accidents."

"But Mac, listen! There's gotta be absolutely no accidents. You mustn't let there be none. You just rock him off." Seidman combined apology, praise, confidence, and encouragement in his tone.

"All right, I see that. Shut up, will ye?" The Ape's temper was frayed.

During the preliminaries, Dawson, Sam and Stuy were up in Stuy's dressing room. Sam was as cheerful as ever. "In less than two hours you'll be champion of this old world thing, Bingo. And I've got everything that belongs or ever will belong to the Horne family on you to win by a knockout."

"He'll save your money for you, Mr. Horne. And don't try and knock me loose when he puts it over, either. How do you feel, Mr. Byng?"

"I'm all right, Alec. I just feel as though I'd like to call it all off and I'm scared to death and my knees may knock together. Otherwise I'm all right. I'll never fight again, Alec." Stuy was in his fighting trunks and shoes, and wrapped in an old football blanket and a bathrobe.

"You're all right, Mr. Byng. But watch him all the time. Both his left and his right is bad. Keep him away with that left of yours, and don't be sure you've got him till you hear the ref counting. Don't let him fool you that he's in bad shape. And stay away from him! Don't infight him. Knock his can off. We stand to win twenty thousand dollars, Mr. Byng." Dawson illustrated each word of his instructions as he talked. He was by far the most nervous of the three.

"You stand to win twenty thou, you mean, Al. Though I don't think the fighter's percentage will be that much."

"You're too good to me, Mr. Byng. But just remember. Keep away from him. Don't let him fool you, and when you get the chance knock his can off!"

Sam, who had disappeared, poked his head in at the door. "Come on. Our number's up. We're at the post. The wheel is going to spin. Come on, you box fighter. I've got a surprise for you, Stuy. Look over where the women are, you mitt slinger, as you go in. See if you can't notice a spot of color."

"You crazy fool. She isn't here, is she?" snapped Stuy angrily.

"She's nowhere else, Bingo." Sam was joyful.

"Who told you to bring her, you fool?"

"Nobody, it was all my own idea. I have them occasionally. Who are you fighting for, anyway?"

"Oh, you crazy damned fool," moaned Stuy impotently. "I didn't want her to even know about it until it was all over. What if I get crowned?" He was so angry, hopelessly angry, that he didn't notice where he was going and jostled into the outside spectators at the edge of the big indoor arena.

"That's all right. She knows all about it. She's here with her father. I explained all about it and you and the 'hard thing' and all. And Stuy, you aren't going to get knocked for a loop or anything because she is here."

They came down a long sloping aisle to the ring amid a roar of applause from all over the house, punctured by shouts of "Oh, you Slammer!" "You'll get him, Byng!" "Kill the Ape!" Sam reached his stool up through the ropes, and Stuy, after bowing, seated himself on it and leaned back, his eyes searching the crowd.

"Over there," pointed Sam. "Are you blind? Wave to her!" Stuy waved where he could see the sheen of Dorothy's hair and a white splash that must be her face.

There was the usual tiresome wait for the champion to appear, and when he came shuffling down the aisle there was another roar. Then the introductions, the referee called the fighters together in the center of the ring for instructions, then the automatic gong clanged and the fight was on. It was so ghastly white in the ring from the light of the banked arcs that shone down on the canvas.

The Ape's chin was sunk on his chest, his shoulders hunched and his hairy long arms out, the left extended, the right curved. He moved with a queer, flat-footed shuffle, and his little blue eyes always avoided Stuy's.

Stuy, as Dawson said, was a heavyweight above his waist. He had terrific shoulders and long arms and thick wrists. His legs were well shaped but not in proportion with his upper body, and his deep chest had the breathing power of a racehorse. His hair was carefully brushed and his face was, as Dorothy had once said, "too handsome."

As they stepped back from shaking hands Stuy's left hand shot out, like the darting of a spear, into the Ape's face. But the Ape's head twisted sideways and his own right whanged against Stuy's ribs over the heart. "Pretty boy!" said the Ape. "You won't be so pretty, pretty soon." He came tearing in with both hands, and Stuy met him with a straight left that brought him up like a poke in the face with a two-by-four. The Ape rushed again, and Stuy sidestepped, stepped in and brought his right up from the hip to the Ape's jaw. It was the old FitzSimmons shift. The Ape swayed groggily and seemed about to fall. His hands dropped low. Stuy shot a left to his head and stepped forward and crossed the right for the knockout, when he felt a terrific jar and heard dimly the ringing of the gong.

On his stool in the corner where Sam and Dawson had dragged him, he was revived with the smell of aromatic spirits of ammonia in his nostrils, Sam dousing him with water, while a handler he had not seen before shot great sweeps of air into his laboring lungs with flaps of a big towel. "Keep away from him until you know you've got him! Keep away from him! Stall and cover up now! Just hang on. He got you with his left last round as you started to right cross him."

Then came the clang of the gong. His stool was jerked out from under him and he was alone in the ring. But he was not alone, for there was the Ape coming toward him where he stood so unsteadily. He must stall and cover up until his head cleared and this hazy feeling left. He protected his jaw as well as he could while the Ape rushed him and showered punches on him. He dimly thought that he'd never seen so many gloves before. His nose felt huge, he knew that it was bleeding badly down onto his chest. How easy it would be to quit! How long was a round anyway? Only three minutes? It had been three hours already. They were in a clinch now, and the Ape was hooking kidney punches into the small of his back. Each one felt like a kick in the pit of the stomach. The referee broke them apart. There was blood on his silk shirt. Stuy covered up again and went into his shell. The Ape slugged away. How easy it would be to quit! Then he'd have peace and this would all be over. No, there was a current somewhere. He must go with the current. That was all that mattered, the steady current. The current that made things move. Dorothy was here, too. Why, he wondered? Then his head began to clear and a plan formed. The gong sounded and he staggered in a drunken zig-zag to his corner.

Dawson bent over him with the ammonia. Stuy muttered between his swollen lips as Dawson worked on the split nose, and sponged the blood out of his eyes. "I'm all right now, Alec. Two can play that foxing game. I'm going to get him this round!"

When the gong boomed, he went out as groggily as before and retreated under the Ape's smashing attack. He could only see out of one eye now, but he did not attempt a counter blow. Just kept in his shell as much as possible and guarded the jaw. The crowd were yelling for the knockout. After a vicious rush by the Ape he slipped to his knees and heard the referee count. He rose at the count of seven, his hands by his side swaying. The Ape stepped close in a rush to finish the job, an evil look on his face. His punch started and Stuy's right hand came up like a flash from below his waist and crashed on the Ape's jaw with the force of a pile driver. The Ape's face convulsed, he swayed and, as he toppled, Stuy caught him again with a bone smashing swing. The referee counted ten, he might have counted a hundred, and then raised Stuy's gloved right hand above his head. Stuy grinned for the first time in a long time.

The auditorium was a bedlam. Sam had his arm around him and was yelling in his ear. Dawson was pounding him madly on the back. And towards the ring were working their way through the milling crowd a red-haired girl and a gentleman in evening dress.

Stuy slipped through the ropes to the floor and Dorothy was in his arms. "Oh Stuy!" she sobbed. "You're so homely and beautiful with your smashed bloody face. And I love you so. Oh why did you take to fighting? Oh I love you so! You're not a philanderer. You're much nicer than the dying gladiator. Oh I'm talking nonsense! But I love you, Stuy. And oh Stuy, you won't ever fight again, will you?" He pressed her close to him and grinned through his gory mush of a face. "Don't worry, dearest. Don't worry."

⛏ ⛏ ⛏ ⛏ ⛏

≥ 12 ≥
Into Our First World

On Saturday, July 30, Hadley left with Helen and George Breaker for a month-long vacation in Wisconsin at the "Home Camp" of Charles A. Brent, twelve miles west of State Line, Michigan, "in the heart of the big lake woods region." She had been there with the Breakers the summer before, had been ill most of the time, and had dreaded going again. But the honeymoon would be at Windemere, and Hadley wanted to train herself for two weeks in the "wilderness."

On her way north, Hadley stopped in Chicago and spent a week with Ernest. Each day, bumbling against her "smelling so funny—an absolutely adorable mixture of cloves and toilet articles and yourself," he took Hadley to the Commonwealth Cooperative at 128 North Wells Street and up to his office, room 205. At night, Ernest kept Hadley up on the roof, talking to her until he "dozed off," then "woke with a start and started talking again." Hadley showed him her "small creamy iridescences," small and lovely pearls given her by a friend for the "cream and lace wedding dress." Ernest, in turn, showed her the poems he was sending to *The Dial*. Once he chilled Hadley with images that lay beneath all his "good guy" talk of the city and his kisses.

> It is cool at night on the roofs of the city
> The city sweats
> Dripping and stark.
> Maggots of life
> Crawl in the hot loveliness of the city
> Love curdles in the city
> Love sours in the hot whisperings from the pavements.

Love grows old
Old with the oldness of sidewalks.
It is cool at night on the roofs of the city.

The last night on the roof, there was "mist and fireworks . . . and quiet stars and feverish city-lighted 'scrapers around." During their lovemaking, Ernest once said he "remembered being born." "I expect you didn't like it too much," Hadley replied. "No refined child would." Ernest told her in vivid detail how frightened he'd been up on the roof during a thunder-storm one night. Hadley leaned over and kissed him "in the sweetest places." When he bought her a dress of dark voile for their "traveling," she showed him her new lace "nighties."

On August 7, Hadley got to Brent's camp in Cisco-Vilas, Wisconsin. While the porters packed her in, she and Helen Breaker walked the trail to Hardin's Lake: "The woods were great, solemn, tall trees, had little firm young green firs and ground stuff, gray and cold and windy." And yet, "the woods are full of light," she said. "The aromatics stand out, too, on a gray day, something the way colors do, though you don't expect it when there's no sun."

With a comfortable and, she knew, expensive fountain pen Ernest had given her on the station platform, Hadley wrote in her best penmanship the kind of sentiments and details of life in Cisco-Vilas she thought Ernest wanted to hear. Friends of the Breakers, Cornelia and Alfred Prim, were there with their "many children." "Their marriage," Hadley wrote, "is a horrible example of what one might decline into if one simply *loved* children." Cornelia Prim drawled so much "you'd think it was a way of enter-taining you . . . until you find it's a serious congenital matter." Mrs. Prim said that she'd "come up here for the summer 'for my children' " so often that Hadley was "awfully anxious to hurt her feelings." Also, Had-ley had heard from a "feminist" friend staying at the former Winston Churchill estate in Vermont: "Letticia . . . allowed that a really sweet husband takes the place of ten intimate friends. 'There's nothing like love's young dream,' she said. 'You can't tell me enough about it.' " "Of course," Hadley said, "that doesn't induce." Nevertheless, "we ought to ramble through this country [Windsor, Vermont] some day. It's covered with houses of rich patrons and admirers of the arts." Remembering her summer there after freshman year at Bryn Mawr, Hadley wrote, "I've got to get over being hurt by old places. And besides, what is there to hurt now? Only people who have been kind to you no matter how wise it was of you to leave them." Unfortunately, scars from the wounds her mother gave her were still tender, and Hadley boldly added, "There is a new arrival, a peach of a looking girl," who "hollared [sic]" as Hadley sat down on the beach bench alongside the lake under a birch tree. "What kind of fishing do you call that?" the girl asked. "You ought to see this black-haired, crimson-tied beauty jump on her husband's back," Hadley wrote. "And he doesn't seem to mind."

While Hadley and Helen Breaker hiked "through bogs and creeky places in woods on high hills over West Bay, paddled on the lake, and tasted and smelled the water and the winds and the pineness again," Ernest sat in the Chicago heat, grinding away at his "mill." That past week, he wrote, he'd had to drive his boss's "dilapidated Chevrolet" all the way back from Toledo, Ohio, fighting the "error that crept into my bum legs." Now he carried around in his pocket not a bottle of wine but a small flask of the throat remedy "Dioxygen." Worst of all, though, was the "maternal–paternal thing." His father had sent him a strange letter, Ernest wrote: "Give Miss Hadley my sincere congratulations and assure her I want to write to her personally, but mother and the girls think it out of form. I have your rifle in excellent condition and keep it clean. . . . Please tell me dear boy exactly what you want and <u>WHO</u> of the family you wish to be present at the wedding. I have been told that you did not wish me to be present, say so to me and I will know it is so."

Grace, for some reason, was playing "the woman scorned":

> It seems a long time since I've heard from you. Here's hoping all of your plans are going well and that <u>SHE</u> still loves you. Have you seen the long list that the "Trib" is publishing everyday of people who won't trade with Marshall Field anymore? You'll be astonished—lots of prominent names you'll find there in the columns of death notices. Tetah tetah tetah—What do you say, Old Stuff?!!
>
> Write to your Mother <u>soon</u> and tell her <u>EVERYTHING.</u>
>
>
>
> [kiss]

Grace also reminded Ernest to bring a gift for his father's fiftieth birthday. "It is the morning after your wedding," she said.

On August 15, Hadley got the familiar manila envelope in the morning mail. There were more of Ernest's "serious" stories inside. In the accompanying letter, he wrote that he'd "like to take the pain of a baby born for you." Hadley didn't know how to reply to that, except to reassure him: "I love you entirely . . . [and] I am very impressed by the stories you are sending me." "I wish I knew," she wrote, "how to work up a subject, elaborate and spread it out clearly but revealingly in its complexities. . . . If one could only feel as if a light broke over many things; if one could find the scheme behind any subject tackled. I found something like that in music a little once, but you've got a magnificent grip on it—a magnificent grip on the form back of the material no matter how strange it is, like icebergs." "You know," Hadley repeated, "there's a tremendous amount of maternals and paternals . . . in our love for each other."

In early July, Ernest had felt so poor in his head and heart that he had thought seriously of suicide. By mid-August, he was terribly depressed again. Taking advantage of Ernest's talent and his urge to please, the new editor-in-chief at the Commonwealth Cooperative encouraged him to take a hand in everything. As a result, Ernest wrote "5000 true and honest words a day," did Mr. Stockbridge's job for him, and single-handedly produced the whole magazine. The price he paid was "blinding headaches" during the day and his worst insomnia since the war at night. Alone at night, he had trouble controlling himself and thought of all sorts of horrible things. From beginning to end, he'd "imagined," he said, "being a woman dying in childbirth." He couldn't eat; he'd lost eleven pounds.

"Where you make your mistake lover," Hadley said, "is thinking the side of the bed on the roof is empty. I must be with you, go to sleep with my arms around you, all warmed by your loving self." Hadley knew that all winter he'd been " 'kissing the chain' working under unbearable circumstances." She was prouder of his character than "maybe any other section of your beloved being."

When Ernest complained that he didn't get her letters at the right time of day (the best time to "replenish my supply of spirit"), Hadley, to help "fill the well" for him, recalled their last meeting in Chicago and hinted that Ernest was not so dependent upon her as he believed:

> Remember how we spent hours in the office where I could watch this strangely impersonal man moving about, arranging, planning, clicking the typewriter, sometimes seeing him through the ground glass window as a shadow, laying a hand on Stockbridge's door handle, motions of head and hand that did the funny things Oin's familiar lines of action do to my heart, then disappearing into the great main office—leaving me feeling a little at loose ends for a moment—just the foolish way I feel without you at all when I've had you along for a stretch. Wonderful times of hand holding and breathing together and, step, stepping, together. Progress through streets, alive with personalities who almost never reach my "Quick," (Rosenfeld) on account of being so selfishly, deliciously engulfed in you and your companionship. Moments of sitting near you in lobbies, streetcars, rooms, with people, just not talking or anything, just loving you so hard, so longing to get hold of you, to love you with my arms and lips—when a certain look came into your eyes that's often there—though I think the look means that "No one need apply."

Hadley reported that she too had been ill the whole time they'd been apart: "fourteen ulcers in my throat, sores in my tonsils, palate, gums, tongue (big white patches)." She'd taken aspirin, gargled often, and "got painted with Argyrole." But the true relief came at night:

> I dreamt last night of longing for a place that seemed to be for myself alone and was looking over a great, dirty city attic with a gabled roof—full of cast off beds and old chests and drawers and things. In the corner was a small sewing machine, recently used. I was briskly planning to put in a north light and a curtain that would pull all the way back . . . or forward, with a train board. The windows on the west looked out on a back yard full of rusty iron. But this was going to be swell. I could put an upright (piano) there and practice all day as far as the landlady was concerned. I had a couple of shelves lined with books sent to me from Fonnie for the big rug and the ranger-wide divan near the stair with thousands of pillows. When I woke with a start, I realized I was going to live with you, but I enjoyed all this so much that I couldn't leave it alone. So taking you along with me, I went back to the same place, fixed up the place for a typewriter table under the window with a light to come over your left shoulder, etc. A way to cook breakfasts and lots of things. And we liked it.

"I like to place myself all around you," Hadley went on, "and make you feel small. . . . Remember lying on your back and me sitting about you in the niche of your hip and the crook of your arm where I could read or talk to you . . . and stroke back hair from forehead and pet wrists or pay um the way we said in cool water." When Ernest wrote that he'd invited his old girlfriend from Toronto, Bonnie Bonnelle, to the wedding, and that Marjorie and her sister Georgiana (Pudge) Bump and Grace Quinlan were coming too, Hadley replied, "I believe you like to tell me those things, or want to, or have to or something." "Anyway," she said, "I notice your skin when you mention the names."

"Sick as we both are," Ernest and Hadley looked forward to their honeymoon as a time to recuperate "from the onslaught of the summer." They wanted "great gusts of perfectly untrammeled living . . . no working except what the fooling is we have to do to run this here Windemere." Two weeks before the wedding, however, something "terrible" happened to Ernest. There would be no living in Kenley Smith's apartment now, he said. That night, Kenley's wife, Doodles, had come around. She'd said she wanted someone to talk to and needed advice. What she really needed, Ernest wrote, he loved Hadley too much to give her. "That's not so terrible nor so surprising," Hadley replied. Didn't Ernest know of Doodles's condition, or about her and Dirty Don Wright? "Of course I remember any number of absolutely improper scenes between Doodles and Wright. . . . One that evidently was completely improper," Hadley wrote, "was when they heard me coming, Wright rushed out from the dining room to meet me, stuttering with terror and laughing hysterically." Doodles sat smug and languid on the couch; Kenley lay reading in his room.

But there was more to Doodles's visit than her proposition, Ernest wrote. She had said to him in anger that he should not be "fooled" by Hadley, that he should ask her about herself and Dirty Don Wright. On Saturday morning, August 20, two weeks before the wedding, Hadley explained:

> At dinner at Kenley's one night (you weren't at the table, you may be sure, or he wouldn't have dared) Wright kept asking me in the most suggestive manner, did I remember one night (my first visit). Did I remember we were sitting out in Nicco Philes's room and I said, 'Blank.' We were walking down State Street and he asked me, 'Blank.' and I answered, 'Blank.' Then I thought all this Blank and these sentences were so ridiculous, and funny, that I laughed and said, honestly, that I didn't remember. And he nodded complacently, as though my laughter had been acquiescence. See? And said, "mighty convenient memory you've got, Hash."
>
> You know I actually believed that man was trying to make out there had been a lot between us. Raked over his memory. You can always think up words, you know, that sound damning and everybody knew meant nothing at all, nothing at the time. Well, I can recall, for instance, coming home from supper and a visit to some bookshop with him, and as we zipped along arm and arm, feeling jolly and congenial, this hobo says to me, 'Well, you and I are getting nearer marrying every day, Hash.' Which remark I poohed off of course, and wouldn't even consider that Wright had intended to marry me. Lord but that would be fun to hold 'agin him, though, as an important statement in the progress of one's acquaintance. Also, I know a lot of familiarity he daily attempted. I suppose because I let him kiss me. So finally I cut out the kissing, as you know. Then, if he hated me so (and I really think Don was quite entertained by me, truth to tell) why the rather unusual invitation to come to Chicago and spend two weeks in a hotel without letting any of you all know? And let him really show me a good time? Huh? How about it? If that was hatred it was abnormally deep? Do you suppose I'd ever do that for a moment? Yeh, I think he hoped I would. . . . I think you'll get Kenley back some day. . . . That's the reason we don't want to do anything too outspoken about the break up.

Ernest wrote back that he'd do two things to Don Wright. First he'd tell Dirty Don that the lovely Doodles propositioned everyone, and then he'd cauliflower his ear and break his jaw. Instead, at Hadley's request, Ernest left Kenley's apartment the next day and moved in with Krebs Friend.

Before he would meet Hadley in Horton Bay, Ernest said he needed that one more fishing trip with his friends. To her surprise, he asked neither

Bill Smith (his fishing buddy for years) nor Bill Horne. Instead, he invited Charles Hopkins, his mustachioed friend from the *Kansas City Star,* and Howell Jenkins, now a confirmed misogamist. For three days, Ernest rose just after dawn, made his buckwheat cakes and coffee, caught his supply of hoppers clinging as if they were dead to the stems of grass in the meadow, caught his trout ("clear, water-over-gravel color, [their] sides flashing in the sun"), carefully wet his hand before touching the delicate mucus-covered skin of those too small to keep, and watched them rest on the gravel and then be "gone in a shadow across the bottom of the stream." Aside from their conventional propaganda (marriage ruins a talented young man, cuts him off from all the best times and from his friends), Ernest discovered that "Hop-Head" and "Jenks" now had little to offer him besides a sure-fire recipe for good coffee.

Ernest got back to Horton Bay on August 27, three days before Hadley was to arrive. He was glad to learn that Bill Horne was already there, staying with Kate Smith on Pincherry Road. His mother, Grace, was there too, and, shuttling from Windemere, she had already made extensive plans. The unused Methodist Church, which looked funereal beside the General Store, had to be stuffed with flowers and filled with people. She delegated bridesmaids Ruth Bradfield and Kate Smith to supply the flowers. Since many of the "best" Oak Park families had declined to make the trip north, she invited almost everyone in the little town.

On September 7, Hadley and the Breakers got to Horton Bay. Hadley's throat was still so sore she could hardly swallow. But since her hair was too long for Ernest, she had Helen Breaker cut it and then washed it in the frigid lake. "Forsaken" came to mind when Hadley saw the church she'd be married in.

The night before the wedding, Ernest discouraged a bachelor party and instead stayed with "Stut" (Kate Smith) and "Horney Bill" (Bill Horne). The three of them lay in the big bed in the front room at Pinehurst and drank and talked. Against an impulse to be sentimental, Bill remarked how stylish it would be if, as Hadley had suggested, all the men wore white flannel trousers. Kate, with gentle cynicism, mocked Ernest's appearance. He'd come to look, she said, like a young, slim Flemish poet instead of the hard, brown, eye-wrinkled, tolerant man she'd expected him to be. Kate said she had hated decorating the church for Mrs. Hemingway, and she had shown it. But for the wedding she would act as though Ernest had been nothing but a friend. In a year, maybe two, Kate said, Ernest would be phoning her to come and "hold the home together."

At three o'clock Saturday afternoon, September 3, Grace Hemingway, dressed in a flowered tunic, a golden sash around her waist, packed Clarence and three of her children into Warren Sumner's fringed-topped, mule-drawn surry. It was a four-mile ride over sandy roads from Grace Cottage to Horton Bay. Nineteen-year-old Ursula, repelled by Sumner's countenance, sat in the rear with Leicester and Carol. (Marcelline, on vacation in New Hampshire, had asked Ernest to reserve her a place at Pinehurst and had gotten no reply.) Clarence, in tails, sat up front with Sumner, made small talk, and sweated though the air was crisp and cool.

The wedding party gathered under the tall elms across from Jim Dilworth's red blacksmith shop. Hadley's matron of honor was her sister Fonnie; the maids were Helen Breaker, Ruth Bradfield, and, bright green eyes over bright green dress, Kate Smith. Ernest's "groom men" (at the last minute he'd refused to select a "best man") were Bill Horne and Kate's brother, Bill Smith. Harriet Connable and her son, Ralph, were there, standing quietly amid the Horton Bay gentry as if they were waiting for a train. Unattended and curious, an assortment of local "kids" clumped giggling about the edges of the crowd. One, Bill Olhe, had interrupted Ernest's letter writing on the steps of Pinehurst the summer before and had been treated to a fable to explain the drawn signature, "Stein."

By four o'clock, the procession to the church was over, the family and guests were seated, and Ernest stood with Bill Horne and Bill Smith in dust-filled beams of sunlight, waiting for the bride. Just as people began murmuring and turning around, Hadley appeared. Even on the arm of George Breaker, who was dressed and beaming like a George M. Cohan dandy, she looked radiant. Ernest's sister Ursula was so impressed that she wanted to applaud, and ten-year-old Carol thought Hadley the loveliest woman she had ever seen.

After a long reception at Pinehurst (the huge wedding cake took forever to cut, and drinks were made by passing the flask), Clarence insisted on taking, in the fading light, as many pictures as he could. Just before dark, John Ketoskey beat Lester Fox in offering the services of his Ford. Ernest kissed his father and shook hands with his mother, and everyone laughed. Then he and Hadley rode down to Grace Cottage and took the rowboat *Marcelline* to Windemere.

Ernest had promised Hadley that their honeymoon would last two weeks. They were ill and tired, he said; they could nurse each other back to health. But from the time they entered Windemere, Ernest searching for a kerosene lamp in his father's room, things went wrong. First, there was a letter on the fireplace mantel from Grace. Ernest pocketed it quickly before Hadley noticed. Later they ate spoiled canned meat for supper. The next day they both came down with what Ernest diagnosed as the "floo."

Toward the end of the first week, when he was well enough, Ernest walked down to Resort Pike Road and hitched a ride into Petoskey for provisions. Unfortunately, he "bumped into a bootlegger" he knew, got very drunk (all the more so for being sick, he said), and bought only four pounds of steak. Hours later, back at Walloon, he found a speedboat moored at the village dock. Bursting off at full throttle, Ernest neglected to cast off from the piling, and the powerful boat skied the debris all the way to Windemere. Hadley, feeling worse than alone with her husband gone, had started out on foot through the woods to Petoskey. Down by the Indian camp, she watched through the trees as Ernest roared by.

Just before the wedding, Hadley had teased Ernest, "When you go to introduce me to strangers, you'll probably be too proud to say, 'This is my wife.' You'll get up something more casual, something like 'I want you to meet my friend, Hadley, the spirit that inhabits the attic room.' Or 'Meet Bacchante; we're living together this year.'" Back at the cottage that night, Hadley said that maybe Ernest's drunken afternoon confirmed her fears. But Ernest asked to be forgiven; they built a deep pine fire against the September chill and laughed about the meat. Then Ernest dragged the mattresses from his parents' separate beds and set them together before the hearth.

Epilogue

The last week of September 1921, Ernest and Hadley moved into an apartment, a fifth-floor walkup in the 1300 block of Clark Street on Chicago's North Side. The weather was dismal cold, the flat dingy, the furniture shabby and stale. A year before and ten blocks away, Ernest had sought security. Now, with a wife and his freedom (he had quit the Commonwealth Cooperative when it seemed certain there would be charges of fraud), he wanted to start his career.

Each morning, Ernest rose at dawn, emptied his chamber pot, and cooked the breakfast eggs in it. Then, on the dinette table, he labored over his Nick Adams novel until noon. Because the grimy kitchen repelled Hadley, they ate monotonous meals at a diner almost every day.

One afternoon in October, Grace Hemingway arrived unannounced. She intended her visit to be inspirational. But, perhaps because of the boardinghouse atmosphere, her harangue on the joys and duties of matrimony did not quite come off. Several days later, Clarence paid an early call. Unfortunately, the eggs were boiling in Ernest's chamber pot, and his stay was brief. Clarence said he had come to protest Ernest's payment of the debt he owed to Windemere. The agreement was the family provisions for two weeks in exchange for Ernest's Marlin .22. True to his word, Ernest had left the weapon at Windemere but had ruined it, according to Clarence, by trying to shoot out a clog in the bore.

There was one visitor to the Clark Street flat who brought good news. Nick Neroni, Ernest's wartime buddy and boxing friend, told of Italy's commander in chief, General Diaz's, upcoming visit to Chicago. There would be a big parade, Neroni said (which he would lead), and afterward the presentation of the Silver Medal for Valor to Ernest by General Diaz himself.

On a rainy Saturday morning at the end of a short parade, Ernest, according to Marcelline (she and Grace and Clarence were in attendance), accepted the decoration with "becoming modesty." With it came an annual pension of fifty lire for life and the honor of being cousin to the king. Listening to the general's speech, filled with patriotic vagaries, Ernest remembered speeches he had heard in Italy "sometimes standing in the rain almost out of earshot, so that only the shouted words came through," or speeches he had read as "proclamations that were slapped up by billposters over other proclamations."

There was one bit of spring in that first season of Ernest's married life. It came from his avuncular friend, Sherwood Anderson. On May 14, 1921, Sherwood, his second wife Tennessee, and the wealthy Paul Rosenfeld (Rosenfeld paying the fare) had sailed to France. There Anderson had met Gertrude Stein, "who in her own large room in the house at 27 rue de Fleurus in Paris" was "an honest to god worker in words. . . . She is making new, strange, and to my ears, sweet combinations of words," he told Ernest. She has the "loving touch in her strong fingers," like women Anderson had watched baking in the brick kitchens of his boyhood. Miss Stein had a sweet and generous aroma, like green, healthy growing things, and had a mysterious smile like the Mona Lisa. Sherwood told Ernest that he had an "undying faith" in what she was up to in her word kitchen in Paris. Was she a salvific woman? Ernest wondered. Sherwood didn't know. But she was making "something sweet to the tongue and fragrant to the nostrils . . . laying word against word, relating sound to sound, feeling for the taste, the smell, the rhythm of the individual word." What did she look like? Ernest asked. "She has red cheeks," Sherwood said, "sturdy legs, and the table was clean." Sherwood, too, had made quite an impression on Miss Stein. She loved his warm, brown "Italian" eyes.

In contrast to Gertrude Stein's Buddha—she was awfully heavy, Anderson noted, and she had the face of an Indian man—he had met a sparrow or a chickadee. She was Sylvia Beach, and she ran a bookstore called *Shakespeare and Company* at 12 rue de l'Odéon. One day he had stopped before the window because *Winesburg, Ohio* was prominently displayed. It was the first evidence he had seen of himself in Paris. Inside he found promotional displays of works by Ezra Pound (arranged by the author himself) and discovered that Miss Beach would personally publish James Joyce's notorious *Ulysses* early the next year.

When Hadley heard that Sherwood Anderson had recommended Paris, she was overjoyed. She knew Ernest respected Anderson's judgment, and she knew Italy was, for Ernest, a mirage. What about all their lire? Ernest protested. It was wonderful that he had saved it, Hadley said. It could easily be converted to francs. Perhaps her concern about childbearing made Hadley want the country of "twilight sleep." No, Hadley said.

He'd give birth before she would, and for him Paris was the place to do it.

Just before Thanksgiving 1921, Kate Smith, Bill Horne, Howell Jenkins, Marcelline, and Clarence said farewell to Ernest and Hadley at the
La Salle Street Station. To Hadley, her knuckles turned white by the cold
pullman's railing, Marcelline yelled, "Put on your gloves."

"I'll be in New York soon," Hadley replied. "I don't need 'um."

Marcelline rolled her own woolen gloves into a ball and threw them
aboard. "That's a going away present," she said. Hadley caught them and
smiled.

Then, with a clank and jolt, the train was moving, and Ernest, his arm
around Hadley's waist, waved a quiet goodbye. Suddenly, Howell Jenkins,
Ernest's five-foot comrade from Section IV, tore off his muffler, wadded it
into a ball, and tossed it to Ernest. "That's my going away present to
you," he said. Perhaps Jenkins did this only to emulate Marcelline. Yet
he may have wanted to express a sense of an ending, his intuition that
for Ernest and Hadley old friends and familiar places were now the past.

In early 1922, a few months after he and Hadley had settled in Paris
in a filthy fourth-floor flat at 74 rue Cardinal Lemoine, Ernest wrote as
though he felt much the same way:

Along with Youth

A porcupine skin,
Stiff with bad tanning,
It must have ended somewhere.
Stuffed horned owl
Pompous
Yellow eyed;
Chuck-wills-widow on a biased twig
Sooted with dust.
Piles of old magazines,
Drawers of boys' letters
And the line of love
They must have ended somewhere.
Yesterday's Tribune is gone
Along with youth
And the canoe that went to pieces on the beach
The year of the big storm
When the hotel burned down
At Seney, Michigan.

For the rest of his life, Ernest would return to Oak Park fewer than
a half-dozen times, his longest stay a week to bury his father. He would

drive through Michigan, stopping to ask directions in Petoskey in 1949. Jim Gamble would get two more letters from Ernest; Bill Horne, a cross-country trip to Wyoming in 1929. Kate Smith would visit Ernest at his home in Key West, Florida, to celebrate the completion of *A Farewell to Arms* and meet a man she would one day marry, John Dos Passos. Agnes Kurowsky would always be ignored.

And yet, in one sense, Ernest did not leave his youth behind that cold morning on the New York train. True to his belief in the artist's work—"Make all that come true again"—Ernest mined those early years for some of his best fiction: "Indian Camp," the story of a cesarean birth and a suicide in a bark peelers' shack where young Nick Adams learns more than he can stand; "The Doctor and the Doctor's Wife," in which Nick shares the humiliation as his "civilized" father (made so by a mother who spends her days in a darkened room) is defeated in a battle of wills by a half-breed sawyer; "Ten Indians," in which young Nick learns from his father that Prudence Boulton is as happy thrashing about in the underbrush with Frank Washburn as she is thrashing about with him; "Big Two-Hearted River," in which Nick rebuilds his war-ravaged mind as he carefully catches his grasshoppers, pitches his tent, casts his line; *A Farewell to Arms,* the story of what Ernest won and lost in Italy in 1918.

There was one story from his youth Ernest was never quite able to tell. In an almost incoherent draft, a precursor of *For Whom the Bell Tolls,* he revealed how much it would have meant if Grace Hemingway had not made him try to earn her love.

As the story begins, the hero—a "tired, fought-out" soldier named Orpen—lies on his stomach behind some cover on a hill. Orpen is keeping watch over a key bridge which should have been blown. Suddenly out of the fog comes a thrust of graycoats. Orpen and the men with him begin to fire, and the enemy withdraws. Orpen himself kills a cyclist. "You pressed the trigger, some one died and somehow you didn't feel bad about it." "Ether in the brain," he decides.

During the lull in the fighting, Orpen thinks of his hands. He had wanted, he says, to be a famous pianist and play at Albert Hall. He compares the digital dexterity needed to "play" the machine gun with that needed by a pianist. Then he recalls sitting in the "music room" at home. His mother would listen while he played Chopin for her. "That's so sweet my dear," she would say. "Will you play some more. I just don't see any sense to Schönberg, my dear. Should I?"

Before he recovers from his reverie, there is another attack, and Orpen is wounded. This happens several times, and each time he becomes more deeply delirious. First, he believes the battle is a symphony for drums. Next, he sees the men in the orchestra rise up and sink down. Then men run at his bayonet.

But his deepest delirium, which is the matter of the rest of the story, is a "dream" that finds Orpen fighting in an ancient war. Shields, swords, and pikes are used. Suddenly, one of the combatants, a big man in a plumed helmet, roars, "Hold! We quench our thirst awhile." Then all the soldiers come toward Orpen. "Hail, O hero," the big man cries. "For thou also kept a bridge well," and he holds out his mailed hand. Orpen grasps it and replies, "How do you do?" "We fare well here O hero," is the big man's answer.

Orpen beholds about him strange faces, strange accoutrements. He knows, because he had read a story like this once, that he is dead. The big man tells Orpen that he is in Valhalla, the Hall of Heroes, higher than heaven, and that all the famous heroes are there (Lord Nelson, decorated with medals and gold brocade, Eric the Red, Drake, Raleigh, Sherman, Khan, Washington, Grant, Bonaparte, Ney, Crockett, Jackson, Custer). In Valhalla these heroes all fight for the fun of it, and no one dies. "There is the fun of killing, but none of the drawbacks of dying."

Soon an absurd quarrel develops among the noble citizens of Valhalla, and they fall to battling with great vigor and with, it appears, great enjoyment. Orpen, however, wants to get out. But he feels no one will understand. "You had to pretend to like it." At one point, George Washington rides up to Orpen and makes a silly joke. Orpen drives his bayonet into Washington's groin. But Washington only laughs, "Great fun," spurs on his horse, and thrusts his sword into Orpen's chest.

Finally, Orpen decides to stop the "hateful game." He says he even wishes he hadn't died a hero's death after all. Soon he withdraws and wanders moodily in a thicket. Then he stops for a time to rest. When Orpen starts off again, there is moonlight, and he finds steps leading down from Valhalla to heaven. He comes upon a country lane. "It looked much like the lane at home to Orpen with great elms meeting overhead. Moonlight dappled the dust of the road and the night was warm." He notes that an arm of the sea juts close to the road, and as he passes Orpen hears voices. "Plenty of bait and we'll start bright and early," he hears someone say. "They'll be running good tomorrow," another voice answers.

"There are the soft sounds of waves and a glowing in the half dark." In this glow Orpen can see a little man walking in a garden with a woman. "This, sweetest one," he is saying, "is my life. The garden, the roses, the smell of honeysuckle on the hedge, the warm night." "And me beside you, Horatio?" the woman asks. "Yes, and you beside me," he says. But now the man (Horatio Nelson) has only a plain black suit on. Suddenly Orpen turns away. "He seemed to know his way without hesitation" to a door. "He turned the handle and entered. A woman smiled at him." "Mother," he said. "I've been a long way." "I knew you'd get here son," she said. "Look!" Then the mother points across the room to the old concert grand piano. She tells Orpen that all his materials are still there. "I've kept them . . . waiting. There is pen and ink." Orpen is delighted because he believes, "Now I can really go on with the symphony tomorrow." But then he remembers. "I got to fight tomorrow in Valhalla—to cut to slice is the greatest joy of man." But his mother only smiles at him "like the mother of all wisdom." Nevertheless he persists. "Today we slashed and slashed. I ran George Washington through as I battled down the road to you." He claims that "the joy of battle was in my heart." Still his mother smiles understandingly.

At this point Orpen becomes angry. He insists that his mother believe he enjoyed the warfare. But when she does not, "somehow before he knew it he was on his knees before her and she was holding his head." Then Orpen confesses, "It wasn't wonderful mother. It was horrible. I wanted to stay and do my music mother. I don't want to be in Valhalla!" Then his mother strokes Orpen's head. "It was like being a boy again," Orpen reveals. "I know son. I know," his mother says.

Orpen's mother now reveals to him that all the heroes who had appeared to enjoy the fighting so much in Valhalla are happily residing in peace at her home. They are all bored with fighting, his mother says; they only go up to Valhalla to welcome a new hero. There are many now, she observes, because of the world war.

After his mother shows him the medals she's kept for him, medals he was awarded for his hero's death, she promises Orpen, "You can stay here and work on your music." Now Orpen realizes he is in heaven and is suddenly so happy that he dances. "It was a curious dance—great high leaps in grace note form with quaver duration. Orpen leapt high in the air— higher than ever before." Soon, however, he experiences a pain in his chest where George Washington had stabbed him. Another, and he is awake. The first words he says, as a small rectangular piece of shrapnel is removed from his chest, are, "Tell them I don't want to go back to Valhalla." A woman's voice replies, "No, you won't have to."

On June 22, 1951, Ernest heard from his sister Madelaine that Grace Hemingway was dying. (He knew that Grace had advanced atherosclerosis; she had been senile for years.) Madelaine, whose care of her mother had been paid for by the annuity Ernest had given Grace since the thirties, asked if he would be coming to the hospital in Memphis, Tennessee.

Ernest Hemingway was in Cuba, at his *Finca Vigia,* his "Lookout Farm," when his mother died on June 28. But he saw to it that the bells at a nearby Catholic church tolled at dawn the day she was buried.

Sources and Notes

Chapter 1

SOURCES

Grace Hemingway faithfully recorded much of what she saw and thought she understood of Ernest's first eighteen years in five "Memory Books." The books date from his birth on July 21, 1899, to July 21, 1917. They are filled with intimate anecdotes expressed with a diarist's candor. Beside her lovely Victorian hand, Grace placed on almost every page of the second and third volumes pieces of childhood memorabilia, so carefully pasted in that they are still secure after eighty years. She included silhouettes of boats, animals, guns, and spears Ernest cut out in 1902; an abstract drawing, loop intersecting loop, in crayon of various colors, Ernest entitled, though he had never heard it, "The Roar of the Sea"; valentines of hearts and paper lace Ernest and "Mary W." made in 1903; a beautifully composed watercolor of a fir tree, the horizon, and a cloud. Grace sealed in an envelope a cutting from Ernest's first "short" haircut, February 15, 1906, with the notation: "He can now never wear long hair again as he is 6½ years and at school. My precious boy, a 'real' boy." Grace enclosed in Memory Book III an unusual letter, hand delivered, dated April 9, 1911, which contained the correspondent's photograph and a popular verse—"I would be true for there are those who trust me / I would be pure for there are those who care"—from one Robert J. Hamilton, who signed himself "friend of boys."

Memory Book V, Grace's record of Ernest's life from "15 years, 5 months (December 21, 1914)" to eighteen years is different from the other four. In it two new voices appear: Ernest's and Marcelline's. By and large, Ernest is gentle toward the family, and humorous:

Dear Folks,
   Please bring home my photos which are on the north end of the fireplace in an envelope addressed to me.
Please do this.

P.S. I pawned my shoes to buy this card.

227

Marcelline is bitterly jealous of him:

> Ernie dear,
> Please come here
> Emily's nice from far and near
> Can't you hear her calling dear!
>
> I'll kiss you again with Joy
> Come to Lacross, my precious boy!
> I've got lots of beaux, but I want a new toy!
> Ernie come!

(Parents' advice)

> Nutsy Ernie loves a Jane
> Jane, she loves another.
> Ernie sits and crys all day
> Runs crying to his Mother.
> She don't love me no more.
> (Weeps)
>
> Never mind dear (Mother tweets)
> Mother loves her precious boy
> Dad's child and parents' Joy!
> Frances knows not a good thing
> When she sees it on the wing
> Love your parents, earn some corn
> Then all the girls will love Sweet 'Oin.

(Marcelline also wrote a story about a fabulous snake—for the *Senior Tabula*, 1916, Oak Park High's literary magazine—which in Freudian terms reads like a case study of sexual repression.)

One other entry is relevant here. When Ernest and Lewis Clarahan returned from a long hike, Grace wrote, "They did not walk much on the way." Next to these words, there is, in Ernest's mature hand, "That is Bunk. We walked 130 miles."

In 1955, Marcelline Hemingway Sanford attended a lecture given at the Town Hall in Detroit by Edward Weeks, a noted scholar. Weeks spoke about twentieth-century American literature and made some comments on Ernest Hemingway's work and life. Marcelline, although she generally resented biographers' intrusions, was so impressed by Week's talk that when he was seated next to her at the luncheon that followed, she was cordial and loquacious. Marcelline spoke of her parents, of family life at Windemere and in Oak Park. Weeks thought her story so "lively and colorful" he urged her to write it. For the next six years, Marcelline did just that. Ironically her book was ready for publication in late 1961, a few months after Ernest had committed suicide.

In one sense Marcelline's work, *At the Hemingways* (Boston, 1962), is very much like her mother's Memory Books. As observant and obtuse as Grace, Marcelline presents the first years of family life with Ernest Hall in the Hall–Hemingway household, portraits of Clarence and Grace Hemingway and of young Ernest, life in "Mother's house" on Kenilworth Avenue, the summers at Walloon Lake, and the years at Oak Park High in rich, unvitiated detail. She challenges her material infrequently. When she does, after a brief struggle, she surrenders to a cliché. Perhaps beneath her self-assurance (she ends her book with an imagined quotation from Grace: "I always said all my children had real ability"), Marcelline knew her prejudices and her limitations. One real insight, however, should not be denied her! "My Grandfather [Ernest Hall] could do no wrong in Mother's eyes."

NOTES

Memorial service for Ernest Hall and six-year-old Ernest's remark, "I'm the son of the son of a better one": Grace Hemingway, Memory Book II, which, along with four others, is in the Hemingway Collection, John F. Kennedy Library, Dorchester, Mass. Memory Books are not paginated by Grace Hemingway.

Biographical information on Ernest Hall: Marcelline Hemingway Sanford, *At the Hemingways* (Boston, 1962), pp. 3–16. Marcelline's account contains several factual errors. For example: "He [Ernest Hall] served throughout the four years of the Civil War," and "When he was offered a pension by the United States Government, he firmly refused it, saying proudly, 'I gave my services to my adopted country. I did not sell them.'" Ernest Hall, in fact, served six months with the First Iowa Cavalry, and shortly before he died he applied for and was granted a War Department pension of six dollars a month for "partial disability." (See pages 10 and 11 in text). For years there had been a rumor in Oak Park that Ernest Hemingway's maternal grandfather was a deserter. His "Certificate of Disability for Discharge," the "First Iowa Cavalry Muster Rolls," and Ernest Hall's "Declaration for Original Invalid Pension" prove that he was not. Ernest Hall's life on the Mississippi, the fact that he lived in Dyersville, Iowa, at the time Mark Twain lived in the downriver town of Keokuk and that both served in Missouri early in the war (see "The Private History of a Campaign That Failed," in *The Great Short Works of Mark Twain,* ed. Justin Kaplan (New York, 1967) pp. 144–62), lightly suggests a source for Ernest Hemingway's intense interest in Twain's *Old Tunes on the Mississippi* and in Twain himself.

Ernest Hall and Caroline Hancock: Sanford, pp. 7–9. It is curious to note that Grace Hemingway, conceived just after the Great Chicago Fire, enjoyed burning what she considered household rubbish. Ernest once rallied her on this account: "Please don't burn any papers in my room or throw any thing away that you don't like the looks of, and I will do the same for you. Much Love, Ernie." See also "Now I Lay Me," in *The Short Stories of Ernest Hemingway* (New York, 1966), pp. 365–66.

Grace Hemingway's childhood and youth: Sanford, pp. 49–53; letter, "Grace Hall-H." to "My Dear Ernest Boy," April 3, 1920: "Your billiard experiences remind me of the days when my father and I used to play every evening. We had a billiard table in our home when I was a girl but Daddy was such a superb player that he always had to give me an [illegible] handicap. Still he was always proud that I could play with him, and we enjoyed each other's company so much."

Clarence Hemingway and Grace Hall's Courtship: Sanford, pp. 55–56; photographs of old Oak Park from *Halley's Pictorial Oak Park, 1898;* "Fathers and Sons," in *The Short Stories of Ernest Hemingway,* p. 489; Anson Hemingway's service record with the Union Army in the Civil War and his application for a pension from General Services Administration, Record Services, Washington, D.C.

Clarence Hemingway's college and medical school career: Oberlin College records, 1890; Rush Medical School records, 1893.

Grace Hemingway and Stephen Crane: Conversation with Edward Stephenson, Hemingway and Crane specialist, Canisius College, Buffalo, N.Y.; portrait of Grace in low-cut satin gown from Sanford, p. 57; photograph of Grace at debut from Memory Book II (inserted just before final page).

Birth of Ernest Hemingway: Sanford, p. 17; Carlos Baker, *Ernest Hemingway: A Life Story* (New York, 1969), p. 3; Ernest's appearance as an infant from Memory Book I.

Life in the Hall–Hemingway household: Sanford, pp. 14–15; Memory Book I; Memory Book II; author's visit to 439 North Oak Park Avenue, July 8, 1979; Sanford, pp. 3, 21; "Now I Lay Me," in *The Short Stories of Ernest Hemingway,* p. 365.

Family life at Windemere: Madelaine Hemingway Miller, *Ernie; Hemingway's Sister "Sunny" Remembers* (New York, 1975) pp. 43–44; Sanford, pp. 68–69; Ernest Hemingway, untitled, unpublished novel (ca. 1927), not paginated by author; "Fathers and Sons," in *The Short Stories of Ernest Hemingway,* p. 496.

Ernest Hall's death: Sanford, p. 103; *Harrison's Principles of Internal Medicine,* 10th edition, eds. Robert G. Petersdorf et al. (New York, 1983), pp. 1628–43.

Longfield Farm: Sanford, pp. 87–88; Baker, p. 7; Ernest Hemingway, heretofore unpublished character sketches (see p. 127) entitled "Cross roads." A most autobiographical writer, Hemingway was especially accurate on "country." He wrote to his father referring representatively to "The Doctor and the Doctor's Wife" (*In Our Time,* New York, 1925, pp. 23–27), that "the country is always true."

Grace's house: Sanford, pp. 103–8; Miller, pp. 5–7; author's visit to Oak Park, Illinois, July 7–12, 1979, for interviews with the current owner of 600 North Kenilworth Avenue, Mrs. Arthur Burns, who has turned the second floor into her own apartment, closed the third, and rented the first. Al Gini, the tenant, has the famous Alfred Eisenstadt photograph of Ernest—"Endurance"—displayed as a poster on the living room wall.

Grade-school years: Leicester Hemingway, *My Brother, Ernest Hemingway* (Cleveland, 1961), pp. 30–31; Sanford, pp. 103–21.

Harold Sampson: Baker, pp. 7–8; Memory Book IV; Harold Sampson's letter to Ernest.

Robin Hood: Baker, p. 15; Sanford, photograph between pages 60 and 61.

Class prophecy: Memory Book III. Ernest revised the manuscript before presentation. All of the "victims" are girls.

Clarence and Ernest in Oak Park: Sanford, pp. 119–20; *The Torrents of Spring* (London, 1933), p. 32.

Birth of Carol Hemingway: Conversation with Madelaine Hemingway Miller, July 18, 1980, en route from Boston to western Massachusetts, where Ernest's youngest sister Carol lives.

Paragraph on mother and father: Excised from published version of "Fathers and Sons." Early draft #383 Hemingway Collection, JFK Library.

Tent at Windemere: Miller, pp. 41–42; Sanford, pp. 99–100; author's visit to Windermere, October 7–10, 1980.

Chapter 2

SOURCES

As with the family history and the story of Ernest's childhood, so Ernest's years at Oak Park High are most intimately rendered by Marcelline Hemingway Sanford's *At the Hemingways* (Boston, 1962), pp. 122–46, and by Grace Hemingway's remembrances in Memory Book V. But there are other sources for these years: men and women who knew Ernest in his teens and still remember him well. The author was fortunate to be able to interview in their homes three of Ernest's fellow students at Oak Park High: Lewis Clarahan, Sue Lowery Kesler Crist, and the renowned biographer and critic, Edward Wagenknecht.

It is difficult to characterize the nature of these interviews. Clarahan and Crist, both lifelong residents of Oak Park, had been questioned so many times that they had created a series of "statements," a presentation, no matter what the question might be. Both were kind, generous, and forthcoming with the stories they had told a hundred times. Fortunately, they also responded to information of which they were unaware, and did so candidly. "So Ernest did get my letter," Lewis Clarahan said, a little hurt after believing for almost sixty years that the mail delivery had been at fault in Milan in 1918. And Sue Crist never thought much of it that Ernest never dated. Yes, he was handsome, she said, but he was a girl's "pal." The ladies' man at school was Morris Musselman, a swarthy boy six inches shorter than Ernest.

Professor Edward Wagenknecht (who makes his some in West Newton, Massachusetts), perhaps because he had not been questioned so often, was spontaneous. Perhaps also because he has a national reputation of his own, Wagenknecht's memory of Ernest Hemingway the boy carried little of the freight of the Hemingway image. Ernest was neither a hero nor a monument, but rather "gentle," "friendly," "civilized." Wagenknecht recalled that he and Ernest (though not together) often enjoyed the plays put on by a stock company—the Chester Wallace Players—and that Ernest was a friend of Reverend Barton of the First Congregational Church. Wagenknecht was class valedictorian at Oak Park High in 1917 (an honor of which, sixty-two years later, he was immensely proud). He remembered that Ernest mentioned—"Wagenknecht [who never threw a ball in his life] Pitches Good Game"—as a warmhearted joke between them and against those who would take athletics too seriously. Wagenknecht still remembers Ernest turning to the class valedictorian with a big, dimpled grin.

Wagenknecht was especially moved when he mentioned attending the Savoy Theater in Chicago in 1918 and saw in the Pathé newsreel a few seconds' footage of Ernest in a wheelchair in Milan. Wagenknecht phoned Marcelline from the theater. Clarence and Grace Hemingway followed that newsreel around Chicago, seeing it in every theater it played in, Wagenknecht said.

The single most valuable work on Hemingway's life in Michigan is Constance Cappel Montgomery's *Hemingway in Michigan* (New York, 1966). With scholastic restraint and in a measured style, Montegomery presents a "country," the history of which includes prehistoric tribes, Indian wars, and Christian martyrdom. (Missionary Father Marquette requested he be buried with his body arranged like the corpses of Stone Age Indians in their graves.) In legend the region is haunted by the Windigo, a cannibalistic man–beast. In the silent autumn forest, one can almost believe this is true. See "Nightmare and Ritual in Hemingway," introduction to *The Portable Hemingway*, ed. Malcolm Cowley (New York, 1945).

There is something of this mood in Ernest's lovely unfinished novelette, "The Last Good Country," in *Nick Adams Stories* (New York, 1972) pp. 56–114. Written during the last years of Hemingway's life, this story marks a return to the controlled lyricism of "Big Two Hearted River" (*In Our Time*, New York, 1925) and the elegiac mood of *A Farewell to Arms* (New York, 1929). Especially in the making of his "country," Hemingway recaptures the ingenuous voice of his youth.

On the author's visit to Horton Bay (August 5, 1979), Bill Olhe, a retired advertising executive and a friend of Bill Horne, spent half an afternoon speaking with knowledge and affection of his five-house town. Then, on a walk down to the bay, Bill spoke about the history of the sand road and the spring that Ernest wrote about in "Summer People." Finally, Bill's small book, *100 Years in Horton Bay* (New York, 1975), proved an invaluable resource.

NOTES

Opinion of Frank Platt: Ernest to Charles Fenton, June 22, 1952.
The Rifle Club: Grace Hemingway, Memory Book IV.
Stocking the Oak Park water supply: Ernest to Fenton.
Growth spurt: Ernest to Grace Hemingway, September 8, 1914; Madelaine Hemingway Miller, *Ernie Hemingway's Sister "Sunny" Remembers* (New York, 1975), p. 49; author's visit to Windemere, October 7–10, 1980.
Disputes with Harold Sampson: Author's interviews with Edward Wagenknecht, July 18, 1979.
On Nantucket: Marcelline Hemingway Sanford *At the Hemingways* (Boston, 1962), pp. 112–14; Ernest to Clarence Hemingway (sent from Nantucket).
High-school contemporaries: Ernest to Fenton: Wagenknecht, July 18, 1979.
High-school football: Senior Tabula (Oak Park High literary magazine–yearbook), 1916; *The Torrents of Spring* (London, 1933), pp. 101–2; Jack Hemingway, interview, July 29, 1979.
Oak Park High swimming team: Senior Tabula, 1917; "Summer People," in *The Nick Adams Stories* (New York, 1972), p. 201.

Ernest reads Marcelline's mail: Ernest to Lewis Clarahan, July 17, 1915.

Learning to box: Jack Hemingway, July 29, 1979; Leicester Hemingway, *My Brother, Ernest Hemingway* (Cleveland, 1961), pp. 29–30; Miller, p. 71; Grace Hemingway, Memory Book V; Ernest to F. Scott Fitzgerald, in *Ernest Hemingway: Selected Letters,* ed. Carlos Baker (New York, 1980), p. 314.

High-school story, "Judgment of Manitou": Tabula (February 1916), pp. 9–10. Not widely known, "Judgment of Manitou," written when Ernest was sixteen years old, anticipates the mature Hemingway voice in its vivid imagery, its taut and rigorous style, and its fatal irony.

High-school play, "No Worst Than a Bad Cold": Unpublished manuscript, Hemingway Collection, John F. Kennedy Library, Dorchester, Mass., #623. During Ernest's high-school years, Longfellow was his favorite poet, and *Hiawatha,* with its lyrical beauty, its themes of love and death in a pristine world, and its powerful mythic overtones, was Ernest's favorite poem. Also in this play there emerges what has come to be called the "code hero"—Paw Paw Keewis—and the "Hemingway hero"—Richard Boulton. The cave, the wooden beaver, the "white eskimo," the "Old Grand-dad-dollar whisky," and the young Indian girl calling to the hero off-stage invite psychological interpretation. Ernest imitated the Longfellow style in his heretofore unpublished adolescent poem, "The Day."

High-school poem, "The Stoker": This is a striking anticipatory work embodying Ernest's nascent conception of the artist's function in society.

Indian friends: Carlos Baker, *Ernest Hemingway: A Life Story* (New York, 1969), p. 13.

Sexual relations in Michigan with young Indian girls: Jack Hemingway, July 29, 1979; "Fathers and Sons," in *The Short Stories of Ernest Hemingway* (New York, 1966), p. 497.

Ernest's "country": "The Last Good Country," in *The Nick Adams Stories,* pp. 57–114.

At Marcelline's party: Sanford, pp. 152–53.

Week at Horton Bay: Ernest to "Dr. and Mrs. Hemingway and family," Monday, 6:00 a.m., September 7, 1917.

The Smiths: "Summer People," in *The Nick Adams Stories,* pp. 197–208; William H. Olhe, *100 Years in Horton Bay* (New York, 1975), pp. 40–41; Baker, pp. 25–26.

Ernest and Clarence Hemingway's farewell: For Whom the Bell Tolls (New York, 1940), pp. 405–6.

Chapter 3

SOURCES

Yale professor Charles A. Fenton wrote one of the first significant studies of Hemingway's life and work, *The Apprenticeship of Ernest Hemingway: The Early Years* (New York, 1954). Hemingway opposed Fenton's work in part because he resented the intrusion into his private life and also because he saw Fenton as an embittered failed artist. (Ernest once offered Fenton two hundred

SOURCES AND NOTES

dollars to fly down to Cuba and say in person the things he had written in his letters.)

Ernest's strongest objection to Fenton's work was that the professor was poaching on his preserve. More than once Ernest warned Fenton off stories of the early years that he himself intended to write. Ernest suggested that to read Fenton's lyrics would make the song no longer his own. Ernest's letters to Fenton include many details of the Kansas City months in the winter of 1917–18. But because he was pursuing a thesis, Fenton neglected the facts that did not fit in.

When Ernest left home in October 1917, he left for good. He was barely eighteen years old. Kansas City was a wide-open town with more vice and corruption than Chicago's South Side. As a reporter for the *Kansas City Star,* he came to know, firsthand, the sordid details. Ernest almost always wrote his letters with his reader in mind. Most often this was a courtesy. But his letters from Kansas City to his parents (the tone beckoning approval) were perhaps his first collection of "stories." These letters, read with their fictional qualities in mind, reveal not only Ernest's acute perception of his parents' personalities and his own special needs but also the paradoxical persona he would develop in his fiction and in his life. To Grace, Ernest is the plucky, cheerful picaro, full of adolescent optimism. For Clarence, he is hardworking, hopeful, boyish, and shyly proud.

Two other sources are indispensable for the story of Ernest's months in Kansas City. The first is the *Kansas City Star* itself; the second, the Missouri Valley Room of the Kansas City Public Library. Besides the reporting Ernest did for the *Star*—identified with few exceptions by Matthew J. Bruccoli in *Ernest Hemingway, Cub Reporter: Kansas City Star Stories* (Pittsburgh, 1970)—three articles contain a wealth of information. The first, printed on Sunday, December 6, 1936, and entitled "With Hemingway Before 'A Farewell to Arms,'" is Theodore Brumback's reminiscence of his first meeting with Ernest, the growth of their friendship, and their decision to join the Red Cross Ambulance Service.

The second is a front-page story in the *Kansas City Times*—the morning *Kansas City Star*—"Back to His First Field." It is an interview with Hemingway and his "new bride," Martha Gellhorn, printed Tuesday, November 26, 1940. Ernest generously lauded the *Star*'s style book ("Those were the best rules I ever learned for the business of writing"); told how he passed the eye test for the Red Cross Ambulance Service by learning from Halley Dickey, who had memorized the test chart; and shrewdly speculated on the results for the United States in the European war.

The third article is a thoroughly researched two-page piece by Hemingway afficionado, Mel Foor. Entitled "Remembering Hemingway's Kansas City Days" (Sunday, July 21, 1968), it traces in a brisk narrative style Hemingway's career at the *Star* and presents Hemingway articles Foor himself discovered. Foor's interviews with old-time staffers at the *Star* produce vivid anecdotes, and his research renders the facts about where and how Ernest lived (including drawings) on Agnes Avenue and on Warwick Boulevard.

Stored in the archives of the Missouri Valley Room of the Kansas City Public Library are photographs of city streets in 1917 and 1918 and a publication, *City of the Future: A Narrative History of Kansas City, 1850–1950,* by Henry C. Haskell Jr. and Richard B. Fowler. The remarkable details of the photographs,

wide-angled shots of the buildings, the advertisements, the crowds on the busiest
streets in town, and the meticulously researched history were most helpful in
learning about Kansas City just before the United States entered World War I.

NOTES

Tyler Hemingway: Carlos Baker, *Ernest Hemingway: A Life Story* (New York,
    1969), p. 32; Baker photo between pages 78 and 79. (In the caption, Tyler
    is identified by his first name, Alfred, a name he never used.)
Crossing the Mississippi: The Nick Adams Stories (New York, 1972), p. 116.
Kansas City Star, interior: Baker, p. 32.
Pete Wellington: Baker, p. 34; Ernest to Charles Fenton, July 29, 1952.
Kansas City "low life": A Moveable Feast (New York, 1964), pp. 18, 124; Baker,
    p. 35.
Ernest's new brown suit burned: Leicester Hemingway, *My Brother, Ernest Hem-
ingway* (Cleveland, 1961), p. 45.
Pete Wellington on Ernest's work: Baker, p. 34.
Friends at the Star: Mel Foor, "Remembering Hemingway's Kansas City Days,"
    Kansas City Star, July 21, 1968.
Theodore Brumback: Theodore Brumback "With Hemingway Before *A Fare-
well to Arms" Kansas City Star,* December 6, 1936; Baker, pp. 35–36; "Big
    Two-Hearted River: Part I," pp. 216–17.
Lionel Moise: Ernest to Charles Fenton, August 2, 1952; Baker, p. 35.
Leo Korbreen: Foor "Kerensky, the Fighting Flea," *Kansas City Star,* December
    16, 1917, reprinted in Foor's article.
"Death Beats Slow Doctor": Kansas City Star, January 8, 1918. The article is
    unsigned, but the style is unmistakable. According to the *Star's* assign-
    ment sheet for January 3, 1918, Ernest's daily routine was "Undertakers,"
    "Hospitals," "General Hospital."
"At the End of the Ambulance Run": Selections from Ernest's article, *Kansas
City Star,* January 20, 1918, reproduced in *Ernest Hemingway, Cub Re-
porter: Kansas City Star Stories,* ed. Matthew J. Bruccoli (Pittsburgh,
    1970), pp. 27–32.
Small pox victim: Bruccoli, pp. 34–36; Baker, p. 34; "God Rest You Merry, Gen-
tlemen," in *The Short Stories of Ernest Hemingway* (New York, 1966),
    pp. 392–6.
Municipal doctor: Baker, p. 34; Ernest to Charles Fenton, January 19, 1952.
Billy Sunday: Ernest to parents, January 2, 1918; for substance of Sunday's
    speech, *Kansas City Star,* January 9, 1918.
Prudence Boulton's suicide: Paul Smith, Trinity College, Hartford, Conn., un-
    published monograph.
Ernest's farewell to family, 1918: Ursula Hemingway to Ernest, February 24,
    1920.

Chapter 4

SOURCES

Before he embarked for Italy as a Red Cross volunteer, Ernest Hemingway spent nine days in New York. During his stay, Ernest wrote a half-dozen times to his parents. One of the first letters included the stunning announcement (understandably stunning to Clarence and Grace) that he intended to marry before going overseas. To his parents Ernest called his fiancée "the Mrs." but to Dale Wilson, his friend from the *Star*, he was more specific. She was the famous young actress, Mae Marsh. Fifty years later, Miss Marsh could not recall the affair. But at the time, Clarence and Grace were convinced Ernest was telling the truth.

As much as Ernest was occupied by his brief liaison with the beautiful movie star, he did have time for some sightseeing. The sights he saw, especially down Riverside Drive near Grant's Tomb (sexual perverts), so distressed him he recalled them in his only extant pornography, a sketch he would never publish, strangely entitled "Crime and Punishment."

For the narration of the train journey to New York and for certain details of Ernest's first time there, the unpublished novel *A New-Slain Knight,* Hemingway Collection, John F. Kennedy Library, offers the most convincing guide.

NOTES

Route from Chicago to New York: Abram Royer Brubacker et al., *The Volume Library* (New York, 1917), p. 441.
Narrative of trip from Chicago to New York, May 1918: A New-Slain Knight, chapters 12 to 15.
In New York at the Hotel Earle: Ernest to "Folks," May 14, 1918.
Sightseeing, typhoid inoculation, and issue of equipment: Ernest to "Folks," May 14, 1918.
Impressions of New York: A New-Slain Knight, chapter 16.
Whores, homosexuals, and perverts in New York: "Crime and Punishment," unpublished short story, #340 Hemingway Collection, John F. Kennedy Library, Dorchester, Mass.
Mr. Lennox: A New-Slain Knight, chapter 20.

Chapter 5

SOURCES

Bill Horne's memories of his time with Ernest in the spring and summer of 1918 were, in 1979, tableaux rather than vignette, episode, or short story. But Bill recalled their trip together across the Atlantic on the old *Chicago,* the service at Schio, their convalescence at the American Red Cross hospital in Milan, their meeting at Bassano, in vivid images with extraordinary texture and depth. Bill's memories were not solicited by questions, nor discovered in rumination; they occurred spontaneously, most often as the story of those days was augmented by Bill's evocative letters (now in the Hemingway Collection at the John F. Kennedy Library and by his souvenir photo album from Italy in 1918.

Bill confirmed that a great deal of *A Farewell to Arms* (New York, 1929) was indeed autobiographical. And he left no doubt that he meant Frederic Henry's wounding, his hospital stay (Bill was at the hospital with Ernest for months), and Henry's affair with Katherine Barkley. In fact, Bill said that the most accurate portrait of Agnes Kurowsky could be found in *A Farewell to Arms*, but strictly modified by Ernest's characterization of Agnes as Luz in "A Very Short Story" (*The Short Stories of Ernest Hemingway*, New York, 1966).

Bill Horne's recollections of the trip across the Atlantic on the *Chicago* are supplemented by details from Ernest's unfinished autobiographical story, "Night Before Landing," in *The Nick Adams Stories* (New York, 1972), pp. 117–24.

For the significant Ernest–James Gamble friendship (Gamble's identity and background have been heretofore unknown), the author's correspondence with Gamble's nephew, Professor Theodore Voorhees of Washington, D.C., was invaluable. Besides the family history he had written and generously supplied, Professor Voorhees "fleshed out" Jim Gamble and in conversations spoke of his uncle and Ernest's relationship and of the letters Ernest had sent to Jim, which came into his hands after Gamble's death in 1958.

The most valuable historical works for this chapter were John Buchan, *A History of the Great War*, vol. IV (Boston, 1922); Charles M. Blakewell, *The Story of the American Red Cross in Italy* (New York, 1920); G. M. Trevelyan, *Scene from Italy's War* (Boston, 1919); Richard Harding Davis, *The Red Cross Girl* (New York, 1916).

NOTES

Weather conditions at Ernest's departure: New York Times, May 21, 1918.
The steamer Chicago: Carlos Baker, *Ernest Hemingway: A Life Story* (New York, 1969), p. 39; ship departures, *New York Times,* May 22, 1918. (For some reason, the *Chicago* was not made part of a convoy although the convoy strategy had been proven for more than a year.)
Trip across the Atlantic: "Night Before Landing," in *The Nick Adams Stories* (New York, 1972), p. 119; Baker, p. 40; Ernest to "Dear Folks," "At Sea, May 1918"; Theodore Brumback, "With Hemingway Before *A Farewell to Arms*," *Kansas City Star,* December 6, 1936.
Gaby: "Night Before Landing," in *The Nick Adams Stories;* "Crime and Punishment"; "A Way You'll Never Be," *The Short Stories of Ernest Hemingway* (New York, 1966), p. 408.
The smell of death: For Whom the Bell Tolls (New York, 1940), p. 254; Ernest to Charles Scribner, August 15, 1940; Ernest to Maxwell Perkins, August 26, 1940.
"Oily Weather": Complete Poems, ed. Nicholas Gerogiannis (Lincoln, Neb., 1979), p. 44.
In Bordeaux: Interview with Bill Horne, July 7, 1979.
In Paris: Ernest to parents from Hotel Florida, 12 Boulevard Malesherbes, June 5, 1918, on YMCA stationery.
Voyeurism: The Torrents of Spring (London, 1933), pp. 138–39. (See Ernest's comments on writing directly from experience, especially when he was young); Carlos Baker, ed., *Ernest Hemingway: Selected Letters* (New

York, 1980), p. 327. (*The Torrents of Spring* is more like the psychologi-
cally revealing ramblings Ernest always kept to himself than any other
published work.)

Trip from Paris to Milan: Bill Horne, July 7, 1979.

Body detail: "The Natural History of the Dead," in *Death in the Afternoon*
(New York, 1932), pp. 135–36.

Trip to Schio: Baker, *A Life Story*, p. 41; *A Farewell to Arms* (New York, 1929),
p. 15; Brumback, "With Hemingway"; Bill Horne, July 7, 1979.

The Italian Front, June 1918: John Buchan, *A History of the Great War*, vol.
IV (Boston, 1922), pp. 261–72.

Red Cross unit at Schio: Baker, pp. 41–42; *A Farewell to Arms*, pp. 12, 33; Bill
Horne, July 8, 1979; Bill Horne's photo albums.

The officers' whorehouse: Baker, p. 43; *A Farewell to Arms*, p. 30.

Tension between veterans and new arrivals at Schio: Il Giornale di Vicenza,
September 27, 1978, p. 11.

Edward McKey's death at Fossalta: Charles M. Blakewell, *The Story of the
American Red Cross in Italy* (New York, 1920), pp. 81–85.

Action on the Piave: Buchan, pp. 269–72.

Volunteering for duty on the Piave: Virginia K. Moseley, "Hemingway and
Horne—Friends from the Front," in *Courier–Review*, Barrington, Ill.,
September 27, 1979.

Fossalta: Ernest to Ruth Morrison, June 22, 1918; Baker, *Selected Letters*, pp.
10–11; "A Way You'll Never Be," in *The Short Stories of Ernest Hemingway*, pp. 402–3; Bill Horne's photo album.

The Piave in July 1918: Across the River and Into the Trees (New York, 1950),
p. 18; Buchan, map of "The Battle of the Piave," facing p. 270.

Visit to Bill Horne at San Pedro Novello: Bill Horne, July 8, 1979; Leicester
Hemingway, *My Brother, Ernest Hemingway* (Cleveland, 1961), photo
between pages 224 and 225; "Now I Lay Me," in *The Short Stories of
Ernest Hemingway*.

Ernest's wounding: Ernest to "Folks," August 18, 1918; *A Farewell to Arms*, pp.
54–55; "A Way You'll Never Be," in *The Short Stories of Ernest Hemingway*, p. 414; Bill Horne, July 8, 1979.

Aftermath of Ernest's wounding: Ernest to "Folks," August 18, 1918; *A Farewell
to Arms*, pp. 55–61, 62–68 (dressing station), 74 (field hospital), 57–59
(James Gamble).

Nursed back to Milan by Gamble: Baker, *Selected Letters*, p. 106; conversation
with Theodore Voorhees and Bill Horne.

Trip to Milan: A Farewell to Arms, pp. 77–78.

American Red Cross Canteen in Milan: Blakewell, pp. 69–70.

Arrival at the American Red Cross hospital: A Farewell to Arms, pp. 81–88;
Henry Villard, "A Prized Specimen of Wounded Hero," *Yankee*, July
1979, p. 74.

First days in hospital: Ernest to "Mom," August 29, 1918; Ernest's nights in hospital, *A Farewell to Arms*, p. 101; Bill Horne, July 8, 1979.

*"Conservative treatment" of Ernest's wounds treated humorously: A Farewell to
Arms*, 96–97.

Chapter 6

SOURCES

In recent years, Agnes Kurowsky granted interviews to Hemingway biographers Carlos Baker (in the sixties), Michael Reynolds (in the seventies), and Bernice Kurt (in the eighties). In each interview, Miss Kurowsky characterized her relationship with Hemingway as "condescending." To Baker, she was the "older sister"; to Reynolds, the tolerant and indulgent nurse; to Kurt, the woman of the world, delightfully afflicted by a charming adolescent. And each biographer took her at her word.

Unquestionably, personal interviews are essential to a biographer. But the sixty-year-old memories of a woman both Hemingway and Bill Horne described as superficial—memories in which she always ascends to a role superior to her young admirer (she never admits lover), where Hemingway becomes, to varying degrees in Baker, Reynolds, and Kurt, enthralled by Miss Kurowsky—should not be accepted unquestioningly.

Fortunately Agnes Kurowsky did leave a telling record of her affair with Ernest in the more than three hundred pages of letters she wrote to him while she served at Florence and at Torre di Mosta. These letters (all of which Ernest assiduously saved) reveal Agnes's love (within the limits of her emotional range), her intention to marry Ernest after he established himself, and her faith in his eventual success. It also seems that her love's "soul is sense," for Ernest, once out of sight was, if not out of mind, out of heart. Both of Agnes's trips, to Florence, to Torre di Mosta, weakened their love. But the second was the beginning of the end.

In Agnes's letters from Torre di Mosta, the tone is quite different. Her letters from Florence are loving, tender, solicitous—they are long because the author, despite her lack of verbal ability, tries to make the reader understand. But Agnes's letters from Torre di Mosta are brief. They are often critical, they are sometimes sarcastic. They are always superior. As Ernest admits in his March 13, 1919, letter to Bill Horne, they intimate "the sad truth which I have been suspecting for some time."

The second most valuable source for the story of Ernest's love affair with Agnes is, ironically, his letters to Bill Horne. Although Ernest does not "run off at the mouth" (there are many lines in his letters to Bill at this time that are blacked out), he does present to Bill a sketch of his affair and of his "Tedeschi-named wife."

The best record of Ernest's World War I experience in Italy is Michael Reynolds's *Hemingway's First War* (Princeton, 1976). Besides his extensive interviews with Agnes Kurowsky, Reynolds includes valuable letters Agnes wrote to Ernest in 1918. He also makes a number of additions and corrections to Baker's *Life*.

NOTES

Early Days at Red Cross Hospital in Milan: Henry Villard, *Yankee Magazine* (July 1979), pp. 72, 77, 134–145, passim. Virginia K. Moseley, "Hemingway and Horne: Friends from the Front," *Barrington* (Ill.) *Courier Review*, September 27, 1979, pp. 28–29, 31, 33.

Agnes's background: Michael Reynolds, *Hemingway's First War* (Princeton, 1976), pp. 183–93.

Procedures at Red Cross Hospitals in war zones in 1918: Charles M. Bakewell, *The Story of the American Red Cross in Italy* (New York, 1920), pp. 86–104; Richard Harding Davis, *The Red Cross Nurse* (New York, 1916); Villard, p. 74.

Agnes at the "Lorenzo and Lucia": Reynolds, pp. 197–98.

Ernest's letters to parents: Ernest's letters here to his parents are remarkably well crafted. As in the Kansas City correspondence, he makes only what they are prepared to hear sound like the truth.

Ernest on his wounding and philosophy of death: Johnny Miller's letters to Ernest, November 16, 1920; in "A Clean Well-Lighted Place," *The Short Stories of Ernest Hemingway* (New York, 1966), pp. 379–83; *A Farewell to Arms* (New York, 1929), pp. 54–57; Guy Hickok, *The Brooklyn Eagle* (May 17, 1925).

Count Greppi: Reynolds, pp. 166–69, *A Farewell to Arms*, pp. 254, 258–63.

Trip to Bassano: "The Woppian Way," unpublished ms. courtesy of Waring Jones; interview with Bill Horne, August 4, 1979; Bill Horne's letter to Marcelline Hemingway, reprinted in *At the Hemingways*, pp. 180–81. (Bill was vague in this letter about the circumstances of his meeting with Ernest in Bassano, most likely because he believed Ernest had gone AWOL (which indeed he had). See Carlos Baker, *Ernest Hemingway: A Life Story* (New York, 1969), pp. 52–53; Agnes Kurowsky to Ernest, November 1918; Ernest to family, November 1, 1918.

Johnny Miller's party: Johnny Miller to Ernest, November 16, 1926.

Agnes, Ernest, and Maurice Blain: Besides the obvious parallels to *A Moveable Feast* (New York, 1964), there is an anecdote worth noting. Ernest's first son, Jack, one afternoon during World War II, sat at the bar of the Algonquin Hotel in New York. Two men there were having a heated discussion. One said the greatest American writer of this century was Ernest Hemingway; the other claimed Faulkner was the best. Jack introduced himself, then said, "My father told me the greatest American writer is Maurice Blain." The taller of the two men said, "I'm Maurice Blain."

Ernest, Agnes, and the influenza victim: Unpublished, untitled story on stationery from American Red Cross Hospital, 3 Via Bachetto, Milano. Ernest also recalls this experience in *Death in the Afternoon* (New York, 1932), p. 139.

"Chink" Dorman-Smith: Baker, pp. 53–54.

Trip to Treviso: Ernest to Bill Horne, December 15, 1918.

At Taormina: Unpublished short story, "The Mercenaries"; conversation with James Gamble's nephew, Theodore Voorhees.

Chapter 7

SOURCES

Again, the letters Ernest wrote to Bill Horne form the backbone of the chapter. They set the mood, the tone; they create the suspense; they reveal the character.

Ernest's letter of March 13, 1919, written the day of his "kiss-off" from Agnes, is the most important document in the text. It helps to create the self-portrait of a broken-hearted young man who, in the Romantic tradition, will fashion his pain into art.

In Ernest's short story "The Mercenaries," he develops what first appeared in his high school Indian play, "No Worst Than a Bad Cold." Paw Paw Keewis, the laconic, cynical Indian tutor of young Richard Boulton, is now the adroit American, Perry Graves. Playing upon the distinctions one of his favorite authors, Stephen Crane, made between courage with imagination and without it, Ernest contrasts the sophisticated French soldier, Ricaud, who had "died a thousand times" and, as a mercenary, expects to die a thousand more, to Graves, whose "gift from God" is his lack of imagination.

Finally, there is the two-day letter Ernest wrote to his friend James Gamble. As long as any other letter of Ernest's that has appeared, it renders his emerging voice as he presents to Jim the "country" he would in a few years present to the world. In this letter Ernest is as much Nick Adams as, outside his fiction, he would ever be.

NOTES

Arrival in New York: New York Sun, January 23, 1919, p. 8; interview with Bill Horne, July 7, 1979.

Days in New York: Interview with Bill Horne, July 7, 1979; Ernest to Bill Horne, December 15, 1918.

Arrival in Chicago: Marcelline Hemingway Sanford, *At the Hemingways* (Boston, 1962), pp. 176–77; Leicester Hemingway, *My Brother, Ernest Hemingway* (Cleveland, 1961), pp. 52–53.

Success with lectures: Ernest to Jim Gamble, March 3, 1919; Sanford, p. 179; Ernest's lecture cards in display case in Hemingway Room of John F. Kennedy Library.

Working room at 600 North Kenilworth Avenue: Author's visit, July 8, 1979, and interview with current resident, Mrs. Arthur Burns.

"The Mercenaries": #573, the Hemingway Collection, JFK Library.

Agnes Kurowsky's letters: Michael Reynolds, *Hemingway's First War* (Princeton, 1976), pp. 201–7.

Ernest's reaction to Agnes's "kiss-off" letter: Sanford, p. 188; Ernest to Bill Horne, March 13, 1919.

Trip to Windemere: Constance Cappel Montgomery, *Hemingway in Michigan* (New York, 1962), p. 90.

Ernest and Ursula: Ernest to Arthur Mizener, June 2, 1950.

Chapter 8

SOURCES

Ernest Hemingway's unpublished "Cross roads" expresses the theme of this chapter; his "Summer People," first published in 1972 with substantive deviation from the manuscript corrected here, is the motif. Back from the war, devastated by Agnes Kurowsky's rejection, Ernest is indeed at the crossroads of his young life.

Characteristically, he retreats to his "country" and calls on his friends. But life had changed for them as it had for him, and by and large they do not respond. One woman, however, does soften this time for Ernest—Kate Smith.

For details of Ernest's stay in Petoskey, Michigan, in 1919, the best published sources are Constance Cappel Montgomery's *Hemingway in Michigan* (New York, 1962) and Ernest's *The Torrents of Spring* (New York, 1926). These are supplemented by the author's visit to Petoskey on August 6, 1979.

For Ernest's stay in Toronto in early 1920, his letters to Charles Fenton in the 1950s offer the best source. For his relationship with his mother, Grace's long letters present a good part of the story. But they must be supplemented by the passage from Ernest's unpublished novel, *A New-Slain Knight* (1927), which is suffused with Freudian suggestions.

NOTES

Ernest and Kate Smith: Hadley's letter to Ernest, see manuscript "Summer People" in *The Nick Adams Stories* (New York, 1972); Kate's poem (on back of letters from Ernest), January 27, 1922.

Grace's trip to New Orleans: Letter, March 23, 1919.

Grace at Longfield: Marcelline Hemingway Sanford, *At the Hemingways* (Boston, 1962), p. 194.

Eva Potter's boardinghouse: Author's visit to Petoskey and interview with present residents, August 5, 1979.

Balmer: Carlos Baker, *Ernest Hemingway: A Life Story* (New York, 1969), p. 62, and Waring Jones manuscript, "The Woppian Way."

Grace Quinlan: See Carlos Baker, Ernest Hemingway: Selected Letters (New York, 1980), January 1, 1920; August 8, 1920; September 30, 1920. Ernest never considered Grace Quinlan a serious possibility for romance. She was a fourteen-year-old girl from Petoskey. She was bright, not unlike his favorite sister, Ursula. For physical details of the town, which hasn't changed much, author's visit to Petoskey, August 5–6, 1979, and October 7, 1980.

Talk at Ladies Aid Society: Baker, p. 66.

Interior of Connable's house: Baker, p. 68.

Toronto and the Toronto Star: Baker, pp. 69–70; Ernest's letters to Charles Fenton, August 2, 1952, and July 29, 1952; unpublished novel, *A New-Slain Knight*.

Grace's metaphorical reference to love: Her famous letter here contains an important quote omitted from the first complete biography (Baker). The thirty or so lines left out are very revealing of Grace's personality at this time and of how she saw her relationship with her son.

Incipient "Hemingway style" in "Crossroads": In a letter to Owen Wister, March 11, 1929, Ernest maintains that the bitterest tragedies are brought on by lack of money; that his life was once shot out from under him, and, as a result, he had to write "very, almost ridiculously, simple stories"; that all his sentences used to go "put, put, put." In a letter to Bill Horne, March 13, 1919, Ernest blames the loss of Agnes on lack of money. Hadley wrote to Ernest on April 20, 1921, "Maybe your work calls for another wreakage, but you're not going to get it from me." Ernest referred again to the

emotional shock that is sometimes necessary to cure a writer's "over-flow
of words," in *Green Hills of Africa*, the one autobiographical book he
published (p. 71).

Chapter 9

SOURCES

As has often been noted, Ernest said that the first time he saw Hadley he knew
he would marry her. But, as the title of this chapter suggests, the Agnes Kurowsky affair had left him worried and a bit afraid. What would happen to him and,
more importantly, to his work if he were to be badly hurt again?

By the fall of 1920, Ernest and Bill Horne had set up a comfortable if tenuous
bachelor apartment on Chicago's North Side. Their plan was to find jobs in advertising during the current economic boom. Meanwhile Bill's savings would
suffice. Things, however, did not work out that way. Bill had jokingly called his
and Ernest's liaison a "marriage" which could only be broken by some "act of
God." Then he added they both knew what that meant—a beautiful woman
(who was probably no act of God at all, Bill added). It was then that Hadley
Richardson came into Ernest's life.

The major sources for this chapter are Bill Horne's dozen or so letters written
to Ernest during the fall of 1920 while Bill was a traveling salesman; the author's interviews with Bill Horne (July 7–8, 1979; August 4–6, 1979; October 7,
1980); and, overwhelmingly, portions of the more than 2000 pages of letters
Hadley wrote to Ernest during their nine-month courtship and Ernest's few extant letters to Hadley (although it is quite clear from Hadley's text that Ernest
wrote at least as many letters to her). It is the author's belief that Ernest's courtship letters will eventually be disclosed.

NOTES

Life at 1230 North State Street: Author's interview with Bill Horne, July 7,
    1979.
Kenley and "Doodles" Smith's parties: Bill Horne, July 7, 1979.
Ernest's opinion of Don Wright: Bill Horne, August 20, 1979.
Kate Smith's introduction of Hadley: Carlos Baker, *Ernest Hemingway: A Life
    Story* (New York, 1969), pp. 75–76. Author's interview with Jack Hem-
    ingway, July 29, 1979.
Ernest and Hadley's first date: Hadley to Ernest, November 5, 1920.
Job at the Commonwealth Cooperative: Baker, p. 76; Bill Horne to Ernest, No-
    vember 12, 1920.
Hadley's family history: Alice Sokoloff, *Hadley: The First Mrs. Hemingway*
    (New York, 1973). Hadley's letters to Ernest, December 27, 1920; July 21,
    1921; and in text, passim. Author's interview with Jack Hemingway, July
    29, 1979.
Kenley and Doodles Smith: Baker, p. 59; Ernest's letter to Charles Fenton, July
    29, 1952; Hadley's letters quoted in text, passim.

Hadley wrote in late November 1920 that Ernest's letters were "running, rippling, and polished, too." The same could be said of what Hadley herself wrote

to him. Unaffected in tone, sonorous, rhythmical, Hadley's style set a standard for Ernest, and it's likely he worked as hard at his letters to her as he did at his fiction. The most significant of Hadley's letters used for the last half of this chapter are cited below.

Ernest's and Hadley's illnesses: Despite their healthful appearance, they were chronically ill with minor yet distressing conditions. Hadley to Ernest, November 25, 1920.

Tone of letters: Almost from the time they met, Ernest and Hadley spoke freely and intimately to each other. Hadley to Ernest, November 25, 1920, and passim in the text.

Ernest reading his writing "hot from the mill" to Hadley: Hadley praises his ability to make rhythm enhance meaning, November 30, 1920.

Hadley's trip to Chicago: Her sister Fonnie strongly advised her not to go. Hadley to Ernest, December 15, 1920.

Details of Commonwealth Cooperative: From the copy of the organization's magazine, Hemingway Collection, John F. Kennedy Library.

Ernest's habit of kissing Hadley on top of her head: Hadley to Ernest, April 1, 1921.

Hadley's offer to "break up" rather than ruin a "good man's chances" with unwanted responsibility: Hadley to Ernest, December 11, 1920.

Ernest to Hadley, December 23, 1920: The longest and most revealing of the two extant courtship letters from Ernest to Hadley anticipates the early short story, "The Idealist in Love," published for the first time in this text.

Bill Horne's layoff: Bill Horne to Ernest, December 18, 1920. Since he would not return to the family house in Oak Park, Ernest knew he must find other lodgings.

Grace in Bishop, California, for holidays: Ernest to Grace, December 22, 1920.

Christmas at the Hemingways: Marcelline Hemingway Sanford, *At the Hemingways* (Boston, 1962), pp. 115–17.

Ernest's Christmas present to Hadley: Ironically, at least in view of his subsequent public image, Ernest took careful note of what women wore and either strongly approved or disapproved of Hadley's apparel. Hadley to Ernest, December 27, 1920.

Ernest's affection for Jim Gamble: Ernest to Hadley, December 23, 1920.

Harrison Williams: Hadley to Ernest, December 31, 1920; Jack Hemingway to author, telephone conversation, May 1983.

Bill Horne's declaration of faith in Ernest's ability: Bill Horne to Ernest, January 9, 1921, characteristically in apt metaphor.

Bill Horne fired from Eaton Axle Company: Bill Horne to Ernest, February 11, 1921.

Ernest's move to Kenley Smith's "Men's Club": Hadley to Ernest, January 7, 1921.

Ernest's reading of Omar Khayyam *before Carl Sandburg and Sherwood Anderson:* Hadley to Ernest, January 7, 1927. Ernest and Sherwood Anderson at Palos Park, a suburb of Chicago, April 3, 1921.

Ernest testing Hadley's love: Hadley to Ernest, January 8, 1921. In fact, the jealousy they could generate in each other seems to have satisfied them both.

Plans for the "bold penniless dash" for Milan: Hadley to Ernest, January 12, 1921.

Hadley endorsing Ernest's plans: Hadley to Ernest, January 15, 1921.

Hadley's dream of an edenic life in Italy: Hadley to Ernest, around January 17, 1921.

Hadley's quote from Chaucer: Hadley to Ernest, January 20, 1921.

Chapter 10

SOURCES

The character of Hadley's letters changed slowly but surely in the spring of 1921 as the courtship developed. The declarations of love, the constant reassurances of sincerity, the painful pleasures of jealousy gave way to a subtle exploration of tastes, attitudes, opinions. Hadley and Ernest began to take a part, albeit through letters, in the details of each other's daily life. And they began to hold each other responsible for nurturing their love. When Ernest hurt Hadley, she would say so, and not in a tone that implied "I already forgive you."

Most importantly, at this time Hadley and Ernest began giving each other, naturally and effortlessly, just what was needed. After years of emotional anemia, Hadley had to be revitalized in spirit. She drew on Ernest's energy, his intelligence, his imagination. For the first time in her life, she revealed herself without fear of condescension or of being misunderstood. Ernest was a good listener, and with Hadley he was genuinely sympathetic. Hadley came alive under his touch. She spoke for Ernest as well when she said that putting the letters in the mailbox was like sending part of yourself away. For Ernest, Hadley offered willingly what he had been denied by Grace and Agnes. Hadley loved him unreservedly. There was no need to earn love as Grace had made him try to do. And, unlike Agnes, Hadley was a serious, intelligent woman with a great capacity for self-sacrifice, especially for the man she loved.

One of the two stories included in this chapter, "Portrait of the Idealist in Love—A Story," is very significant. Although the bulk of the work is a letter, Ernest reminds the reader in the title that it is indeed a story. When read in conjunction with Ernest's letter to Bill Horne, written the day he learned Agnes would not marry him (pp. 113–14 in this text), it suggests that despite "the crash of smashing ideals" something of the idealist survived.

The major source for this chapter is Hadley's letters to Ernest dating from late January to mid-May 1921.

NOTES

Heavyweight Championship fight: Ernest bet almost all he had saved while working at the Commonwealth Cooperative on the French champion, Georges Carpentier. Jack Dempsey was the odds-on favorite. To Ernest, Dempsey represented much of what he disliked about America of the twenties. He thought Dempsey a vulgar brute who did not raise violence to art but rather made violence barbaric. The author was fortunate to have known in the mid-sixties a gentleman of eighty-five years, Delbert Dextrase, a one-time fight promoter in New Bedford, Massachusetts. Carpentier was Del's favorite fighter, and Del, a Frenchman himself, followed Carpentier's career closely. Del saw the Dempsey–Carpentier fight, and he told me that Carpentier was clearly the better boxer but that Dempsey was just too strong. Ernest, at twenty, knew enough about boxing to see that Carpentier had little chance. But his prejudice overcame his judgment. Hadley to Ernest, June 29, 1921; Ernest's article in *Toronto Star*, June 21, 1921; Hadley to Ernest, July 2, 1921; Hadley to Ernest, July 7, 1921; Ernest to Howell Jenkins, September 16, 1920; Ernest to Grace Quinlan, July 21, 1921.

Ernest's chronic suffering from minor but distressing ailments: Hadley to Ernest, January 20, 1921; Hadley to Ernest, May 13, 1921.

No sympathy from Grace: Grace to Ernest, January 19, 1921.

Hadley beginning to "come alive": Hadley to Ernest, January 22, 1921.

"Poison" in Ernest coming from parents: Hadley to Ernest, January 27, 1921.

Ernest as "truly" religious: Hadley to Ernest, January 27, 1921.

Source and value of Ernest's special talent: Hadley to Ernest, February 19, 1921.

Hadley's worry that Ernest will "gyp" her as he did Kate Smith: Hadley to Ernest, February 7, 1921.

Men–women roles: Hadley to Ernest, February 11, 1921.

Emotional chaos Agnes's rejection had created in Ernest: Hadley to Ernest, February 17, 1921.

Hadley's gift of her hair to Ernest: Hadley to Ernest, February 19, 1921.

Ernest's fear of being intimidated by Hadley's intellectual friends: Hadley to Ernest, February 19, 1921.

At the Richardsons' home: Ernest's three-piece suit, Hadley to Ernest, March 6, 1921. Ernest's "ash-can" build, Hadley to Ernest, April 12, 1921. Scrapbook left, Hadley to Ernest, March 16, 1921. Songs played, Hadley to Ernest, February 11, 1921. French blouse, Hadley to Ernest, February 17, 1921. Hadley coming into her room to get things, Hadley to Ernest, February 19, 1921. Daily routine, Hadley to Ernest, February 19, 1921. Hadley's attacks of nerves, Hadley to Ernest, February 19, 1921. Orpheum theater, Hadley to Ernest, March 16, 1921. Ernest and Hadley are each other's child, Hadley to Ernest, April 1, 1921.

Ernest would "despise" Hadley if she did not keep a clean house: Hadley to Ernest, April 8, 1921.

The heroine of The Red Lily *achieving a "fourth dimension":* This insightful observation was probably the foundation for Ernest's belief, as he wrote in *Green Hills of Africa* (1935), p. 27, that literature could achieve a fourth and possibly a fifth dimension. It is difficult to know exactly what Ernest meant by this, but most critics suggest he must have meant something about time. Hadley, however, in her letter to Ernest dated April 8, 1921, makes it clear that the fourth dimension to which she refers is the workings of fate to bring about what she would later call "destiny" (Hadley to Ernest, April 21, 1921).

Hadley on marriage: Hadley to Ernest, April 8, 1921. Marriage is a trap biologically and socially, Hadley believes, but the way you get furthest.

Ernest "stale": He writes he needs a woman to get him going again. Hadley's reply, April 13, 1921.

Ernest begins first novel: Hadley to Ernest, April 20, 1921.
Relationship between the Agnes Kurowsky affair and Ernest's writing: Hadley to Ernest, April 20, 1921.
Hadley on "destiny": Hadley to Ernest, April 21, 1921.
Hadley on marriage again: Hadley to Ernest, April 22, 1921. Here, to express her feeling about marriage, Hadley uses the partnership metaphor.
Clarence expecting to die soon: Hadley to Ernest, May 1, 1921. Clarence had recently discovered that he had diabetes (which was very difficult to control with the insulin available in 1921), and he suffered from severe angina. In fact, Clarence lived for seven more years. The rest of the family did not learn of Clarence's illness until early 1927. Marcelline Hemingway Sanford, *At the Hemingways* (Boston, 1962), p. 225.
Hadley about herself: Hadley to Ernest, May 5, 1921. Hadley's lack of experience in the "world" must have been one of the most frequent themes of Ernest's letters. Hadley defends herself here as elsewhere by arguing for depth over breadth.
Ernest worried about competition from Hadley in art and even in fishing: Hadley to Ernest, May 6, 1921.
"The Ash Heel's Tendon": Unpublished early short story, #254 Hemingway Collection, John F. Kennedy Library.

Chapter 11

SOURCES

The essence of this chapter is irony. Hadley, worried for years about mental instability, about her "white nights" of anxiety and depression, about her lesbian tendencies (of which she had none), about her physical weakness, her breaking under stress, became, as the wedding date drew near, a paradigm of grace under pressure. Ernest, at every opportunity, distressed Hadley with his concerns about the marriage: What would his friends do without him? What about his "duty" to Kate? What about his freedom to go where he wished and do what he chose? What about the responsibility (and competition for Hadley's love) a baby would bring? Ernest tormented Hadley by reviving his relationship with Kate, by continually mentioning other women in his letters, by pretending it was perhaps in his best interest to take advice from people he neither respected nor liked and who were against the marriage (the Charles family), by constantly complaining about his job and his health, by threatening suicide.

From June to September 1921, Hadley gave Ernest, through her insight, wisdom, and art (many of her letters not only offer reason and guidance but are beautifully evocative), "loving protection and protecting love."

On the other hand, Hadley did upset Ernest by going to dinner—where "you eat in funny little screened-in houses and fell you are meant to take some devilish advantage of their privacy, but never do"—with one Dr. Tony Day. Later the doctor took her up on Letzminger Road to "look at some picnicing places."

Nevertheless, in Ernest's short story "The Current," which he sent to Hadley, the hero is clearly not the boxer, "Slam Bing," who wins his girl by winning the championship, but the girl herself, Dorothy Hadley, whose ideals make a man of a playboy.

On the train to St. Louis: Bill Horne to Ernest, "Grubstake Letter," March 2, 1921; interview with Bill Horne, July 7–8, 1979; Hadley to Ernest, May 24, 1921.

Days in St. Louis: Hadley to Ernest, May 24, 1921; May 25, 1921; June 2, 1921; June 3, 1921. Interview with Bill Horne, July 7–8, 1979. Bill recalled boiling spirit of nitre on Hadley's stove and condensing the alcohol vapor. But Hadley had friends with "connections," and Bill didn't have to keep this up for long.

Going out in a rowboat during a storm: Hadley to Ernest, May 20, 1921. Some of Hadley's details suggest she had been reading Stephen Crane's "The Open Boat" (probably because Ernest had recommended it), and her images make one suspect she is recounting a dream.

Dr. Tony Day: Hadley to Ernest, May 25, 1921.

Ernest loves Kate, but, paradoxically, Hadley must understand that he only loves her: Hadley to Ernest, June 2, 1921.

Hadley's mother: Hadley to Ernest, June 3, 1921.

Hadley contemplating suicide: Hadley to Ernest, July 7, 1921.

Ernest's fear of storm: Hadley to Ernest, June 3, 1921.

"Bad news" from Dr. Schawb: Hadley to Ernest, June 4, 1921.

Ernest not wanting children for a long time: Hadley to Ernest, June 6, 1921.

Marriage plans: Hadley to Ernest, June 7, June 8, June 9, 1921.

The Rapallos: Hadley to Ernest, June 7, 1921.

Hadley worried about giving birth: Hadley to Ernest, June 8, 1921.

"Manifesto for one": Hadley to Ernest, June 10, 1921.

Hadley's opinion of Kate: Hadley to Ernest, June 18, 1921.

Hadley overwrought: Hadley to Ernest, June 20, 1921. Ernest had asked her to come to Chicago, and threatened to take up with Kate again if she did not. Unfortunately, Hadley had no money to travel on.

Hadley on the value of "openness" between lovers: Hadley to Ernest, June 22, 1921.

Ernest and Kate's love affair: Hadley to Ernest, February 7, 1921. There is a curious passage in this letter: "My dear, if you've any faith in the thought being suggested do yo'on Kate leave poor Mrs. Dickey alone or there'll be trouble brewing and Dickey'll inquire in anger who is the father of this child? It wouldn't be good for Kate to get the reputation ever especially in cahoots with a man like yourself, being a father ever having been a father. So cover your tracks and beat it ex Dickey while the going is good." This passage seems to suggest that there was a child borne by Kate and fathered by Ernest. The author has found no corroborating evidence.

Hadley's ideal life: Hadley to Ernest, June 24, 1921.

Hadley's purpose in the marriage: Hadley to Ernest, June 25, 1921.

Hadley on Doodles Smith: Hadley to Ernest, June 26, 1921.

Advice to Ernest on practicing writing conversation: Hadley also warns him about lazy writing, "slipping with technical ease into poor psychology." Hadley would make a significant contribution to Ernest Hemingway's artistic creed. Hadley to Ernest, July 27, 1921.

Special Delivery letter in answer to Ernest's mention of suicide: Hadley to Ernest, July 7, 1921.
Hadley's difficult weekend in Chicago: Hadley to Ernest, July 13, 1921.
Hadley's dream of married life: Hadley to Ernest, July 17–18, 1921.
Hadley's light criticism of Ernest's poetry: She found a word, "Swats," "dripping and stark." Hadley to Ernest, July 20, 1921.
Ernest's wedding gift to Hadley: Hadley to Ernest, July 23, 1921.
"The Current": There is no direct evidence that the story that concludes Chapter 11 is the story of which Hadley writes. But to the author the circumstantial evidence is convincing. (Theme: woman sets ideals, man lives up to them. In doing so he becomes a man, man wins woman. Name: Dorothy Hadley. Hair color: auburn. The best friend: Sam Horne for Bill. The ending: " 'Don't worry, dearest, don't worry,' " thematically echoing the last words of Orpen's dream; see pp. 223–25.) Here as in the later story a suffering man has earned his dispensation. He may leave off the struggle now. In his life Ernest had finally won the woman he needed. "The Current," unpublished short story, Hemingway Collection, #352, John F. Kennedy Library, Dorchester, Mass.

Chapter 12

SOURCES

The seven days Ernest and Hadley spent together in late July and early August 1921 at 100 East Chicago Avenue was probably the finest time of their courtship. During the day Ernest took Hadley down to the Commonwealth to watch him work and to keep him company. Nights they lay on the roof in a single bed; Ernest read his work to Hadley; they talked and talked. Sometimes Ernest was frightened by the brief but violent thunderstorms that would roll in toward dawn. He and Hadley would cuddle under the blankets, under a tarpaulin. With Hadley there, Ernest could enjoy both the fear and the comforting which would follow and be as happy as a well-cared-for boy.

Hadley, however, approached the next weeks of her life with apprehension. She hardly felt the outdoor type. And she imagined northern Michigan to be rustic and primitive, challenging to her recently won self-confidence. With this in mind, she accepted the Breakers' invitation to spend a month camping in Wisconsin. It would be good training for the honeymoon at Windemere.

The major source for this chapter is Hadley's letters to Ernest, dating from August 7 to August 23. Important minor sources are the author's interview with Bill Horne, July 7–8, 1979; an untitled fragment of an intended short story by Ernest, which begins, "Last night Stut Horney and I . . ."; the author's conversation with Carol Hemingway Gardner (Ernest's youngest sister), July 19, 1980; Guy Hickok, "Hemingway First Lives Wild Stories; Then He Writes Them," *Brooklyn Eagle*, May 17, 1928, p. 12; Marcelline Hemingway Sanford, *At the Hemingways* (Boston 1962), pp. 209–10; author's interview with Bill Ohle, Horton Bay, Mich., August 5, 1979.

NOTES

Hadley's week with Ernest in Chicago: Hadley to Ernest, August 7, 1921.

Hadley's experience at "Brent's Camp": Hadley to Ernest, August 7, 1921.

Grace on Ernest's upcoming marriage and strange suggestion that she may soon die: Grace to Ernest, August 7, 1921.

Ernest wanting to take the pain of birth for Hadley: Hadley to Ernest, August 8, 1921.

Hadley as originator of Ernest's famous metaphor comparing great literature to an iceberg: Hadley to Ernest, August 8, 1921.

Hadley's illness: Hadley to Ernest, August 14, 1921.

Hadley on Doodles Smith: August 18, 1921.

Ernest fishing with Howell Jenkins and Charles Hopkins: "Big Two Hearted River," in *The Short Stories of Ernest Hemingway* (New York, 1966), pp. 221–32.

Night before wedding: Unpublished short story, "Last Night Stut Horney and I . . . ," #546 Hemingway Collection, John F. Kennedy Library, Dorchester, Mass.

The Wedding: Conversation with Carol Hemingway Gardner, July 20, 1980; interview with Bill Horne, July 7, 1979; interview with Bill Ohle, August 5, 1979; Marcelline Hemingway Sanford, *At the Hemingways* (Boston, 1962), p. 209.

Honeymoon: Guy Hickok, "Hemingway First Lives Wild Stories; Then He Writes Them," *Brooklyn Eagle*, May 17, 1928, p. 12; conversation with Carol Hemingway Gardner, July 20, 1980; author's visit to Windemere, October 7, 1980.

Epilogue

SOURCES

Ernest's life took on a transitional quality in the fall of 1921. Both Leicester, in *My Brother, Ernest Hemingway,* and Marcelline, in *At the Hemingways,* record how bored and frustrated Ernest and Hadley were in Chicago. They had made many plans during their nine-month courtship; they had many dreams. Now it was time, they felt, for Ernest to start his career. But the moves that had seemed so simple and easy to make when written about in letters required a self-assurance neither Ernest nor Hadley yet possessed. In short they needed someone with their interests at heart to tell them what to do. Grace of course volunteered, and so in a way did Clarence. But Ernest and Hadley took only one person's advice seriously. Sherwood Anderson, who had just returned from Paris a few months before, told Ernest that in that city Ernest could gain the one thing most valuable to an artist—his freedom. France was a "civilized" country, Anderson said, Paris a tolerant, exciting city. Many of the best young artists lived quite well there on five dollars a day. Besides, it was the place to make connections with people who could influence publishers. Anderson wrote for Ernest a letter of introduction to Gertrude Stein.

Sherwood Anderson's characterization of Gertrude Stein in "Four American Impressions: Gertrude Stein, Paul Rosenfeld, Ring Lardner, Sinclair Lewis," *New Republic,* October 11, 1922, pp. 171–73, is one major source for this epilogue. The other is an untitled rough draft of a Hemingway short story about a wounded soldier and what he dreams in his delirium. Written some time between the Spanish Civil War and World War II, the story anticipates *For Whom the Bell Tolls* in its setting and, on a symbolic level, its dramatic tension. Because the story of Orpen the soldier seems to be the raw material of Hemingway's subconscious and is highly autobiographical (particularly the dream), it may be suggestive of inner conflicts that troubled Ernest throughout his life.

NOTES

Clarence and Leicester's visit to Ernest and Hadley: Leicester Hemingway, *My Brother, Ernest Hemingway* (Cleveland, 1961), pp. 74–75.

Grace's visit to Ernest and Hadley: Carlos Baker, *Ernest Hemingway: A Life Story* (New York, 1969), p. 82.

Ernest, General Diaz, and the award: Marcelline Hemingway Sanford, *At the Hemingways* (Boston 1962), pp. 210–17; *A Farewell to Arms* (New York, 1929), pp. 184–85.

Ernest and Hadley's departure for Paris: Sanford, p. 212; Ernest to Howell Jenkins, December 26, 1921.

The artist's task—for Ernest it was "Make all that come true again": *Death in the Afternoon* (New York, 1932), p. 272.

Index